RON McMILLAN

Ron McMillan has been travelling since 1979, when he spent time in Germany working on Formula One cars, which he maintains was not particularly glamorous, since the workshop was a grimy factory in Bavaria — and the cars were toys. The following summer saw him in Germany again, where demolishing the roof of a metals factory sixty feet above swimming-pool-sized vats of boiling acid was only slightly less perilous than working alongside three Liverpudlians, all of whom were called Frank.

After two years in Australia and New Zealand (funded by dishwashing, driving and digging ditches), came fifteen years in the Far East. He began in Korea as a part-time English teacher and full-time student of Tae Kwon-do; then, amidst the flying rocks and tear gas shells of nationwide student demonstrations in the run-up to the 1988 Seoul Olympics, became a freelance writer and photographer for newspapers and magazines in Asia, Europe and America. During a decade based in Hongkong, he visited Mainland China on assignment nearly fifty times, lied to men carrying guns in at least a dozen different countries, and made five 'tourist' visits to isolated North Korea. The resultant photographs from North Korea graced the covers and inside pages of *Time*, *Newsweek*, *L'Express* and the *New York Times Sunday Magazine*.

On his return to Scotland in 1998, he took on a domestic travel column for *The Herald*. He also wrote and photographed travel and business stories for magazines including the inflight titles of Cathay Pacific Airways, Korean Air, Thai Airways and Japan Airlines. In the autumn of 2005, he spent five weeks in Shetland researching the first travel narrative to be written about the islands since 1869. *BETWEEN WEATHERS – Travels in 21st Century Shetland* is the result.

Ron McMillan is now a correspondent based in Bangkok, Thailand, where a vibrant live music scene allows him to indulge his passion for playing blues harmonica rather badly.

BETWEEN | WEATHERS

Travels in 21st Century Shetland

RON McMILLAN

Foreword by Aly Bain

Sandstone Press
Highland, Scotland

BETWEEN WEATHERS
Travels in 21st Century Shetland

First published 2008 in Great Britain by Sandstone Press Ltd, PO Box 5725, One High Street, Dingwall, Ross-shire, IV15 9WJ, Scotland.

Editor: Robert Davidson

ISBN-10: 1-905207-20-4
ISBN-13: 978-1-905207-20-6

Designed and typeset in ITC Giovanni by River Design, Edinburgh.

Printed and bound: Totem S.C., Poland

SANDSTONEPRESS
CONTEMPORARY QUALITY READING
www.sandstonepress.com

CONTENTS

Acknowledgements

Heartfelt thanks are due to everyone at the Visit Shetland Tourist Information Centre in Lerwick, and in particular to Stephen Simpson for his unflagging professionalism.

I am indebted to travel guides Elma Johnson, Allen Fraser and David Murray, as well as to Shetland Amenity Trust and the Shetland Islands Cruisers.

Brian Smith and Joanne Wishart of Shetland Museum and Archives responded to a slew of enquiries with saint-like forbearance, and David Kosofsky, Mark McTague, Charles Martin, Tom Slover, Peggy Myron, Roberto De Vido and Allen Fraser offered valued editorial advice and encouragement.

Brian Johnston of Shetland Times Ltd supplied the map adapted on page ix, and the family of Rhoda Bulter kindly granted permission to quote her poem 'Da Clearance' on page 208.

Thanks go to Basil Pao and Stella Lai for the cover design; and to Aly Bain for his generous foreword.

Gratitude is also due to Robert Davidson, Moira Forsyth and Iain Gordon at Sandstone Press, for their patience and considerable assistance throughout the writing process. Any remaining errors in the text are, of course, entirely of my own making.

Lastly, I thank the people of Shetland, who forged a special place in this traveller's heart.

Dedications

This book is dedicated to my father, Tom McMillan,
to my late mother, Ellen McMillan, and to the two ladies
in my life, Ae Shim and Shona. And no dedication would
be complete without a wee wave to my Aunt Sadie McPhail.

Colin 'ViKing' Fraser — Aberdonian, Liverpudlian,
sooth-moother and proud Shetlander — passed away
in September 2007. A fine friend sorely missed.

MAP ADAPTED BY KIND PERMISSION OF SHETLAND TIMES, LTD

MUCKLE FLUGGA

HERMANESS

UNST

BALTASOUND

BELMONT

GUTCHER

FETHALAND

YELL

NORTH MAVINE

FETLAR

COLLAFIRTH

ULSTA

ESHANESS

TOFT

MAVIS GRIND

BRAE

WHALSAY

VOE

SYMBISTER

PAPA
STOUR

WEST BURRAFIRTH

WEST MAINLAND

WALLS

VAILA

LERWICK

FOULA

SCALLOWAY

BRESSAY

ST NINIAN'S

BIGTON

MOUSA

FITFUL HEAD

SCATNESS

SUMBURGH

THE SHETLAND
ISLANDS

FAIR
ISLE

Foreword

This is a refreshing and entertaining look at my native islands. It has all the more value as the author is a much travelled journalist. It would be impossible to describe Shetland without giving the weather its place. Ron McMillan does this to sketch in the background to present day Shetland.

The Oceania, sister ship of the Titanic, was grounded on a reef off the island of Foula on 8th September 1914. Her skipper, Henry Smith, realising that she could not be floated off, said she would be there as a monument for all time. A local man commented, "I'll give her two weeks." They were both wrong - she was gone in three. This was a ship the length of two football pitches.

In the days of open six-oared fishing boats, when a fleet turned, heading for shore at frantic speed, there was no sense of competition – they were rowing for their lives. They would cut their long lines in full awareness that the lairds who owned the boats and gear would expect full compensation.

Life for past generations of Shetlanders could be extremely harsh, and the author reflects that during the Clearances the families whose roofs had been burned off their cottages might look back from New Zealand or the Americas years later and think that it was the best thing that ever happened to them.

Shetland today is a place of much happier circumstances. There is comfort and prosperity, a good social life, a great musical tradition. Incomers are made welcome and many have put down roots and raised families. There are, of course, many weeks when the weather is memorable for all the right reasons.

Above all, however, this is a book about people. Ron McMillan looks at Shetlanders with a sharp but affectionate eye and his style has a wit which makes reading this book a pleasure.

As for the Shetland character, when a writer as widely travelled says that Shetland is the best place in the world to thumb a lift, he has said a great deal.

Aly Bain
Edinburgh 2008

PROLOGUE: GETTING THERE

I: Northward Bound in a Force 8

Late on the night before I drive to Aberdeen to set out on a lengthy trip among distant northern isles, a button marked 'Gale Warnings' on the Met Office website draws my computer cursor like iron filings to a magnet.

Click.

> GALE WARNING SUNDAY 25 SEPTEMBER 2154GMT 74
> VIKING NORTH UTSIRE
> GALE NOW CEASED BUT SOUTHERLY GALE FORCE 8
> EXPECTED LATER.
>
> FORTIES CROMARTY
> SOUTHERLY GALE FORCE 8 EXPECTED SOON.
> FITZROY
> SOUTHWESTERLY GALE FORCE 8 EXPECTED SOON.
>
> FAIR ISLE FAEROES
> GALE NOW CEASED BUT SOUTHEASTERLY GALE
> FORCE 8 IMMINENT INCREASING

I am about to take my first long ferry ride in years, and there are Force 8 or 9 gales to look forward to. This does not sound promising. The long drive north is spent consoling myself with the truism that weather forecasting is more about scientific theory than real life, and so when at last the North Sea coastline opens up before me, I studiously disregard ten different shades of grey-black cloud hanging over murky waters.

'NO ACCESS TO OUTER DECK DUE
TO EXTREME WEATHER CONDITIONS'

So says the sign on the inside of the NorthLink ferry door, in fading red capitals and behind a wooden frame affixed so solidly that it may well be a permanent fixture. Considering last night's forecasts, this is either bad news or worse.

My cabin is neatly compact and complete with ensuite facilities. Despite having dimensions and finish that are reminiscent of 1970s caravans, it is comfortable and private, and even features a miniature work surface that passes for a desk. Behind fifteen inches of faux veneer desktop is a disconcertingly sharp mirror with frightening auto-ageing properties; the face staring from it looks a little like me, only older. Between us sits a telephone from which I can talk to any other cabin on the ferry, but which might not be such a clever idea, since I know not another soul on the boat, and telephone stalking is not something I need added to an already chequered résumé. Next to the phone squats a solid brick of so many white sick bags that they beg to be counted. There are forty-five. Even in a cabin fitted out for double occupancy, could there possibly be a need for more than forty sick bags in the course of a 14-hour ferry ride? The thought that I might be about to find out is not a comforting one.

Forget the caravan slur, because my cabin now feels like a budget Tokyo hotel room, circa 1990, complete with tiny bathroom (though not the remarkable all-in-one-moulded-plastic floor, walls, ceiling, fittings, shelves, bath and other plumbed furnishings that used to have me awe-struck in Japan), and I am very glad to be berthed here — and not facing a long night trying to grab sleep in a lounge chair next to a gang of pissed-up poker players.

BBC Radio Two, leaking softly from invisible speakers, informs me that Western Isles and Irish Sea ferry services are subject to cancellation due to stormy weather, but there is no mention of the

North Sea or of this ferry, the NorthLink service bound for Lerwick in the Shetland Islands, Britain's northernmost island group. The Skipper breaks in with a chirpy airline captain impersonation to deliver a 'welcome aboard' speech and goes on to confirm that we will encounter gales up to Force 8 or 9. This, he says, means things 'could get a little bit rough'.

Now I really am worried. When a career mariner whose daily remit is the wild water between Aberdeen and Shetland says things could be a 'little rough', the whiff of understatement is overpowering.

At least he solves one mystery that has been bothering me ever since I first set eyes on this slab-sided modern ferry. According to him, the MV Hrossey's name is pronounced 'Rossi', as in the motorcycle racer, Valentino Rossi.

Hrossey is the Old Norse name for Orkney, the other group of northern islands served by the Hrossey/Rossi. The Hrossey featured in news stories from 2002 when, newly-introduced on the route by NorthLink, she departed Lerwick one stormy November evening bound for Aberdeen. But instead of mooring at her destination the following morning, the Hrossey limped back to her starting point in Lerwick, after no fewer than forty-two uncomfortable hours at sea. She had ridden out a force 10 storm in the lee of an island after something broke loose and damaged an outer door in the fo'c'sle (a peculiar maritime word that I have a feeling might be pronounced 'Rossi').

'They just hit a lump of water and something broke off,' opined one salty commentator in a newspaper report. With NorthLink being new to the service which until recently had been operated for so many years by P&O, critics heaped derision upon the company's management, even if passengers interviewed by the press seemed content with the free food and drink provided throughout their stalled journey. Stuck offshore in a force 10 storm, and they are not only able, but happy to take advantage of free food and drink? These Shetlanders must be made of tough stuff.

One passenger, Alan Kirwan from the island of Whalsay, even expressed anger over 'sensationalist' media reports that dubbed the trip a 'voyage from hell'.

'We had no problem with the sea, no problem with the crossing.

It was enjoyable, considering the circumstances,' he was quoted in The Shetland Times, which neglected to pick up on the fact that there *was no crossing*. Perhaps they felt unqualified to contest his claims, as the Hrossey odyssey was in fact Mr Kirwan's third non-voyage from hell marathon trip in under twelve months. Twice before in 2002, while the service was still operated by P&O, he suffered journeys of thirty-seven and thirty-nine hours, throughout which ordeals a more parsimonious P&O managerial policy saw passengers given ONE free drink each.

The Aberdeen harbour basin that once heaved with the workboats of a booming but doomed North Sea fishing industry sits placid as the late September evening hunkers down. Centuries of continuous port activity have preserved its city-centre location, mere yards from the regional capital's shore-based attractions, yards worn shiny by the footfalls of generations of sailors hurrying ashore for that much-anticipated tryst with strong drink or favoured brassy whore or both.

Next to the Hrossey is a sturdy craft out of Kiel that was surely christened by a committee of non-movie-goers. *Poseidon* is a working boat with an aft deck shadowed by a sleeping crane in a fetching shade of anti-rust orange.

They call Aberdeen the Granite City, and right now it fades into a darker-than-granite world. Above it, the sky is the colour of old lead fishing weights.

There is something visceral about the rumbling vibrations that pulse through a major vessel on the brink of setting off to sea. Engines awaken and growl themselves to operating temperature, and ropes as thick as Popeye's forearms slip from pierside bollards to smack into black water rainbowed with diesel. Then the higher-pitched whine of deck winches kick in, main engines raise their tempo, and we're off. Slowly.

More rig supply vessels lie up double- and triple-parked against the harbour basin, their only signs of movement imparted by the Hrossey's bow wave that sets them off in sequential bobs that are absorbed by mooring ropes exactly set up to allow just enough but not too much movement. The vessels are dark and lonely for human activity.

We cut through the glassy inner harbour at what feels like walking pace, an impression lent credence by huge letters that unfold along the wall of a breakwater: 'Max Speed 5 Knots' — less than six miles per hour, or a brisk walk for an Olympian. As the Hrossey clears the breakwater end, its mighty engines are set free, and from giant funnels spumes a soot cloud that corkscrews downwards, intact, to near the surface of the water, where it holds momentum, rolling parallel to its source. While I watch, my eyes play tricks on me. Four or five times, sleek shapes course from the surface, through the soot, and back to the depths. Bottle-nosed dolphins, even more grey than all that is around us.

The sky is grey, now with a shrinking golden torchlight beam spread across a western horizon saw-toothed by a city skyline speckled with tungsten lights newly-summoned to confront the impending gloom. More grey again is a sea already flecked with tiny bubbling crests. And greyer still, in among the mini-crests and the black soot, sweep the acrobatic sea creatures.

A tannoy announcement says the bar is open, and that it will remain so throughout the trip. The same announcement includes, however, one bit of bad news for the heavy drinkers: alcohol sales will stop at 3 a.m. This may be a concession to the need for passengers to get 'fit' enough to drive ashore at Lerwick, four hours later.

With darkness descended like a shroud, and the swells not *too* bad, the bar seems like a better idea than the 'casino' — a bare room with two bored drunks throwing money at an equally bored Blackjack dealer whom I last saw selling coffee and sandwiches. I recall he seemed a lot happier dealing toasties.

About a dozen bar customers sit at tables, their drinks on non-slip rubber netting mats, clever technological concessions to the needs of a bar that at any moment can find itself a long way from horizontal. I buy a drink, sit at a near-empty table, and explore the impressive disaster-avoidance qualities of the rubber mat. Just as notable are solid brackets that fix table legs to floor, and shiny steel hawsers that stretch between the bottom of every seat and U-brackets set into the carpet. The designers of the Hrossey *had to* have been Boy Scouts in an earlier life.

My tablemate is an engineer on his way to service machinery in

Shetland, and whose first job tomorrow morning is at a fish-processing plant. A naïve enquiry as to whether such work might have its rough moments inspires graphic tales of machinery innards overflowing with writhing hordes of maggots. Judging by the smile on my companion's face, this could be a tale he relishes inflicting upon unsuspecting victims.

Before long, the weather worsens enough to make watching a meaningless football match on television an even greater threat to my physical wellbeing than the engineer's stories. I weave along a rotating corridor and settle in for the rough ride in the only position from which past experience tells me I can almost deal with sea-sickness. The foetal position.

II: Mainland, the island

I awake feeling foolish. It is early morning, and I pop from a dreamless sleep unspoiled by gale-tossed seas, my worst fears unwarranted. I don multiple synthetic layers and climb up to a rear deck that, unlike the side decks, is open to passengers. This may be because it is more sheltered, but is more likely a function of the need to provide *somewhere* for smokers to huddle and shiver.

Whatever storms failed to stir me from slumber are consigned to meteorological history, and the Hrossey powers along the eastern side of Shetland's largest island, confusingly called Mainland. (There is no such confusion in Shetland, where locals never refer to mainland Scotland as mainland anything. Instead it is simply known as 'south' — or, more accurately, 'sooth'.)

One hour out from Lerwick, the moon is a canted melon slice in an azure sky sparingly dusted with cirrus. A bone-brittling southerly pursues us parallel to the Mainland coastline, which from a few kilometres away is a jagged wave of black rock washed soapy white by the invading swell. As I stand tipping slowly towards hypothermia, the island appears low-lying, seldom reaching more than about thirty metres above the churning sea. Its late September tones offer barely a hint at the green of a summer already despatched to memory, and presage the inevitability of a long winter.

I lean on a metal hand rail as chilled as the inside of a meat locker, and face the numbing draught. Straight ahead, peering from the post-dawn haze is a ramped island like a colossal door wedge rising to a near-vertical cliff at its seaward edge. West of the wedge's thin end soars the shoe-box rectangular cliff-face of another island, which I think is Bressay. I sweep the seas with my binoculars. Not a single other vessel graces the jagged horizon.

Shetland tourism industry officials intent on drawing travel junkies like me should tear up the glossy brochures filled with contrived photographs of studiously fashionable couples running hand in hand through Atlantic surf. Instead, they should pump out a million copies of a booklet already sold by the Shetland Islands Council. It is called Shetland in Statistics, and every statistic within it sends up another alluring beacon to travel-lovers.

Of Shetland's one hundred-plus islands, only fifteen are inhabited, and those by a total of just under 22,000 souls.

There are twelve puffins and eighteen sheep to every human resident.

Shetland's combined coastline is 1,460 kilometres, roughly the distance from London to Rome, or Chicago to New Orleans. An astonishing 400 kilometres of this is made up of cliffs, including the highest in occupied Britain — over 370 metres of vertical rock on the remote isle of Foula.

It is closer to the Arctic Circle (640 kilometres) than to London (965 kilometres), and closer still to Bergen, Norway (380 kilometres).

Sitting at a latitude equal to that of Anchorage, Alaska, its 1,470 square kilometres are peppered with over seven thousand recorded archaeological sites, some of which pre-date the Pyramids of Giza by fifteen hundred years.

Eight hundred species of flowering plants are rained upon two hundred and sixty-nine days a year, yet Shetland's total annual rainfall is similar to that of Devon — a thousand kilometres away on the 'English Riviera'.

Number of non-business visitors in 2000: **19,625**.

Number of (non-business) British visitors to Spain in the same year: **10.7 million**. (Last number sourced on the Internet.)

Until the late 1980s, Shetland was not only all-but missing from British consciousness, it was entirely absent from television weather bulletins — literally off the map. In some ways, it might as well still be.

Travel excites me. Any travel. Almost thirty itinerant years have implanted in me a *need* for exploration that dishes up fun, escape, adventure and even the odd scrap of professional reward. This trip is devised to deliver all of the above by spending over a month wandering a group of islands whose place in history pours scorn on its perceived remoteness. An archipelago whose geographical isolation has surely contributed to what it is today, an offshoot mini-society with independence in its veins and thousands of years of history forever hovering in its near-past.

Ahead of me stretch a few autumnal weeks, set aside to do what I love best. My goals are entirely non-specific. There is no quest to cover every mile of road or visit every community, and I suffer no pressing time restrictions. No kitchen appliances feature in my luggage, and I harbour no ambition to completely encircle every coastline or tick off every possible destination on any list, because there are no lists made up for this trip. My uncomplicated goal is to travel wherever the notion takes me, to explore as many islands as is practicable and encounter as many Shetlanders as I cross paths with. Along the way, I will surely learn something about a prosperous northern community that sits on the outer fringes, not only of British, but of European consciousness.

LERWICK AND WEST MAINLAND

I: A Czech welcome

Bressay Sound is an eight-kilometre north-south sea corridor that separates Mainland from the island that provides not only the corridor's name but also a broad buttress of shelter from the brutal forces of the North Sea. It is the most easily accessible naturally protected harbour in Shetland and the location of Lerwick, its capital. The Lerwick name comes from Old Norse, and means 'Muddy Bay', but this morning, only crystalline waters lap at a shoreline thick with buildings.

As we nose through the Sound, the sun breaks cover over the shallow hills of Bressay, eclipses the blue pre-dawn light, paints Lerwick with a cosy post-sunrise glow that is entirely at odds with the temperature, and casts a cartoon-like Hrossey shadow that reaches out for the shoreline of a capital as prettified as a 19th Century watercolour.

William Hickey was less impressed when he sailed into Bressay Sound in 1780 aboard the Dutch East Indiaman *Held Woltemade*. Lerwick struck him as '*the most wretched town I ever beheld, principally consisting of fishermen's huts with only three or four houses fit for a human creature to inhabit.*'

Granted, this is not the sort of quote that appears in tourist brochures, though he did go on to say that '*the inhabitants received us with the utmost good nature and hospitality. The herrings were the finest I ever tasted.*' Talk about being damned with faint praise: your town's a midden, but the people are bearable, and the herring's just dandy.

In historic terms, the herring Hickey savoured represented far more than a fine repast in a wretched town.

Lerwick may be the capital today, but at only four centuries old, it is one of Shetland's infant communities. Two hundred years before the *Held Woltemade* sailed into Bressay Sound, Lerwick was only just evolving, and thanks mainly to the herring.

Annual shoals of migrating herring were first exploited here in the late 16th Century by Dutch fishermen, who quickly identified Bressay Sound as a place of sanctuary when they were not out chasing their pay packets. More than four hundred years ago, where Lerwick is today there was not even a village, let alone a township.

An annual influx of Dutch fishing vessels for six weeks every summer awoke Shetlanders to all-new trading opportunities, and soon locals set up booths where they bartered knitwear and bird feathers for highly valued tobacco and strong liquor. The resultant mini-flood of hard drink drew increasing ire (or was it envy?) from some of the more conservative locals and in 1625 the Court in nearby Scalloway, then Shetland's capital, issued an edict that the booths be demolished.

Commercial enterprise of course prevailed and the fledgling community of Lerwick grew steadily to a population of seven hundred at the end of the 17th Century, and over the following hundred years, it doubled again. But the real boom, when the population leapt from fourteen hundred to three thousand, occurred in the first third of the 19th Century, as a new merchant class evolved.

Four hundred years after the Dutch inspired the birth of what is today Shetland's only real town, Lerwick remains the northernmost town in Britain. Its population numbers just under seven thousand, and fully half of Shetland's nearly twenty-two thousand inhabitants live within sixteen kilometres.

The Hrossey creeps ashore and ties up precisely on schedule — to the minute. This is not something we expect in Britain. In mid-Tokyo the trains on the Yamanote Circle run so frequently that at times I suspected there may only be one train stretching the entire length of the line; in Switzerland you can set your cuckoo clock to the bus schedules and even the much-maligned French can run immaculate public transport networks to a precise timetable, but not us. Stand in the grand Victorian concourse of Glasgow Central Station and listen to the litany of excuses for late or cancelled trains, and you wonder how the Second City of the Empire ever got an Industrial Revolution up and running.

So when the Hrossey ties up at its destination after nearly twelve hours in a North Sea Force 8 gale, on time to within sixty seconds, I tell myself it bodes well.

This is only my second visit to Shetland. The first was a few years ago and comprised several days on a Press junket, whisked around in a minibus on a tight schedule so liberally sprinkled with alcohol that much of the trip occupies a black hole in the memory banks.

I do recall being surprised to discover that, even up here, many bar staff spoke with an Antipodean twang. Whether it was the bastardised-over-the-generations criminal class cockney of the Sydneysiders or the stilted vowels of the Kiwis, the bars of Lerwick rang to the cries of Australasia. Even then this put a lie to the British misconception of Shetland as an embodiment of remoteness; the notion of Shetland's isolation is one that I will discover to be about as far-removed from the truth as, say, 'Reality TV' is removed from reality.

The first person I meet on Shetland soil, Visit Shetland's Marketing Manager Misa Kotkova, is a case in point.

She and her partner meet me at the ferry terminal, having risen early to extend a pre-breakfast welcome. Her partner Donald works in the local government accounts department, collecting Council tax and rates. Which, he concedes wryly, might not make him the most popular guy in Shetland. He has willingly dragged himself from home to pick up this stranger, an act of kindness that he clearly thinks nothing of, and which, over the coming weeks, I am going to learn *is* nothing in this hospitable land. He is a big guy with the build of a rugby player, and standing beside him, partner Misa is almost as tall. She is startlingly blonde with skin of porcelain perfection and she looks me straight in the eye with the confidence of youth.

OK, so I made up that last bit about the eyes. At easily six feet in shoes as flat as a sheet of newsprint, Misa has to stoop to shake my hand, and throughout our conversation I must strain my neck to maintain *any* eye contact. My lack of stature is something to which I have long become inured (until I was fifteen I thought my first name was 'Wee'), but Scots of my generation have little experience of women the height of Rob Roy, and if Misa was not so sweet, she would be intimidating.

Given our present location, her blondeness could be easily mistaken for Norse heritage, but Misa hails from the Czech Republic. She came to Shetland two years ago to work in a hotel, ended up staying, and now works to promote Shetland tourism.

Donald drops us at the Tourist Office, where I learn that I arrive at the worst possible moment in years, on the very day that the entire staff transfers to cramped temporary premises while their Information Centre undergoes renovation. Despite the pressures of decanting one large workplace into a much smaller temporary substitute, welcomes and handshakes are extended across overflowing boxes and packing crates of maps and pamphlets and souvenir tea towels, and the friendly front office staff tell me just to make myself at home. I leave them to their travails and head out for a wander.

II: Da toon

Despite what self-interest groups may claim, large swathes of urban Scotland are either dead or visibly dying, gripped by terminal decline brought on by the reversal of economic fortunes that once fed and watered entire communities on the back of the Industrial Revolution. My own home town, only a handful of miles from Glasgow, not so long ago rattled to the din of textile weaving and thread making and shipbuilding and car manufacturing. Today, not one core employer industry survives, leaving behind an extended community without a reason for being, a formerly skilled artisan workforce deprived of ever-evolving technical demands that once generated the jobs that fostered the skills that kept the community truly alive. In a community so absent of challenge, upward social mobility is no more than a pipedream. Within recent memory, many of the town's breadwinners were time-served engineers and craftsmen whose trades and skills were vital to local and national economies. What remains now is a compartmentalised dormitory town for the unemployable and for a middle-class service sector that toils to sell each other things they neither need nor can afford. From skilled craftsmen and women in great demand to supermarket check-out specialists working temporary contracts. It is no wonder that large areas of Scottish (and other British) towns reek so badly of depression.

Only occasionally in Scotland have I found, to self-cancelling delight and chagrin, towns that have managed to escape this post-industrial, post-Thatcher gloom. Communities that, in the main due to geographical location, cling contentedly to roles played and prospered from for centuries. At the opposite end of the country from Shetland, Dumfries is one such town. Dumfriesians may once upon a time have envied their industry-driven counterparts, but the absence of a manufacturing base meant the county capital clung to its role as a regional centre of local government, markets and transportation, one that it maintains today.

Lerwick shares such a life-giving raison d'être. As the port for the ferry link to Aberdeen, it is the funnel through which pour the majority of visitors and trade exchanged with mainland UK. The port is also a big player in the fishing industry, with enormous pelagic trawlers routinely tied up at Shetland Catch, a north harbour fish plant and significant source of well-paid local employment. Also, as the central seat of the Shetland Islands Council, Lerwick citizens by the hundreds — Donald among them — enjoy job security virtually unknown in the archipelago's outer reaches.

With more than half of all Shetlanders living within fifteen minutes' drive, 'da toon' (the town, in local-speak) is Shetland's centre of local trade and shopping and entertainment. Commercial Street, a pedestrianised central lane that picks its way between buildings that backed directly onto the harbour before 19th Century reclamation works extended the waterfront sixty-five metres out into Bressay Sound, is like a snapshot of days long gone in much of Britain. Odd-shaped family owned shops with display windows like oversized 1960s living room windows peddle clothing or eyeglasses or photography services or household goods from within premises they have occupied for generations.

Every self-respecting sea port has a fort to buttress its sense of self worth, and Lerwick's is immediately above the north end of Commercial Street, set square atop a modest rock face that once fell straight into Bressay Sound, but today looks out across reclaimed land.

The present structure was built in the 1780s, at the height of the American War of Independence, when Britain faced the combined naval forces of France, Spain and Northern Europe, aided and abetted by American privateers led by the Scots-born Father of the American Navy, John Paul Jones. Jones only adopted his third name as an adult — to prevent Scots confusing him with himself; under his birth name of John Paul, he was accused of murder, and when cleared of the charge, he added 'Jones'. Perhaps people were easily confused back then.

The fort never saw any action before the Treaty of Versailles in 1783, and it later stood as an uninvolved sentinel during the Napoleonic Wars of 1792-1815.

Long before the Americans or Napoleon posed threats real or imagined, Britain was at war with Holland. Not once or even twice, but three times in the second half of the 1600s.

This means the nation was at war with the Dutch at the very time when the nascent community of Lerwick welcomed an annual summer influx of several hundred fishing vessels from Holland. The locals never let the small matter of international conflict get in the way of trading bird feathers for baccy and hard drink. This surely must have put the wind up a few starched shirts in London, but then, as now, London was a long way away.

The original stronghold, where now sits Fort Charlotte (named after the wife of George III when it was re-built in the 1780s) was constructed during the first Dutch War (1652-1653); that fort was razed and re-developed into a pentagonal structure during the second Dutch War (1665-1657), at the astounding cost of £28,000, the equivalent of tens of millions in today's money — for a few walls and some cannons. Military overspend, anyone? Nearly four centuries later, as an acceptable commercial practice, such overspend has gone global.

The other end of Commercial Street dog-legs towards the waterfront, past Victoria Pier, where an oddball selection of small craft snuggle within an inner harbour. From there I wander south to the lodberries, the last remaining coastal buildings with Bressay Sound lapping against their outer walls.

Dating from the 1700s, the few surviving lodberry buildings (from the Old Norse *hladberg*, a location suited to loading or unloading boats) served as trading houses, complete with sail-in basements for small craft called flit boats. In the centuries before commercial piers, flit boats 'flitted' back and forth from cargo ship to shore, transferring goods straight to the lodberries, which had warehouses on their upper floors. In urban Scotland, 'to flit' still means to move house; and to do a moonlight flit is to do an overnight runner from your landlord. Today, the lodberries make bijoux residences that are not so much on the coast as in it.

The trail south hugs the shore of the Sound, between two grand, almost gothic structures that both bear the name of Anderson. Funds for the Anderson Home for Widows and Anderson High School came from the deep pockets of Arthur Anderson, Lerwick native and founding shareholder of the P&O shipping empire.

Passing beyond the High School (which has a roll of over one thousand students, some of them boarders from the more remote islands), is Shetland's first ever purpose-built road, constructed in 1781 to connect Fort Charlotte to a point at the southern end of Lerwick bay called The Knab.

Jakobsen's Shetland Dictionary defines *knabb* as a *'projecting knowll, rock; now only used as a place name.'* The spelling may have changed, but the Knab is indeed a projecting rock headland of sandstone cliffs that stand firm in the face of everything the North Sea can throw its way.

I pause where the town cemetery occupies a pronounced slope facing the sea, with steppes cut out to accept long rows of grand memorials. Adjacent to it, a huge landscaped extension of empty steppes makes me wonder if the Council's coffers are so replete that it throws large sums at the not-yet deceased. In the existing cemetery, a disturbing number of memorials are to young servicemen who met their ends during a variety of conflicts in distant corners of the world.

The short walk out to the Knab is rendered a struggle by a powerful south-westerly that has birds hovering hesitantly over their nesting points in the pitted brown sandstone cliffs. Beneath them, the sea rolls and swells like a giant waterbed patterned with hundreds of two-tone seabirds. Where ocean meets vertical sandstone, formidable waves thrash the cliff faces, and on sheltered stone plinths loll clusters of fat grey seals.

This is Lerwick harbour's South Mouth, and as the arrival gateway to Shetland's incomers over the centuries, its very own pejorative has burrowed into the local lexicon — *sooth-moothers*.

The south-westerly pummels the Knab with surf that is not so much boiling as frothing. Dizzying movement in the air above the cliff edges is sea froth so aerated as to become soaring flurries of foam that tumble over cliff edges and race across ramped, grassy knolls as if in the clutches of miniature thermal fairground rides.

Beyond the Knab the coastal path narrows and rounds the point before clinging to clifftops that dip and soar towards the neighbouring suburban bay of Breiwick.

I huddle in the relative calm that is the lee of a drystone wall and look across the Sound to Bressay, and to a landmark that is partly responsible for me being here.

During the Press trip to Shetland, we enjoyed a boat excursion around Bressay on the Dunter II, a custom built aluminium-hulled tour boat operated by Jonathan Wills, a native of Bressay well-known both for the strength of his convictions and for the unabashed willingness with which he shares them. Wills is a naturalist and wildlife expert with a keen eye for colourful historical context, and towards the end of the tour he manoeuvred his beloved craft through a narrow crevice in the rocky coastline into what he told us was 'Orkneyman's Cave'.

The name, he explained, came from an Orkney fisherman who, in the early years of the 19ᵗʰ Century, hid himself and his craft inside the cave to escape the attentions of a Press Gang cutter intent on adding him to the British Navy's crew roster. While he lay deep within the cave, his boat floated away, leaving him trapped on a ledge for several days and nights. When he was eventually rescued by Bressay fishermen, according to Jonathan (giving off more than a whiff of storyteller's licence) the hypothermic Orkneyman was put to bed with a Bressay lass to revive him. Thus, said the Shetlander from Bressay, the Orkneyman was a winner on two counts, since he not only got himself a Bressay wife — he never had to return to Orkney.

Hearing this while bobbing on chilled North Sea waters inside a daunting cave on the edge of an under inhabited Shetland island, I was struck by how *real* the tale was to Jonathan. This was almost certainly because he had heard the story decades earlier from his ageing grandfather, who himself probably heard it from *his* grandfather, and who may even have been alive around the time of the story's origins.

Shetland's capacity to relate to and draw from its own history is so deep-rooted that stories from two centuries ago survive, largely through word-of-mouth, with their significance unquestioned precisely *because of* how they have been handed down by trusted elders.

I had never before been anywhere in Britain with such a sense of involvement in its past. Shetland's complex social history is so much a product of the archipelago's geographical isolation — and yet so patently nothing at all to do with isolation, so inextricably involved is Shetland in the narratives of so many distant lands. In a dark cave under the Bressay coastline, the germ of an idea was incubated, to return to these shores and learn more about what makes Shetland's history such a part of its present.

And here I am.

III: Fellow itinerants

The walk back into Lerwick lays out the town's architecture like a tableau of extremes. Grand Victorian sandstone mansions wear extravagant bay windows and the roofline frills so often aspired to in today's bolt-on conservatory. There are slabbish roughcast-coated terraces and semis from the 60s and 70s, their dormer windows coloured by teenage calls to anarchy; and post-1950s Town Council utilitarian boxes, seemingly devoid of even a nod toward aesthetics. In fact, very little of the architecture on view holds much in the way of aesthetic appeal, leading me to wonder if the Shetland climate dictates that function over form is the *only* pragmatic design principle.

Back on Commercial Street, I slip into a coffee shop and order up a caffeine hit that arrives in a cup big enough to keep goldfish in. At the next table a local woman, accent as thick as fog, talks with a man who sounds to me as if he comes from somewhere near Aberdeen.

'*I was takkin ta an ald maan,*' she says, '*an' he sayd werr in for a fool wintur.*'

The man appears confused.

'*Severe winter,*' she says, adjusting her dialect to order. The Aberdonian nods and smiles, but looks none the wiser.

I pick up a sandwich and head out to the pier. The sky is vivid blue, the light is as sharp as a glossy magazine spread and locals, oblivious to the chill wind, wander around in shirt sleeves. I wrap up tight and walk out past a gleaming lifeboat the colour of freshly-squeezed orange juice to a bench that sits in the shelter of a concrete shed near the pier end.

There, I unwrap my lunch and pop into the world of the Shetland Times. It is that old-fashioned print institution, the community newspaper that *everybody* reads and discusses, and a mine of local information, a striking amount of it Council- or court-related. In the court stories this week are hints at the numbers of Shetlanders whose roots lie elsewhere in Scotland. This week, a Falkirk man is fined for shouting obscene threats down the phone and a Fraserburgh man denies assaulting a woman. But the award for Recidivist Of The Week is claimed by a Shetlander who, despite being only twenty-six years old, has already been banned from driving four times — and was recently arrested on a fifth charge of driving while banned. The defendant, current residence listed as 'prisoner in Aberdeen', was pulled over by the police in his home village, after a fellow-local reported him.

Another story rates unemployment at the astonishingly low level of 1.7%, with only 229 people in the whole of Shetland unemployed; this might well explain Shetland's attraction to people from Falkirk and Fraserburgh.

Over the top of the Times, I see three middle-aged men who, from the contents of two plastic bags proceed to make a table of a box-like structure that overlooks the entrance to the small boat harbour. From one bag, they pull a bottle of wine, a corkscrew and three gleaming long-stemmed glasses, still in their boxes. From the other emerges steaming portions of fish and chips. At this point, if from their trouser pockets they were to produce high-backed chairs and silver service cutlery, I would not be in the least surprised.

They are from an oil industry vessel that is tied up metres away across the narrow harbour mouth. The three of them have been calling into Lerwick for nearly thirty years, and the pierhead wine and dine ritual has become an ironclad tradition savoured on every visit

— rain, shine, or whatever else the northern climate throws their way. The last time they were in town, they occupied the bench I just sat on, and consumed their treats as they sheltered from snow blown horizontal by gusting winds. Today, shore leave extends only while skippers change over; time enough for the ritual fish supper washed down with a satisfying New World Chardonnay — and maybe a couple of quick pints before re-boarding and setting out for another few weeks of twelve-hour shifts inspecting pipelines at the bottom of the North Sea.

On the opposite side of Commercial Street from the shore, dauntingly steep cobbled lanes, or closes, take foot traffic from the waterfront up to the prosperous area of town known as Hillhead. Laid out in the late 19th Century in the showy manner of Victorian planners to the well-heeled, Hillhead paints a broad-brush picture of how the moneyed trader classes once lived. Expansive north-south avenues named for figures from Norse royalty run between grand sandstone villas, with occasional, almost grudging breaks for geometric parks and extravagant houses of worship, many belonging to denominations that I have never heard of. My own favourite church building is the one with the big sign outside that says:

Closed all day Sunday

St. Ringan's was built in the 1880s, and for over a century, served Lerwick's United Free Church community. It is now one of the prettiest libraries I have ever set foot in, and boasts a superb collection of books on Shetland. The conversion to worship of the written word has been achieved with taste and imagination. Bright, cheery light streams from towering stained-glass windows, and a modern mezzanine structure where once may have perched the choir or a grand fluted organ, is now packed tight with Shetland books. In the body of the kirk, Shetlanders of all ages browse the shelves; families scatter towards reading matter of choice and bow-legged infants run snakes-and-ladder courses around adults' legs and among shelf towers. This is my kind of library, and for the next two hours I lose myself in texts devoted to Shetland through the ages.

In the evening, the waterfront exerts its magnetic pull once again, and at seven o'clock I shelter from light rain in a darkened doorway, enveloped in an aromatic vinegar cloud from a huge bag of chips. I watch teenagers pull thirty-year-old Mirror sailing dinghies out of the water and onto a floating pontoon in the inner harbour. With six months of short days looming, they squeeze every last twilight minute out of a receding autumn evening, and local knowledge and youthful detachment see them glide in from the Sound just in time to get everything wrapped up and tied down as full darkness falls and onlookers' chips start to congeal in the cold. They walk off, coiled ropes and polished oars tucked against squeaking waterproofs and grime-soiled lifejackets. It is a long time since I sailed in a dinghy, but the intervening years have done nothing to disabuse me of the conviction that it delivers easily the most exhilaration you can experience at under five miles an hour. I envy them their memories of tonight.

The dreaded shadow that is 'progress' has caught up with the first bar I wander into. Six years ago it was a working man's harbourside den with gritty nailhead-blackened wooden floors scored by workboots, high bar edges smoothed to the grain by thousands of man elbow hours and a décor clotted brown by years of nicotine fog. Today it is a refurbished glass-and-synthetic stab at modern respectability, recessed tungsten lighting and all. When I last experienced its atmosphere of macho repressed violence, it made me think of the old Glasgow gag about being searched at the door and, if you didn't have a gun or a knife, they gave you one. But I would still swap the Thule Bar of today for the old one in a moment.

Unsurprisingly, a few hundred quid's worth of glass and plastic has failed to bring about a tidal change in clientele. About twenty years ago, a family friend bought a tough pub in Central Scotland, and after gutting and renovating the Lounge Bar, he hosted an opening party with live jazz music that drew equal numbers of well-dressed invitees and bemused regulars in dungarees who drifted through from the Public Bar. My Dad was getting a drink when one local nodded at the musician holding makeshift stage in a vinyl alcove and said:

'Who the hell's that?'

My Dad, impeccable working class roots notwithstanding,

allowed pride in his own jazz credentials to surface:

'That is only Martin Taylor, one of **the** premier jazz guitarists in the world.'

The local's expression was unchanged.

'So whit the fuck's he daein' here?'

The sight of a u-shaped bar lined by men wearing blue soccer jerseys with foreign names on the back has me wondering what is going on in the newly-refreshed Thule, until I recall that Glasgow Rangers are playing a Champions League match in Milan. The rash of Rangers colours provides the instant reminder that there is nowhere in Scotland free of the cancerous social divide that is the rift between Glasgow's two big clubs, Rangers and Celtic — collectively known as the Old Firm. The last time I walked through Glasgow city centre on the night of an Old Firm encounter, the streets were a walking minefield of supporters of the winning team, chanting and bellowing, one collective maniacal drunken eye alert to passersby not smiling broadly enough. Glasgow might be the only city in the world where, for several months of the year, being set upon for *not singing* is a very real danger.

At least tonight Rangers are playing Inter Milan who, thanks to being Italian, might not be too well represented in a bar in Shetland. A quick look around confirms that there are no Inter Milan fans. Then a glance at the big TV confirms that there aren't any Inter Milan fans at the game, either. Milan are being punished for crowd trouble at an earlier fixture, and the game, played to an empty stadium, is so quiet that three thousand kilometres away in a bar in Lerwick, I can hear the players talking to each other.

Or at least I can when the big Norwegian folded against the bar next to me takes a break from moaning loudly into his beer. He emits a stream of drunk man's oratory, addressing everyone in the room but nobody in particular, sending out slurred verbal smoke signals that, the moment any bystander pays a moment's heed, will stick to him like glue. I resort to the only reciprocal tactic, the one that grants me deadpan X-ray vision, a vacant unfocussed look that never rests on another face for longer than a split second. I maintain a phizog so vacant I might as well be watching the Queen's Speech on Christmas Day. I sip at my drink and keep a vague eye on the widescreen television, and slowly pick up on what is bothering the big guy.

I recently visited Norway, so the memory of how astoundingly expensive it is to drink beer in a Norwegian bar remains painfully fresh. My neighbour, experiencing things in reverse, is surely in the middle of an evening of excess inspired by the fact that, for the price of a couple of Norwegian bar beers, here he can get hammered.

A few minutes of the match that is being so avidly followed by the fans in blue supplies a hint at what might be bothering him.

'This fokking game is fokking crrrap,' he tells his beer, often.

A barman the size of a Kodiak bear wearing a wool cap like a tea cosy with the holes sewn up scans him with a wary eye. Although only an arm's length away, he maintains a remoteness that effectively raises an impregnable barrier to correspondence that does not relate to sales of alcohol, cigarettes, or a limited selection of arterial threats posing as potato-based snacks. It is a skill unique to the bar trade, and takes a bartender of medium intelligence about twenty minutes to acquire.

'Fokking crrrap.' The heavy-jowled head swivels suddenly and catches me unawares. 'I am Norweeegian. I am from Trondheim, you know. Trondheim. My home town is fokking Rosenborg — I mean my fokking home town is Trondheim.' He takes a break to dip his head down in slow motion to meet the upward-moving glass half way. Perhaps experience has taught him not to trust the beer to find his mouth with only the assistance of his hands. I have no choice but to wait for him to get to the point, which he does as soon as he recalls the name of his beloved football team.

'Rosenborg! My team is Rosenborg, and we are playing tonight also.' He flicks a banana-sized finger at the television. 'And we must watch this fokking crrrap. Hey you, barman, why not we switch to see Rosenborg for a few minutes, instead of this crrrap?'

The Kodiak bear in the knitted cap opens his arms at the squad of Rangers jerseys hugging the bar, and with a mastery of understatement that I do not normally associate with giants in woollen caps, says:

'I don't think so.'

Drunk or not, the Norwegian knows an impasse when he sees one. In one long slurp, he drains his glass of a quantity of beer whose purchase price in Oslo would pay a house deposit in Pnomh Penh and wanders off in a gait that, despite an impressive element of randomness about it, eventually leads him outdoors.

He is correct. It is crrrap, and so, remembering that I am new in town and have research to undertake, I drain my glass and head out into the night in search of knowledge — and perhaps another beer or two.

I do not have to go far, as Captain Flint's occupies the upstairs of another old harbour front building. Downstairs is a general store-cum-bakery with an eclectic selection of tightly-packed wares that would not be out of place in a corner store in Brooklyn.

Flint's is entered by way of a ground floor corridor that dives deep within the building to a stairway that doubles back on itself so that I emerge, like a stage magician's assistant, from a broad black hole in the middle of the bar floor. Nobody seems to notice, which makes me think I might need to work on my entry. I am swallowed whole by the gloom of an interior that might, if I could see anything other than the glow of large television screens, be painted black.

There is thankfully no sign of the big Norwegian, but as my eyes adjust, I see that the whole place *is* full of football fans of yet another pair of stripes. The joys of satellite television mean that a different live game captures the attention of the crowded bar. There is not a spare seat or place at the long bar to be had, because Liverpool are playing Chelsea, and Flint's is filled with the clashing twin tones of inner London and Merseyside, many of them from a large oil industry vessel that has been tied up in Lerwick for a week.

When a space at the bar with an empty glass in front of it appears, I have to be quick. I order a drink from a barmaid wearing enough make-up to paint a canal narrowboat twice, and only then do I get the impression that I may be standing next to the only person in the entire bar who cannot care less what is going on in a packed stadium in middle England.

Lone drinker bar etiquette, so long as the guy next to you is not a Norwegian delivering a monologue to his beer glass, dictates polite nods and at least a token exchange of dialogue. I look at the guy to my left, who returns my nod and says,

'Y'ahrright?'

'Not bad,' I reply. 'Not watching the football?'

'Norra foochin' chance, pal. Foochin scousers.'

In an earlier lifetime I spent a summer in Germany pretending to be a carpenter and fooling nobody, working alongside a squad of Liverpudlians. It was long hours, stupidly dangerous work, far too much to drink between shifts — and a crash course in the Scouse dialect.

If this guy was a stick of rock candy, you could break a limb off him and find 'Liverpool' in red letters. But he hates Liverpool the football team, which can mean only one thing.

'Are you a Toffee man then?'

'Foochin roit.' (Translation: 'Well spotted sir, indeed I am.') The Toffees are Everton Football Club, also from Liverpool, and relations between the two sides could almost match Glasgow's Old Firm equivalents for enmity. All around me, Liverpudlian and Cockney accents are joshing each other with good humour, but my new neighbour has no say in the ribald exchanges, not being a supporter of either team, and certainly not wanting to be heard backing up the jibes of rival Liverpudlians.

As he tells me his name is Ken he reaches out and we shake hands, which is reminiscent of King Kong reaching out to Fay Wray. I am relieved when the handshake is gentle, because I need that hand for other things, like picking up my pint for a start. Ken is a commercial diver from the vessel in the harbour, and like every commercial diver I ever met, he chain smokes industriously. Long hours in claustrophobic decompression chambers apparently turns every diver into a hopeless nicotine addict. Lerwick is a frequent stopping off point for the support vessel, so Ken has been here many times.

'For such a small place, it's orright, like,' he says, 'Nice people, norra lorra bother with the locals.' He shrugs big shoulders at some of the fellow crewmembers. 'Mow likely t'ave bother wi' dese foochers, I tell yer.'

I ask him if he has managed to explore much of Shetland, and he shakes his head. 'I been out ter the Co-op a coupla times, but that's abbarit.' The Co-op supermarket is about a half mile away from where his boat ties up. He sees my surprise.

'I tell yer, after a few weeks on that foochin boat, all you wanner do is get foochin tanked.' He finishes his pint and waves to the bar staff for more tanking fluid.

Only when I am most of the way up the cruelly steep hill to my Bed & Breakfast does it occur to me that I have been on Shetland soil for a full day, and apart from a couple of staff at the Tourist Information Centre and a teenager working in a chip shop, I have yet to talk more than five words to a native Shetlander. A mental note is made to fix that tomorrow.

IV: Hitch-hiking revisited

I stand at the front end of a lay-by on the outskirts of Lerwick and keep a watchful, even bashful eye on the sparse traffic heading north out of town.

What now feels a very long time ago, hitch-hiking used to be my main mode of long distance transport. In 1978 I thumbed my way from Glasgow to a Yugoslavia still held in one shaky piece by the ageing Tito; I went on to hitch back and forth across Europe multiple times, and later navigated large parts of Malaysia, Australia, New Zealand and Japan in the same way. Getting out of town was always the hardest part of any journey, yet somehow I managed to depart, among many others, Brussels, Luxembourg, Munich, Zagreb, Monaco, Kuala Lumpur, Tokyo and two different Perths — one each in Scotland and Australia.

But I last played the hitch-hiking game during the who-cares indifference of my mid-twenties, so at first I am painfully self-conscious, especially when vans full of working lads respond with mocking grins and thumbs-ups over the traditional dashboard detritus of bashed Coke cans, crumpled cigarette packs and faded tabloids.

Thirty minutes and about a third of all Shetlanders pass by before a minibus stops outside the lay-by, blocking the traffic. A friendly face half obscured by a walrus moustache looks out at me, but says nothing.

'I'm going to Walls, are you going that way?'

'No,' he says.

'No?'

'Going north.' He is apparently a man of few words — but I am not about to let him get away. He can free me from a spot where prospects of a lift are grim, and take me a few kilometres to somewhere else. Anywhere else. I hustle self and backpack aboard while a small traffic jam gathers behind him in a state of graceful calm that is alien to city dwellers like me.

I am only with him for a few minutes, and when he does talk it is in a Shetland accent so dense that, no matter how hard I try, I am fortunate when I catch even one or two words.

He drops me at the turn-off to west Mainland and before departing, some noises that I take for kind words of encouragement fight their way through the moustache and I thank him and park myself under the road sign that says 'Walls 19'. Nineteen miles. About thirty kilometres. I may be hitch-hiking for the first time in over twenty years, but at least this time, if no lifts materialise, I could just about walk to my destination.

I am under the Walls 19 sign for a few minutes before a car stops; the driver is only going over the next hill — three kilometres at most — but it is in the right direction, so I happily hop aboard for a couple of minutes until he drops me at a tiny side road just as a bus pulls up behind us. It takes me a while to wrestle bag from back seat, and to find the bus still sitting there, the driver not about to leave until he is certain that his services are not required. Where I come from, bus drivers routinely refuse to stop for anything less than a body in the road, and here a bus driver is waiting for *me*. A wave and a hitch-hiking gesture inspires either a warm smile or an acknowledgement of my madness.

First time visitors to Shetland are invariably struck by its almost total absence of trees, but unlike the Scottish mainland, here there is no relief from the treelessness, not even the partial consolation of hills contoured by massed ranks of commercially-farmed pines or firs. Yet it is surprising just how quickly my outsiders' eyes adjust to what is initially written off as barren topography, an ease that surely has something to do with Shetland having been this way for well over a thousand years.

Scientific pollen studies indicate that, around 3000 B.C., Shetland was covered in dense woodlands of willow, alder, birch, hazel, rowan and aspen. The beginning of the end of all this was marked by the arrival of Neolithic man, and for ensuing millennia the woodlands suffered an incessant onslaught from Neolithic and Bronze Age settlers in constant need of wood for heat and cooking, and land for the grazing of animals. By the time the Vikings arrived in the 9th

Century A.D., only isolated pockets of woodland remained, and they did not last long.

Another key element in the several-millennia-long equation was climate change that brought about the formation of dense peat coverage throughout the islands, its acidic soil unsuited to growth of anything taller or less hardy than heather. Nor does the tree-unfriendly tale stop there, as widespread sheep farming over recent centuries has seen huge areas of the islands close-cropped relentlessly by livestock. Even if seedlings are painstakingly protected from sheep, they have a hard time surviving high winds laden with suffocating levels of salt. Seventeen percent of the Scottish mainland is covered with trees. In Shetland, tree coverage is so thin as to be statistically negligible.

Despite all of this, the scenery around me looks *so* natural. After more than twelve centuries, Shetland has grown into the treeless look, a bit like how your Grandma grows into a new hairdo.

Stretching towards misty horizons in every direction are stark bare hillslopes that tumble towards coastal shorelines. The hillsides are interleaved with slender fingers of gleaming water, Shetland's 'voes', or ribbons of ocean inlets that sometimes slice into the landscape from opposite directions to points where their inland extremities almost touch.

When Ice Age glaciers melted about ten thousand years ago, sea levels rose sharply and inundated hundreds of Shetland river valleys, creating fresh new coastlines high up on what before were hillsides. Where coastal farms and hamlets now overlook sea-water voes were once high slopes looking down over river valleys.

In hitch-hiking terms, I am on a roll. When a lady in a small car stops, I am hardly in the front seat before she sets off at the pace of a rally racer. She quizzes me about my visit, and within minutes volunteers the names and telephone numbers of people she thinks I ought to talk to, including her own Mum.

She drops me about eight kilometres along the road in a hamlet of four or five buildings, where again my luck holds. Inside two minutes I am not only back in a vehicle, but I am on first-name terms with the driver. He is the engineer I had a drink with on the ferry from Aberdeen, the one with the maggot stories I have been trying to forget ever since. He soon deposits me at the cut-off for Walls in the wilds of west Mainland, with hardly a house in sight and for company only a few free-ranging sheep, mouths hung low over gravelly roadsides, scouring the terrain for nourishment like vacuum cleaners hoovering up dust.

A sign says Walls is now only two miles away, and I consider walking for just long enough to allow a white van to pull up before I even get my thumb out. Three minutes later I am at my destination, and feeling good about the weeks ahead.

V: Two-time sooth-moothers

By far the biggest community in west Mainland, Walls is a light dusting of houses spread across a coastal landscape where twin North Atlantic voes curve around the island of Vaila. Walls is said to be a corruption of the Norse *vaas*, meaning 'the place of voes', a thesis supported at least in part by local pronunciation. To say Walls to rhyme with 'falls' is to mark yourself as an outsider barely off the bus, or not, in my case. Around here, the word is pronounced — and even sometimes written — Waas, with a hard 's'.

Deep-reaching inner voes make for a natural harbour that is a haven from the wilds of the Atlantic, only a couple of kilometres away on the other side of Vaila.

With the kind help of Shetland Amenity Trust, I have arranged to stay at a camping böd, sort of an unmanned, bare-bones youth hostel, but without the crotchety poly-lingual warden or the American teenagers strumming mistuned guitars and murdering Amazing Grace through dauntingly-white teeth.

The böd (from Old Norse for booth, or tent) is a restored village house with a dozen or more neat pine bunks and a basic kitchen area. By basic I mean it has a sink and a long table with benches and nothing more. The whole building is mine — there is evidently not a lot of budget tourism in west Mainland in late September — so the only thing to be done is to spread out like I own the place. In a kitchen as conveniently chilled as the inside of the refrigerator that it lacks, I fashion a late lunch of pasta and tinned fish, then don waterproofs and binoculars and head out on foot.

Between the böd and the water sits a neat church with an

adjoining graveyard that, like the one in Lerwick, has a large extra space laid out as if in preparation for an upward surge in the death curve. The graveyard is so perfectly tidy that to sully it with my boots would be unseemly, so I browse a few headstones from the other side of the stone wall; a distressing number of the recently interred have passed away in early adulthood, including a young fisherman 'lost at sea off Vaila', almost exactly a decade ago. During the Press trip to Shetland a few years ago, we visitors were bussed to the rather fine Burrastow House Hotel a few kilometres past Walls, where we dined luxuriously at a long table in an even longer conservatory. After coffee, desserts, cognacs and the last of vast reserves of fine wine, the hotelier surprised us with a midnight boat ride around Vaila Island. It was mid-summer, so we savoured a twilight dream voyage on seas barely stirred by a warm June breeze. I recall the journey with vivid alcohol-embellished pleasure, but a few years on, it sobers me to think that the same waters claim lives and wreck families.

Across the narrow voe is a commercial marina, filled with the sea-going equivalent of pick-up trucks, sturdy aluminium work boats moored bow-first against a floating pier. A few hundred metres in the other direction is a stout jetty with one fishing boat tied to it. Beyond that, a muscley-looking workhorse with stout metal containers strapped to its foredeck pushes a fat wake ahead as it slips in from the open Atlantic. This may be the ferry from Foula Island, one of the most remote communities in Europe, twenty-five kilometres out in the North Atlantic. Foula is high on my destination wishlist, but I have been told that atrocious weather has prevented the ferry from even leaving the island for the last couple of weeks.

A woman emerges from a nearby house and casually throws a rubber ball along the road. A canine dervish flashes from the gate behind her and chases the ball down in a matter of seconds. Its owner asks if I am staying at the camping böd, which makes me wonder if perhaps the smell of tinned fish has given me away. By now the four-legged thing is trying to tempt me with a ball soaked in dog slaver, but only at my third attempt to dislodge it from his foaming mouth does the cunning creature feign defeat. I feint a hard throw, and he gives me a look that says 'D'you think I've never had that trick played on me before?', then fires himself rocket-like after the flying ball almost before I think of throwing it. He is back again inside three seconds. We repeat the ritual, and again the mutt is back before I finish furtively wiping its spit from my hand. The fun-loving little devil could do this for hours, and the limits of my dog-loving masquerade are exhausted. While I talk to his owner, he pogos around me like a saliva-flecked Brillo pad.

The nice lady indulges him with a knowing shake of the head and confirms that the boat tying up at the pier is indeed the Foula ferry.

As I walk towards it, the New Advance has bulky metal containers lifted from its decks with a crane. Piled high onshore, boxed supplies with names written in black marker await loading; I notice that the same names keep cropping up, which is hardly surprising since there are fewer than three dozen people on Foula. I ask the crane operator who the skipper is, and he points me to the man with the trim grey beard, who shakes my hand and introduces himself as Willie Tulloch, an Orkneyman serving as relief skipper. He apologises for the chaos, confirms that this is the first time the ferry has made it to Mainland in two full weeks, and says that even today, I 'wouldna hae enjoyed the trip too much.'

He tells me that the forecast does not look good for sailings in the next few days but promises to call me on my mobile if things change. As an afterthought, he asks where I will be staying on Foula, and when I mention the possibility of camping, his crewman snorts and says,

'I've seen many a tent torn to pieces on Foula.'

They assure me that a crofthouse Bed and Breakfast is the only sensible option, and Willie supplies the phone number of a lady proprietor. I walk away feeling as if, without setting foot on the island, I have already met the welcoming committee.

A community as spread out as Walls needs a focal point, a role assumed by a combination shop/post office/petrol station, an Aladdin's cave of consumerism with everything from magazines and soap powder and mooring rope and candles and canned goods to a selection of wines from as far away as Chile. It is run by Kevin Smith and his wife, two-time sooth-moothers enjoying their second spell in Shetland, and who come from Colchester in Essex, or almost as far from Shetland as you can get without departing Britain's shores. Today is the first anniversary of the day they took over the shop. I wonder aloud what made them twice swap life on the outer edge of the London commuter belt for life on the outer edge of civilisation, and Kevin laughs.

'We love it up here. The lifestyle, the people, everything about it. And the schools are great.' He is plainly convinced, and who am I to argue with a man who loved Shetland so much that he moved here with his entire family, twice.

Darkness arrives early in October at sixty degrees north, and the little community shrinks into itself. The last bus to Lerwick departs at around six o'clock, the shop closes for the night, and the absence of a pub or anywhere else to rub shoulders hangs heavy on this committed town-dweller. I spend a solitary evening toying with more pasta, reading a truly awful best-seller that some well-meaning swine left on the böd mantlepiece, and listening to a BBC radio broadcast that emanates from London but might as well be from another planet. When I switch off the radio, the böd offers up silence so complete I can almost reach out and touch it.

I awake early wishing for silence, but instead lie cocooned in my sleeping bag listening to what sounds like shovels-full of gravel crackling against the böd windows. At eleven o'clock I am still indoors. Outside, rain is not so much falling as flying like shrapnel clouds driven by a southerly gale. The voe is empty, the roads are deserted and there is not a pedestrian in sight. And to think that I came here to meet people.

Shortly after lunch the rain slackens, albeit almost imperceptibly, so I wrap myself in waterproofs and walk through the village and out towards the western headland. I stroll a weaving bitumen trail that reaches out towards farmsteads on a hillside overlooking Vaila, and that soon leaves most of the buildings behind. Homes become spread out until they are hundreds of metres apart, and the landscape looks like the pictures in an amateur photography magazine feature where an effects filter washes the scene with incongruous tones that go together like blue trousers and brown shoes. The sky is the monochromatic grey-black of rain clouds waiting for the perfect moment to open up on me, and the west Mainland hillsides are streaked a hundred shades of yellow-green. Amidst it all is the primary colour intrusion of an old-fashioned red telephone box, and in front of its leaden door, stepping stones rattle in a fast-moving stream of run-off that scythes through mud and grass.

There is not a soul in sight, but everywhere I look, animal life busily munches at plant life, and I speculate upon the possibility of an obscure caste system being inflicted on west Mainland sheep. Some are cooped up in tidy fenced fields, yet others are free to roam the road in search of sustenance. One field's occupants are of every colour imaginable; paper-white, off-white, yellow-white, desert brown, tan brown, muddy brown, muddier brown, dark brown, black brown and plain black. Like a UN Congress meeting breaking up and heading for the bar, they cut a neat procession across the green of the field. I wait for a welly-booted farmer or an attentive sheep dog to crest the hill behind them, but there is none.

Most of the fields have modern fencing, but others are marked out by stone walls with the look of centuries past. Dotted around them are odd stone enclosures, many of them well-crafted drystone circles about a metre tall and no more than two metres in diameter. Intact examples show that they used to form complete circles, unbroken enclosures without gates. Nearby, much larger enclosed pens are rectangular in form. A logical explanation for them eludes me, so when a farm truck laden with straw bales lumbers my way, I take a chance and wave it down. Inside sit two wind-whipped faces popped from near-identical genetic moulds, but a generation apart. Being hauled to a stop on their own narrow roadway by a Gore-Tex-encased tourist does not faze them one bit, and the elder farmer is happy to tell me that the enclosures are 'planti crubs', or plant circles, in which farmers once grew kale feedstock for their animals. The planti crub walls kept the animals out and provided shelter from the elements. He tells me that farmers used to drape nets over the tops of the crubs, supposedly to protect the plants from frost. The roll of his eyes tells me he thinks his ancestors were a few bales short of a haystack. He explains that the bigger enclosures were part of the same process, and are called planti yards. Seedlings were raised in the crubs and re-planted in the yards. Many of the enclosures are several hundred years old, and have long fallen out of use.

I hike on through sheep country, and take advantage of hard-won elevation to look out over ocean bands that wrap around Vaila like fat fingers bejewelled with the neat patterns of floating aquaculture works. Fish and mussel farming are big employers in Shetland's pristine waters, and evidence of their importance to west Mainland bobs throughout the voes. At one fish farm, a rust-bubbled barge that might have started out life on the Rhine serves as a floating shed; at another, the workplace is a down-at-heel cargo ship; at a third, an honest-to-goodness warehouse lords over a custom-built pontoon so vast that it might command its own postcode. Like all the other farms, it is deathly quiet, like a western movie set left to desiccate in the Nevada desert, except these are in the North Atlantic and the rain is coming down in sheets.

Not that the rain seems to bother one villager I see on the way back to the böd. Without breaking rhythm, he waves to me with one hand while with the other he uses a long powerbrush to wash the slab sides of a forty-seater coach.

As I approach the böd, the low-lying sun peels back cloud cover to suffuse the terrain with a warm glow. Landscape photographers and artists flock to Shetland from as far away as the Mediterranean to sample this magical light. Looking out over gleaming specular waters and polished shores washed by the luminous warmth of a low northern sun, the attraction is palpable.

I continue past the böd, choose between two bold road signs that point to places I have not seen on any map, and walk for ten minutes to what turns out to be a private home. The road ends there, and in the distance lurks Burrastow House Hotel and yet another view over the Isle of Vaila.

The fields here are marshy, heavy with run-off, and striped by herringbone indentations, complete with a spinal line that runs directly from the terrain's high point to its lowest edge. The opposite of irrigation channels, these ditches are to allow water to run *off* the land and towards the sea. A tightly packed single file sheep procession navigates its way across one set of ditches; like a thick woolly rope being flicked from the far end of the line, a bump in the convoy runs along its length as each animal, in turn, takes to the air over the waterlogged ditch.

PAPA STOUR

I: Stone sentinels

Before I can even set out to visit the first outlying island of my trip, I have to make some telephone calls.

The importance of roles played by Shetland's inter-island ferry skippers is demonstrated by how local ferry schedules include their home numbers, and my first call is to the captain of the ferry to Papa Stour, who puts me down for tomorrow's 9 a.m. trip. Next, I speak to a Walls taxi man whose number I get from shopkeeper/postmaster Kevin Smith. The ferry to Papa Stour leaves from remote West Burrafirth, more than sixteen kilometres from Walls, and west Mainland's sparse resident head count means that, a mere two days into my adventure, I have to forget about hitch-hiking. The taxi man promises to pick me up at eight o'clock.

My third call is to a farmer on Papa Stour whose travellers' hostel is the island's only visitor accommodation. I use the telephone box outside the Walls shop, and on the fourth or fifth ring my call is answered:

'Mr Strickland here.'

This strikes me as rather proper, coming from a sheep farmer on an island with fewer than twenty full-time inhabitants, but it is only much later that I learn exactly *why* his telephone manner is so stiff. Mr Strickland confirms, in clipped middle-England tones, that I will be welcome at the hostel, that he will pick me up from the ferry pier, and to look out for a red pick-up with a silver back.

When Pat the taxi driver's MPV pulls up the next morning fifteen minutes late, I try not to fret too much, since after forty years in the west Mainland transportation business, it could be that Pat has a decent idea of how long it will take us to get to West Burrafirth. He is the chap who waved to me yesterday while washing his coach in the rain; he provides bus services to and from schools in Lerwick, and drives his private hire taxi at other times. Today, in order to help me fulfill my rendezvous with the Papa Stour ferry, his wife will do the morning bus run.

Five minutes into the journey, we take to a thin tarmac strip like a metallic grey ribbon thrown over the dark side of the Moon. Mainland is an island at most lightly populated, but Aithsting district's paucity of inhabitants is almost complete. We roll through countryside with minor tonal shifts from rusty tussocks to grey-black moorland to blue-brown peat lands occasionally broken up by eruptions of cloudy grey granite, and by a horizon-swallowing multitude of miniature lochs and tinier lochans carved by passing glacier traffic of distant eons. Freshwater dimples mirror a muted sky that stifles the terrain like an old army blanket. This is lonely country in an underpopulated land. For the duration of the trip, the only movement is in the wind-lashed clouds scudding across the horizon. Not a living soul is in view, and I no longer feel quite so bad about not hitch-hiking.

West Burrafirth is the name attached to two neighbouring west Mainland locations, neither of which seems all that much in need of a name. One is a rocky headland pointing north towards the uninhabited island of Vementry; the other is the port that hosts the impressive modern ferry that serves the historic island of Papa Stour.

To call this dot on the map a port is to afford it a sense of station at odds with what unfolds as we drift down the gentle hill to the coast. Four or five homes are well spaced around the innermost reaches of Burra Firth. From their midst extends a two-pronged concrete pier that glares from the gloom like Grandad's new false teeth adrift beneath the sofa. West Burrafirth has no shop, no pub, no community hall, and neither doctor's surgery nor medical clinic. There is, however, yet another red telephone box. Mobile telephone signals get patchy this far from Shetland's idea of urban civilisation.

At the smaller of the piers, a handful of tiny fishing craft rock unattended, and at the other, the bulky bright roll-on, roll-off ferry boat is the sole focus of human activity. Pat smiles at the look of surprise on my face; Papa Stour, population about twenty, has under three kilometres of paved roads. Its shiny ferry *Snolda* — from the old Norse for 'pinnacle' and named for Snolda Stack off the west coast of the island — can surely carry more vehicles than exist on the whole of Papa Stour.

The *Snolda* noses out through the firth, gathering speed gradually while alongside us the firth's southern coastline jumps from flat enough to host the occasional waterside residence to stark cliff faces that are home only to avian life of a toughness that can eke out an existence from tiny wind-thrashed ledges high above the Atlantic.

Papa Stour's name comes from old Norse, means 'the big island of priests', and is thought to derive from Celtic missionaries who lived there as far back as the 6th Century. Fifteen hundred years ago what constituted 'big' may well have differed from today, because as well as being low-lying, the island is only three kilometres across. Yet its coastline is so deeply indented with multiple voes and 'geos', deep clefts in the clifflines brought about by the brutal forces of sea erosion, that it is over thirty-four kilometres long.

Throughout the forty-minute crossing, the island occupies almost the whole western horizon while the *Snolda's* rumbling diesels work hard to counter fierce tides that rush the strait between Mainland and Papa Stour. It is hard to believe that, not so long ago, men routinely faced these frightening waters in flimsy oar-powered wooden *yoals*.

We bear north and keep a respectful distance from a variety of rock formations that stand off the island. Some are no more than wave-lashed reefs, others are miniature steep-sided islands, and yet more are stone pinnacles standing high in ever-moving waters. Academics with nothing better to do dispute the veracity of claims that the Saharan Tuareg have multiple distinct terms for different types of sand, but coming from a nation whose local dialects overflow with descriptive terms for rain, I am a believer. Shetland, with its nearly fifteen hundred kilometres of often fearsome coastline and several thousand years of maritime heritage, boasts a diversity of names for rocks sticking out of the sea, and even a simple map of Papa Stour fronts up an intriguing selection.

Brei Holm is almost big enough to qualify as a small island of its own; less poetic-sounding are Lambar Banks, coastal platforms that, like most of the rock features in the area, go back to the Devonian geological period, between 360 and 400 million years ago. Back then Shetland lay near the equator, on the edge of a broad depression called the Orcadian Basin, and was host to giant lakes that expanded and contracted according to the climate of the time. Fossilised remains of ancient fish life lie today where lakes receded 400 hundred million years ago, and for that reason, Lambar Banks is strictly protected.

Red Stacks, rough-edged stone sentinels at the entrance to sheltered Housa Voe, are further evidence of when the Earth's crust was cast summarily upwards by the clashing plates of the Continental Drift, as is Maiden Stack, which takes its name from history of a more recent nature, real or imagined.

After the Vikings took over Shetland in the 9th Century, the islands belonged to the 'Lairds of Norway' (actually the Danish royal family) for about six hundred years until they were returned to Scotland as part of a defaulted royal wedding dowry in 1469. But the returns did not include Papa Stour, which remained under Scandinavian control well into the 17th Century.

Also known as Frau Stack, Maiden Stack — which still has the low remains of walls perched on its top — was supposedly the place of imprisonment of a Norwegian nobleman's daughter. In a tale to match Snow White for both implausibility and cloying sentimentality, the fair maiden was put there not only because she refused to marry the Norse beau of her Daddy's selection, but because she even had the temerity to fall in love with a local peasant fisherman. Sentimentalists will be warmed to learn that legend declares she was rescued from her cruel place of exile by her daring young suitor, with whom she escaped and of course lived happily ever after. Given the typical life spans of Shetlanders five or more centuries ago, this might have been another couple of years.

Bruce Jamieson is the second-in-command of the *Snolda*. A seaman for nearly forty-five years — since a few weeks before he turned fourteen — his solid frame more than fills his blue Shetland Islands Council overalls, and a bushy salt-and-chilli-pepper beard nurtures an ever-present smile. He patiently explains to the landlubber why the *Snolda* is taking such a w-i-d-e line around all the rock formations at the south mouth of Housa Voe. We are heading roughly north-west, and looking out to our left until a powerful lamp at the inner end of the voe, with an industrial-strength lens to focus its beam along a precise line, turns from red to pinkish-red; only then does the skipper swing the boat around to the south-west until the beam sits dead ahead and unblemished white in colour. On either side of the safe course, one of two colours becomes visible: a green beam means you are pointed left of your target, and a red one that you are pointed to the right of where you want to be. Only while the beam remains white, is it safe to head directly for the lamp.

'It's not such a big issue in the daylight,' says Bruce, 'But try to sail in here at night, and it's a different matter altogether, with low-lying land all around that is invisible in the dark.'

Another reason for the lamp is yet one more rock feature, the most feared of all. A *'baa'* is a submerged slab of pitiless geology that hunkers just below the water's surface. Out beyond the mouth of Housa Voe sit Housa's Baas, which lurk out of sight except when extreme weather comes in from the north-west and breaks over them. At any time and under any conditions, they are capable of doing mortal damage to any craft.

So we round the holm and savour the stacks and afford the baas maximum respect before we slip into the inner calm of the same protected Housa Voe that drew the priests here fifteen hundred years ago and set course for the concrete pier. From the vantage point of the ferry, I can pick out no more than a half-dozen homes, including one that looks better-suited to a London suburb than to a wild North Atlantic island, a bright white modern home that sits with an unbroken view of the voe and all beyond. The few other houses in view are more utilitarian and more suited to their environment, with natural stone colours and low roof designs.

II: To Kirstan's holl and back

The one car waiting at the pier is a red pick-up with a silver back. Leaning against it is a very tall man with a beard so dark and all-enveloping that only from straight in front is it even possible to see

the glint of sharp intelligent eyes. I shake hands with Mr Strickland
— who says I can call him Martin now — and we set off on the few
hundred metres to Hurdiback, his farm-cum-backpacker hostel. We
hardly leave the pier behind before another car comes the other way
on a road that is only wide enough for one of us. It stops and waits
until Martin backs around a corner to a point where the track widens,
then drives past without its driver offering even a glance in Martin's
direction. Stories abound about Papa Stour's modern community
troubles, and perhaps I have just seen evidence of it.

A proud element of Papa Stour's history is the undisputed
provenance of the earliest extant Shetland document, one that with
the unfair benefit of seven hundred years of hindsight sits like an
ominous portent over relations in the community. It was written in
1299, and remains in fine, legible condition in the Arnamagnaen
Institute in Copenhagen.

Its subject was a dispute between a local woman, Ragnhild
Simunsdatter, and Thorvald Thoresson, the Shetland Governor at the
time. The document records a bitter confrontation that took place in
the *stofa*, or best room of the farm belonging to Duke Hakon
Mangusson, who later rose to the throne as King Hakon V of Norway.
It relates how Ragnhild accused Thorvald of being a 'Judas' to Duke
Hakon. This allegation of corruption against a man who held the
important role of 'sysselmann', or Royal official responsible for
gathering revenues due to the Crown in Norway, was all the more
significant for having been made at a Royal farm, hence its careful
recording in the document of 1299. (Later, Thorvald's statement of
rebuttal was ratified by the Shetland *Lawting*, or parliament, at
Tingwall. Any ordinary soul who has ever lodged a claim against
persons in positions of authority will understand how *that* works).

Martin pulls into a rain-spattered farm yard guarded by a noisy
black mongrel that does its powerful best to dislodge the fence post it
is chained to. Thankfully the post holds, and Martin shows me to the
spacious traveller's hostel with its glorious outlook towards Maiden
Stack. The narrow strip of yard in front of the building is thick with
ducks and geese — and even thicker with their slick waste. I remove
my boots before setting stockinged feet indoors, lest I sully the
spotless interior with a cocktail of avian droppings. Outside,
barbecue-charcoal clouds tumble into the voe and lumber ashore,

dumping their contents as they go. From the hostel window I watch the entire sky blacken and emit powerful raindrops that plummet like incendiary devices and throw up explosive spatters of bird waste. This might be a good time to put the kettle on.

It takes a couple of hours before the storm packs up and leaves just as rapidly as it arrived. A new set of cotton wool clouds graces skies of a deep blue that reflects off the ocean and renders the world a better place, while the fields in front of Hurdiback acquire a lush freshness entirely out of kilter with either time of year or latitude.

Caution prevails and I pull on the full protective rain gear, but once I get outdoors, it remains redundant for at least a couple of minutes.

I am no more than two hundred metres from Hurdiback when yet another rapid reversal of light and shade and cloud and colour swamps the landscape, and soon after the rain commences, the only guide to the island I have, a tiny tourist map, disintegrates between my fingers. I depart the island's only road, let myself through a modern alloy farm gate, and trek west through rain as potent as any deluxe hotel power shower. I decide to do a few minutes' token exploration before I will surely retreat to a kettle still warm from the last coffee I rustled up while hiding from the weather.

On the approach towards the uninhabited western half of the island, a complex voe opens up to my right, reaching in to a stony beach marked with driftwood and omnipresent glowing plastic debris that will likely still be there in a few million years when the rocks have eroded to dust. Despite pointing almost due north, the voe is called West Voe, possibly because it lies west of where most Papa Stour islanders have lived over the centuries.

Man divided the island into two distinct sections more than seven hundred years ago. Some of the most fertile grazing and cropland in all of Shetland, Papa Stour's 'in-bye' land, lies on the eastern third of the island, facing the island's most sheltered port in Housa Voe; it is isolated from the western part of the island by a man-made 'hill dyke' or turf barrier that runs north-south from West Voe to Gorsendi Geo — from the Old Norse *garōsendi*, or 'the end of a dyke'. The dyke in place today dates from the mid-19th Century, but it is thought that a dyke existed here to protect farms such as Martin Strickland's

Hurdiback as far back as medieval times, as documents (not least the one of 1299) firmly suggest these farms were well established by the turn of the 14th Century.

West of the dyke, the terrain morphs abruptly from green and fertile to virtually barren and strewn with loose rock cover. Centuries of turf being peeled from the western part of the island to feed livestock and heat homes in the eastern sector ended in the mid-1800s with the western area stripped bare of topsoil.

The abundance of rocks west of the dyke is not all down to turf stripping. The field of rain-washed boulders that threatens my ankles is classic glacial moraine topography, a terrain peppered with the geological detritus of Ice Age glaciers that streamed over here more than ten thousand years ago.

Apart from boulders, the terrain is so topographically indistinct that the incessant downpour that I walk through, once it hits land, need not take even the most basic of twists or turns. Water drains from the landscape in thin unbroken sheets that wash over entire hillsides. With the sheen of water curling around the edges of my boots, I push on.

My trail turns south-west until soon it overlooks Hamna Voe, a far-reaching inlet that swells from a narrow opening to a rounded rocky-shored inner bay that is as calm as a lake, never mind that only a few hundred metres away, the North Atlantic rages unabated.

Temptingly accessible to vessels on the run from heavy Atlantic seas, and because its south-west-facing aspect and the expanse of its inner calm provides sanctuary to storm fronts from most points of the compass, Hamna Voe has long been sought out as a protective bolt hole from severe storms.

But its offer of protection comes at a dreadful price. Vessels seeking refuge in the inner calm of the voe must first survive not one, but two deadly obstacles. The first, a horrid skerry offset slightly north of the voe mouth, is relatively easy to avoid, so long as visibility permits, which itself is anything but certain in these waters. The real danger awaits further within the voe, where a low-lying set of rocks called Tiptan's Skerry has over the centuries been the ruination of vessels from Holland, France, Germany and Norway.

As if the elements alone were not enough to contend with, at times there was yet another source of peril, this one man-made. Beyond the mouth of the voe is 'Johnnie Wearie's Holl', a name with a sinister story behind it. One night in the 1780s, when ships of the hated Royal Navy Press Gang were known to be scouring Shetland for new recruits, islanders spotted a vessel struggling in heavy weather, and using lanterns, lured her directly onto coastal rocks. She struck an offshore obstacle called Mid Baa and was thrown onto the coast at Kalsgio Tang, killing all aboard. Islanders scouring the wreckage for salvage prizes were in for a shock: instead of the expected Press Gang cutter, they discovered a Dutch Brig. On one of the bodies they found papers that indicated he was the ship's captain, named Jan Weerij. To this day, the cove where his broken body lay is known as Johnnie Wearie's Holl.

I sit on the broad, heavily-pebbled shoreline at the deepest inland point in Hamna Voe and cast my binoculars towards Tiptan's Skerry and beyond.

Outside the jaws of the voe, a low-lying island blocks giant swells roaring in from the west. Swarta Skerry is formed of pinkish rock, but endures such a beating from Atlantic breakers that from where I sit it takes on a black outline that is haloed by afternoon backlighting. The waves grow in intensity, and every few minutes the halo turns to an inundation as tons of aerated water streams over the top of the skerry and into the voe, where its forces gradually subside until eventually they reach the inner shore at my feet as wide-spaced ripples in the cold blue-black bay.

Bobbing comfortably among the swells is the giant head of a seal, watching me intently. It lies on its back like a fat bloke lounging in a hot pool at the sauna, and has facial features like a very large dog, and which make it a common or harbour seal. Through the binoculars I watch it languidly roll over, dip beneath the surface momentarily, and emerge with a sizeable fish flapping helplessly in its powerful jaws. The fish disappears down the seal's throat as quickly as it is plucked from the sea, and I scan the bay and find three more seals casually scouring the bay for dinner.

Around the voe's inner edges are multiple signs of days long gone when Papa Stour's population was nearly twenty times what it is today. When the turf from beyond the hill dyke ran out in the 1870s, island inhabitants dropped from over 350 to about 250 in only ten years. Nowadays, the only habitations are east of the hill dyke, but here, the flat land on three sides of Hamna Voe is marked by the remains of dwellings and the remnants of whaling station buildings long-ago stripped of every last scrap of precious wood.

There is an oft-quoted line that says an Orcadian — someone from Orkney — is a farmer with a boat, but a Shetlander is a fisherman with a croft, and it is true that the Atlantic has been the true lifeblood of Shetland for centuries. In the late 1800s, every able-bodied man on Papa Stour worked 'the *Haaf*', a summer season of long-line fishing conducted from flimsy open boats.

'*Sixareens*' were clinker-built of wood and up to about nine metres long, with no shelter or superstructure, powered only occasionally by a rudimentary square-rigged sail and most of the time by six strong men hauling heavy oars. Designed for offshore conditions, *sixareens* worked wild waters up to sixty-five kilometres from land for days at a time, with their crews of six or seven men baiting and setting and reeling in eleven-kilometre-long lines of barbed hooks entirely by hand.

The *Haaf* was not only brutal in practice, it was an act of survival borne of men who often found themselves in eternal debt. Local landowners, alert to the seasonal nature of farming and fishing income, set up their estates in a way that saw tenants fall into inescapable debt cycles. Lairds owned the boats and the fishing equipment and the shop that sold the farmer/fisherman everything his family needed to feed his family. They took payment for homes and farmlands in kind, according to terms that often saw tenants unable to eat much of what they grew. The same bosses owned the fish curing businesses vital to the processing of the catch.

Deaths among the *Haaf* fishermen were commonplace, and in the unforgiving role as 'company bosses', landowners were sometimes known to exact payment for lost tackle and wrecked boats from the widows of fishermen lost at sea.

Theirs was a business model that certainly allowed thousands of Shetlanders the means to feed their families, but it was also one without much room for sentimentality; little wonder that today it is hard to find a Shetlander with a kind word for the Lairds of old.

Resident numbers on Papa Stour received a temporary boost when a Mainland-owned herring curing station opened in 1885, but by then the writing was on the wall for the once bustling island. Herring curing had to be done locally because *sixareens* and sailboats were too slow to get the catch to Lerwick while it was still fresh. But when steam power arrived, catch processing became centralised, outlying regions' work on the *Haaf* vanished, and Papa's population plummeted.

By the 1930s, the population had dropped to one hundred, but it reached crisis point in 1970, when inhabitants numbered only in the mid-teens. A national press campaign announced that anyone in search of an alternative lifestyle would arrive to a free house and a handful of sheep, and drew idealistic young long-hairs from all over the country, and who quickly brought with them the nickname 'Hippy Island'.

The newcomers got more and less than they bargained for. For a start, there was more isolation then they could ever have imagined. Only three-and-a-half decades ago, mains electricity and running water were distant dreams for the people of Papa Stour. A few of the more resourceful arrivals stayed on, keeping the school open and the community alive for years, but today, only two residents remain from the days of the hippy influx. The population is just under twenty, and bilious inter-factional feuds have drawn derision from British newspapers and Mainland Shetlanders alike. In an act that embodies the adage about cutting off your nose to spite your face, factionalism recently prompted one family to remove their children from the school, condemning it to closure. Things do not look good for Papa Stour.

And yet, the sense of solitude and the proximity to history stir this visitor's soul.

I wade around Hamna Voe's pebbled shoreline to the bouldered remains of a roadway that once reached out to long-gone communities on the inner edge of the bay. It is one of Shetland's 'meal roads', the archaeological legacy of a make-work scheme instituted throughout Shetland after famine followed crop failure in 1846/47. The islands, Papa Stour included, received a network of new roads, and hungry locals received a pound of barley meal for every day laboured.

Here, all that remains of the meal road's decayed skeleton are parallel lines of boulders that peter out towards the foot of Maun's Hill, and which I debate scaling in search of a viewpoint. The rain has hammered at me constantly for the last hour, and I am beginning to weary. But just as the notion of returning to warm and dry Hurdiback starts to gain appeal, the rain ceases abruptly, the sun pops from between parting clouds like a stage star at curtain call and the incessant wind tugs at moisture-beaded rainwear. I take on the barren, rock-peppered hill, and celebrate conquering all sixty metres of its elevation by adding a tiny shard of moraine rubble to the hiker's cairn at a summit so gently rounded that it is almost imperceptible.

In thirty years of seeking out viewpoints, I have never known such a modest climb to open up a vista so rewarding. Below me, Hamna Voe makes a panoramic seascape of grey-blue ripples broken shaving-foam-white over the black peril that is Tiptan's Skerry. Beyond the voe, the topography hints at the fertility of the island's farming heartland, and on the other side of that, Mainland runs dark with the rain that moments ago left me drip-drying on the hillside.

South-west, across kilometres of undulating Atlantic, the stage backdrop outline of Foula Island lurks, its mighty peaks and soaring cliff banks caressed by whispery white stratus.

Behind me, Papa Stour's cliffs are laid out in a display that makes it abundantly apparent why an island so small can have a coastline so extensive, and the pocked moraine gives way to sparse, well-cropped turf land that offers slim pickings for lean-looking sheep. I give a wide berth to the first inlet I come to, a coastal gash called Nort Lungie Geo, hemmed in on three sides by sheer cliffs. At the geo's innermost point squats a small rocky beach, and the naïve town-dweller in me is dismayed to see two sheep stranded at the foot of the cliff face. They must have fallen down the impossibly steep, heavily eroded dirt banking. I step marginally closer to the cliff edge and realise there are not a couple of stranded animals, but a dozen. I am contemplating searching for a crofter to alert to his animals' plight when the entire flock stops scouring the rocky shore and cast their glassy eyes up at me. Then, with an air of collective guilt, they trot up the 60-degree dirt slope and vault the cliff top overhang with ease.

They walk briskly in a single file so tight that it dawns on me why animal trails here are so impossibly narrow, like the tracks from a one-wheeled barrow. Could it be that centuries spent on clifftops have genetically conditioned the sheep to avoid ranging around haphazardly, like sheep?

I have come this far because no self-respecting traveller can set foot on Papa Stour without going the extra rain-soaked mile to cast an appraising eye over Kirstan's Holl. What sounds like an intimate part of the island slattern is in fact a spectacular coastal feature that, thanks to the same forces of nature that for millennia have made Papa Stour what it is today, continues to evolve. There are innumerable geos and inlets on the island where sea caves lead to subterranean channels, some of them even navigable by small craft in suitable weather conditions. Which, at Kirstan's Holl, would be any day other than today, as its inlet faces directly at the onrushing south-westerly.

Even before I see it, I can hear subterranean sucking and roaring as fat waves charge the broad inlet, turn to foam around the storm-battered stack in its middle — and fire down the underground channel beneath the cliff, to crash to a halt in the Holl itself, a formerly underground chamber whose 'roof' used to be a depression in the land that held a small lochan — and that suddenly drained into the chamber in 1981. I take no chances, and watch incoming waves batter against the end of the Holl from a point well removed from the roof of the channel that feeds it.

North of the Holl, the coastline becomes even more dramatic, with the tall cliffs whipped by foaming waves that sweep around Aesha Head and Aesha Stack. The sun has once again faded from view behind slate-grey clouds and now casts a cold blue light over sixty-metre precipices pummelled by ocean waves that have soared unhindered since they were conceived, somewhere out towards Canada. I pause near the cliff tops to take a photograph, thankful that at least the stiff onshore gale threatens only to roll me inland, and not towards the edge of the abyss. [Only weeks later do I learn just how potentially deadly this naïve assumption was. Shifting winds combined with Shetland topography can bring about completely unexpected gusts from the opposite direction of the prevailing wind; for a few minutes, perched on the cliffs of north-west Papa Stour, I was an unsuspecting lost-at-sea accident waiting to happen.]

To the north-west, I can only just make out the fire and brimstone of waves exploding over the Vee Skerries, deadly low-lying rocks that only had an unmanned lighthouse installed in 1979, following the December 1977 wreck of the 122-ton Aberdeen trawler *Elinor Viking*, and the near-miraculous rescue of its crew by a British Airways helicopter manned entirely by volunteers.

In 1930, the men aboard another Aberdeen trawler, *Ben Doran*, were not so fortunate. When the fishing boat foundered on the Vee Skerries in atrocious weather conditions, it took a lifeboat from Orkney three days just to reach the scene. Even though the last of the trawler's crew were still visible clinging to the wreckage, the hellish seas thwarted all attempts at rescue, and the entire crew were lost. Mourn the dead, certainly, but spare a thought for the brave lifeboatmen who had to leave them there to perish.

I arrive at Hurdiback thoroughly worn out, more than a little damp and struck deeply by the beauty and grandeur of this lonely underinhabited isle. In a little over three hours I have covered nearly two-thirds of the island, felt touched by the lives of untold hundreds of past residents and players in a variety of historic, sometimes tragic happenings. Yet in the same three hours, I have not encountered a single living soul.

III: A new hat for the fractious pastor

The next thirty-six hours are like being an extra in the Twilight Zone.

In weather every bit as unsuited to hillwalking as yesterday's, I take a shorter trek, this time north from Hurdiback, again in heavy rain that is propelled by gale bursts against my face. It is difficult at times to see the end of my nose, let alone where I should place my next footstep. I make it to a small cairn at the high point of the headland of North Ness and add to it a flat piece of sandstone, polished smooth by the elements and smaller than a credit card. The surrounding turf is speckled with far heavier rocks, suggesting that mine will not be there for long. I sit in the cairn's scant lee, in awe of what stretches out before me. This place is an assault on the senses and fertile food for the imagination; how could Norsemen in open boats a thousand or more years ago ever deal with these seas, this climate, this landscape of random inward coastal gorges that could just as easily provide absolute sanctuary as they could throw up deadly baas and even deadlier sixty-metre precipices?

In two-and-a-half days on Papa Stour I share not one word with islanders outside of Hurdiback, and grab but limited conversation with my host Martin, who is one of only two live residents I actually see, the other being the driver of the car who blocked our way on the first morning. Martin's wife Fay remains a low voice from deep within the croft house; not enamoured with their names appearing in national Press coverage of recent island shenanigans, she declines to sit down with me; I fail to even set eyes upon her, and only when I make the excuse of returning a borrowed book do I manage to engineer the briefest of doorstep dialogues with her husband.

He and Fay are animal lovers who ran a smallholding and an animal rescue centre before moving up here from their native Lincolnshire five years ago, full of idealistic anticipation about life on their own farm on a beautiful, peaceable island. For a while, they lived their dream, but before too long found themselves in the cleft stick of a feud between two island factions — both of them incoming families from England — disputes that have cut the tiny community in half and destroyed any hope of a cohesive, caring village society. In the population of about twenty, there are only four Papa Stour natives, and evidence suggests that some of the incomers may have arrived weighed down with emotional and behavioural baggage. Baggage of the sort that must have seen their old neighbours in England break out the bubbly when they headed for faraway Shetland — and that has seen the ruination of any notion of the island as a haven of tranquility.

The big white house next to Hurdiback belongs to the pastor of a small church in the south of England, by all reports a fractious character, a focal point of the feuds who found himself more central to one particular episode than even he could possibly have wanted. After he allegedly shot a dog belonging to another family, he had a bucket of dog droppings dumped on his ministerial noggin by a rival who wound up in court for his actions. Because the island schoolteacher made a statement to the authorities, the wife of the man who was soon convicted of the odiferous assault pulled her kids out of the island school, thereby condemning it to closure. The poor schoolteacher apart, we are not exactly talking about the most reasoned of creatures here.

The dogshit dumping was only the most notorious event in a long running stand-off, and because he is identified by some, rightly or not, as an ally of the pastor, Martin Strickland remains a target. His stiff manner on the telephone when I called from Mainland was down to crank calls he receives even now, months after the unpopular pastor and his family packed their bags and returned to England. Telephone abuse among a community of five or six homes. Work that one out if you can.

A peaceable paradise Papa Stour is not, and day to day intimidation remains common. Martin has returned to his parked car to find it firmly blocked in by a rival vehicle. This, on an island with only a sprinkling of cars, and no shortage of places to park them. If he comes up behind certain other drivers on the island's narrow roads, they slow to a crawl to spite him. The incident on the day I arrived, when another vehicle stubbornly forced Martin to back up, was nothing unusual.

This moronic schoolyard bully pattern has attained such national notoriety that Martin recently fielded a call from a graduate student in Wales who wants to visit Papa Stour to research a thesis on its factional strife. If the student does make the long trek north, I hope he has more luck finding people to talk to than I have.

The only time in five years that Martin ever saw all the people of Papa Stour in one room was to debate the recently-completed improvements to the island pier and the building of a simple waiting room — the only shelter available to anyone waiting in often ferocious weather. At the meeting, half of the residents were against the modernisation, and vehemently so, because they felt it would encourage an influx of incomers. This at a time when depopulation threatens the island's very existence, and when there are only four 'native' islanders. This means that, with no apparent notion of irony, at least six incomers voted to present every barrier possible to fresh incomer blood arriving on the island. I pity the poor innocent hopefuls who opt to move into the state of bitterness that has taken over this gorgeous island landscape.

Sadly, Martin and Fay have given up on their island idyll. Hurdiback is on the market, and they hope to leave the island soon to explore the back roads of France in their camper van. When I ask if he minds that I will be writing about all this, he says he doesn't care, since he and Fay will be long gone.

When it is time for me to catch the *Snolda* back to Mainland, Martin takes me down to the pier and bids me well. I wish him good luck and happy trails in France, when the time comes.

[A few months later, the Stricklands were indeed gone; newspaper reports related that newcomers from Wales took over Hurdiback and spread word that anybody who wanted ducks or geese were welcome to come and take them away. The big white pastor's house was also sold, again to incomers from England. Sadly, its new tenants soon found themselves in the news, when one newcomer spent time in a cell in Lerwick, and the rest of the family moved back to England. After that, things only got worse. In early 2008, the largest family on the island – the only one with any children – departed the island for good, taking the population down to single figures for the first time in at least fifteen hundred years. The tragic soap opera that is modern-day Papa Stour lives on.]

I leave on the *Snolda* uncertain of what the next few days might hold. A telephone call to Willie Tulloch, relief skipper of the Foula Ferry, tells me that the weather forecast precludes them sailing anytime in the next few days, which puts the kibosh on hopes of swapping one of the most isolated communities in Shetland for *the* most isolated one. Which leaves me with Plan B, except there is no Plan B.

During the trip back to West Burrafirth, I get a break. Bruce Jamieson mentions that the *Snolda* has a special commission for tomorrow, a rare trip down the length of south Mainland and beyond to Fair Isle. I ask if passengers are permitted and in return get a confused expression. *It's a ferry, Ron — what do you think?*

So long as I can get myself back to West Burrafirth before daybreak tomorrow, I'm on.

I get to spend another quiet night in the Walls camping böd, and take yet one more early-morning jaunt across the stark moors of west Mainland in the company of Pat the taximan. When I tell him I am joining the *Snolda* on a trip to Fair Isle, he is so visibly enthused that he manages to buoy my own spirits.

I am fast learning that Shetlanders are obsessively *au fait* with the latest weather forecasts, and Pat is optimistic that I have picked a great day for the long trip south. I hope he is right, even if there remains one niggling doubt: the same forecasts prompted Skipper Willie Tulloch to keep the Foula ferry safe in its island berth.

In the meantime, I am treated again to the views I savoured when I was last in Pat's MPV. Even in the pre-dawn near-light of early October, it looks like a different land. The sky is awakening to a brightness and clarity that I have hardly seen since I arrived in Shetland, and it floods the landscape with bright shining cheer.

It's *déjà vu* all over again when we slip down into a West Burrafirth as isolated and asleep and devoid of life as it was four days ago, complete with the sole area of activity, the *Snolda*, moored precisely where it was before. The familiar blue-overalled crewmen tend carefully to the peculiar needs set by a round-trip to an island over eighty kilometres away in the volatile watery folds of the North Atlantic.

FAIR ISLE

I: North Atlantic woes

The *Snolda* rumbles its way out through the firth on a westerly course that takes us towards Papa Stour and to the left turn at the headland that will point us southwards for the five-hour run to Fair Isle.

Behind us, the sun is about to rise above the undulating west Mainland horizon, but before it does, the entire sky, unblemished save for stray wisps of ice-crystal cirrus, turns luminous tangerine. Then the white orb that signals a new day peeks over the skyline and west Mainland hillsides go from black silhouettes to muted three-dimensional landscapes in varying shades of grey-green. The ferry's powerful engines push us steadily through indigo waters broken up by marching white wave tops and a pale wash that expands behind. Roiling patches of aerated phosphorescence dance amidst the blues and blacks while in the distance the land recedes and the tumbling ocean steps in to dominate the ever-expanding panorama.

The skipper, Hubert, invites me up to the bridge, so I climb the precipitous metal steps to the bridge deck and let myself into the cabin, where he and his number two Bruce Jamieson are ensconced in plush suspended chairs that would not disgrace a private jet. Spread out in front of them is an array of computerised displays straight out of a 1990s James Bond movie, and dominated by a bright yellow and blue rectangular monitor that details not only the land and seascape for miles around, but the *Snolda's* ongoing progress courtesy of satellite navigation systems. As Bruce stands up to usher me into his seat, there is a thud-thud from somewhere near his knees. He bends floorwards to open a mid-cabin hatch, and a callused hand pops up clutching three steaming mugs of tea. Bruce passes them around, then reaches down to collect a plate of thickly buttered toast.

I sip tentatively at the tea and politely decline the toast. The bridge is elevated enough to give the men in control a command of the seascape ahead, but the same elevation magnifies movements imparted by the seas, so I am at the end of a flicking lever that already wants to destabilise me from the inside out. And yet, Hubert and Bruce are in vocal agreement that we are *verrrrry* lucky to get conditions so favourable for today's sail.

Bruce flicks a switch that sends a thin intermittent splish-splash of fresh water down the salt-encrusted cockpit windscreen. Then with another switch he fires up sweeping screen wiper blades that take on their own controlled sideways rhythm. So the boat and the washers and the wipers go buck-lurch-splish-sweep-twist-dive-splish-soar-swoosh-splash-sweep-lurch while I try forlornly to find something to focus my mind on, *anything* that might reduce the sensation of being caught in an industrial-sized tumble dryer. I am failing miserably when Bruce says:

'Mind, when we round the point and away from the lee of the firth, it could get a wee bit rough.'

Could get rough? What is this right now?

It is nothing, apparently. A few minutes later Hubert puts fingertips to automatic pilot, a digital readout blurs through many degrees of change, the *Snolda* sweeps left and quickly emerges from the twin shelters of Burra Firth to the east and Papa Stour to the west, and just as quickly I grasp how comparatively fine conditions were just a few minutes ago — when I was already beginning to suffer the vile grip of seasickness.

The first thing I see as we round the vertical rock walls at the outer edge of the firth, as the bow of the *Snolda* swings into the Sound of Papa, is a western horizon that writhes with energy. I should hardly be surprised. If the *Snolda* was to head due west from here, and so long as Hubert's James Bond navigation systems helped him clear the southern tip of Greenland, the first landfall would be the Labrador coast in northern Canada, nearly five thousand ocean kilometres away.

I excuse myself from the bridge with a limp line about how some fresh air might do me good. Hubert and Bruce's expressions combine understanding with perhaps just a hint of amusement, and amidst rolling and pitching that could flick me over the low handrail in an instant, I carefully negotiate the perilously steep stairway down to the cargo deck.

Less than an hour into the journey, and the unmitigated misery of sea sickness looms large. The prospect of only another five hours to go offers scant consolation.

II: You meet the nicest bank robbers on Fair Isle

For the next few hours I endure raging *mal de mer* from a perch on a frigid metal hatch on the ferry's cargo deck. The warm shelter of the passenger cabin is but a couple of steps away but entirely out of the question, not least because I cannot be sure of getting back out in time for distressingly unpredictable bouts of explosive vomiting.

I undergo periodic episodes of wholesale sufferance at the ship's rail, facing the twin liquid hazards of flying sea spume and soaring, aerated, personally-generated spew. More than once, I fail to avoid either, and discover an unexpected but very welcome benefit of my expensive Berghaus waterproofs.

The hours that follow are filled with stomach-clenching wretchedness and unrelenting nausea, yet I would not have missed them for the world. The journey is so spellbinding that not for a second, seasickness or no seasickness, do I wish that I was anywhere else.

The bluff cliffs of west Mainland recede as we plug south-south-west at something like 10 knots which, from where I perch at deck level, or a bare metre-and-a-half above the rolling sea, feels *rapid*. Speed, I know, is entirely relative. In terms of sheer sensation, 250 kilometres an hour on a German autobahn does not even come close to wearing a trapeze on a canted sailing dinghy at one-twentieth of the velocity. Right now, ten knots, or about eighteen kilometres per hour, feels *fast*.

The deck at my feet pitches every which way, the most discomfiting being when the boat rotates along its axis, dipping first one siderail in the streaming seas, then the other. Frigid streams of North Atlantic sweep in through openings at the lower edge, to be spat across the cargo deck and ejected out the other side a split second before *that* side dips underwater and the whole process reverses itself afresh. Add in the pitching as the *Snolda* negotiates its way up and over a relentless procession of waves and gravity-heavy troughs, and the scope for ongoing nausea is endless.

Foula Island pops up on the western horizon, closer and clearer than I saw it from Papa Stour or Mainland, but still maintaining its remote, almost two-dimensional form. Its gigantic cliffscape looks cut from black card, stark against the western sky and encircled by malevolent seas. From where I am, it is easy to understand why the Foula ferry has hardly ventured out in weeks.

As I sit feeling leaden and useless, I expect sneaking signs of amusement from the carefree crew as they skip sure-footedly around me, but instead I am the object of touching concern and sympathy and hot drinks that they encourage me to get down, and that remain neither hot nor down for long. Advice on fighting sea-sickness tells you to look towards, but not *at* something in the distance, to embrace an object on the horizon, but not to focus upon it. And so for a long time desperation makes me watch but not stare at the southernmost point in Mainland, Sumburgh Head, as it retreats slowly into the distance until at last it looks more like an island than the long tall headland that I know it is.

I glance in the other direction and it finally registers that Foula, too, is actually retreating, so I stick my head out into the breeze to look forwards where, sure enough, Fair Isle is beginning to take shape. I may feel wretched, but time is flying.

I always arrive at new islands with a burning sense of anticipation, and as Fair Isle grows in stature ahead of me, my excitement is well-rewarded.

The skies part and the sun arrives to cast a welcome blush over an island that could do justice to the opening paragraphs of a Tolkien story. From sea level, it presents a verdant vision ringed by formidable precipices. And what cliffs they are. Even the small ones are over sixty metres tall; in places, a hundred metres of rock climbers' dreamscapes leap from a coastline strewn with boulders the size of houses. Vast sea cave cathedrals loom shadowy black, and deep within coastal geos, miniature precipice-enclosed crescent beaches, inaccessible without a boat, look as if human foot might never have marked their sands.

Sheep Rock is a towering adjunct to the main island linked by an un-navigable knife-edge ridge of crumbling rock, with cliffs over sixty metres tall at either end. Its upper reaches are sloped like a giant emerald-green ski jump to which, incredibly, islanders used to transport sheep to graze. From a landing point on the seaward side of the Rock, whole flocks were manually hoisted on ropes, one by one up a sixty-metre cliff to the fertile slopes. At the season's end, the whole exhausting and treacherous exercise was repeated in reverse. This centuries-old practice only came to an end in 1977.

On maps, Sheep Rock appears joined to Fair Isle by a causeway, and so when, just after World War I, government authorities on the UK mainland noticed that its spacious area of fertile land was for some reason uncrofted, they summarily assigned the land to a house in the southern part of the island, with no idea that it was all-but inaccessible. The house they assigned it to is now Stackhoull Stores, the island's only shop, but for decades, it was known to islanders as Rock Cottage, in an ironic nod to the ignorance of bureaucrats in faraway places.

Soon the *Snolda* rounds a robust man-made breakwater, creeps to a berth in the cliffscape notch that is the harbour of North Haven, and the crew set about the job they came all this way to do. With the ferry's own crane and a cargo net woven from hefty rope, they pluck from the pierside a van too large for the island's regular ferry, the *Good Shepherd IV*, which sits far above the high water mark on a purpose-built ramp, like a royal ruler on her throne.

I have booked accommodation at a croft guesthouse, and belatedly follow the host's instructions to give her a call when approaching the island. I am skeptical about getting a mobile phone signal at a sparsely-inhabited dot of land mid-way between Shetland and Orkney, but I get through immediately. Kathy Coull tells me 'someone' will pick me up shortly, which strikes me as a little cryptic, but in the complete absence of public transport, I am quite content to believe her.

I stand on the pierside and photograph the *Snolda* crew swinging several tonnes of van through the air, and it has hardly set tyres to the ferry's cargo deck before an ageing Peugeot pulls up beside me. Three doors spring open to disgorge middle-aged men clad in khaki and with expensive Zeiss binoculars swinging from neck straps.

Kathy sent them, and they're the bank robbers.

Or so they soon tell me, jiggling with laughter at the label fellow bird watchers have attached to them due to how they swoop down on birding locations in the car brought purposely all the way from England, screech to a halt with the doors flying — and leap out primed for action, binoculars brandished like high-powered weapons.

The robbers are ardent bird watcher comrades, regular guests at Kathy's B&B, and their welcome could not be more spontaneous or warm. They are in their forties and fifties, yet they exude the energy and zest of teenagers. After the chilled solitude of Papa Stour, this is reception enough to warm the cockles of one recovering sea-sickness victim's heart.

Peter is a driving instructor from Land's End whose ambitious goal is to create a video DVD of **all** British birds, as well as another DVD on the ten 'specials', avian migrants that make Fair Isle a Mecca to birdwatchers (he requires three more to complete the set). Phil, a disgustingly fit rock-climber who is pushing sixty, is a retired steel industry worker from Rotherham. And chatty Mel is a self-employed tipper truck driver from Derbyshire who combines his long-running passion of bird watching with a newer lust for digital photography.

They are near the end of a two-week bird watching holiday, and although they freely admit it has been a failure in terms of fresh sightings and specials logged (not a single one so far), they seem not in the least discouraged. There is always next year, and the bank robbers already know they will be back. Like committed fishermen, to venture out and make the effort is the activity they savour; catching — or in the case of bird watchers — spotting their prey is simply the icing on the cake.

They take me to the home from home that is the crofthouse B&B operated by Kathy Coull, a cheery soul originally from the borders region of Scotland, and a 12-year Fair Isle veteran. Kathy combines running the island's best B&B with teaching visitor groups traditional wool spinning and textile skills using wooden spinning wheels and other time-honoured hand tools; Fair Isle is world-renowned for the quality of its wool and its distinctive woven designs, and Kathy passes on her skills to spinning enthusiasts from all over the globe.

The bank robbers take their binoculars for walks in different directions, their ears ringing with Kathy's warning not to be late for lunch. The island has a shop but no restaurant, and its only bar is an informal affair in the hideously ugly (but vital to the island economy) Bird Observatory near to where the *Snolda* dropped me, so accommodation at Kathy's guest house includes three meals, and as many cups of tea or coffee as we can drink.

Kathy flits around a kitchen with an idyllic view over the south end of the island, complete with the slightly comic figure of Mel pacing towards the coast, his short legs swallowed by giant green wellington boots. She tells me that her daughter Charlotte is due to fly back from Anderson High School in a couple of days, for her first visit home in several weeks. She talks of the 'boys', as she calls the bank robbers (at least two of whom are many years her senior), with something akin to maternal pride. Regular customers, often together and sometimes for over two weeks at a time, they have become more like family than paying guests. They help out around the croft (the B&B is also a working farm, and only yesterday they repaired the shed roof), and when they fly out tomorrow, they leave behind their trusty imported Peugeot for Kathy's private use.

The robbers come back, on time, and as soon as we sit down to the dining table for a home-cooked lunch the wretched agonies of my seasickness are forgotten. The three friends exchange rapid-fire banter in the manner of companions who have spent thousands of comfortable hours together, and Mel uses a piece of bread to clean his plate so meticulously that it could almost go back on the shelf unwashed.

Lunch finished, teas and coffees soaked up, and it is time for my first experience of 'twitching', as bird watching is sometimes called — usually by people who fail to appreciate its appeal. This particular twitcher trio have got the bug in a big way. Mel wears an electronic pager on his belt and subscribes to a bird watcher network that sends out alerts to subscribers about sightings all over the UK. When the pager beeps, even when he is up to his boot-tops in icy water, he pauses to squint at it and announce in excited tones that a purple-pimpled potboiler has been spotted in western Snowdonia.

Alright, I admit it. I made up the bit about Snowdonia.

Fair Isle's huge debt to bird watchers dates back to the late George Waterston, an Edinburgh ornithologist who, on return from service in World War II, bought the island in 1948 and soon after established what was to become its world-renowned bird observatory. Nearly sixty years on, the Observatory is known to birding enthusiasts world-wide — and attracts over four hundred of them to visit annually. Because of its northern position, and being forty kilometres from the nearest land, Fair Isle attracts rare avian species on trans-continental migrations. In turn, the birds attract the twitchers, and the money they put into the island economy is of vital significance.

At the island's North End, the bank robbers explore the cliffs around one of Fair Isle's two 19th Century lighthouses built by the Stevensons, relatives of Robert Louis Stevenson, author of Kidnapped and Treasure Island. That it is only a modest structure is with good reason, since a lighthouse at the top of a 130-metre cliff does not have to be in the least grand. While it may not be tall, it is of *very* sturdy construction, and again with justification. Even though the cliffs here are gigantic, when storms come from the right direction, the lighthouse is battered by rocks hurled up by seas of dimensions and power beyond the imagination.

The robber trio stroll perilously close to overhung cliff edges, binoculars at the ready, and the sighting of a spotted flycatcher raises spirits, if only momentarily. In birdwatcherspeak, it might merit a 'tick' — a bird well-known but not seen here before today. At the other end of the scale of exclusivity is a 'lifer', a bird never before seen by the twitcher marking the log book. I don't have to spend a long time with birders before I begin to understand that their hobby has a lot to do with the assembling of lists.

In the island's more fertile south, we splash through soggy ditches in vain search of something called a lancey. In seventeen days, the robbers have not had one rare sighting, because this year — like last year — the wind direction is wrong. The migrating flocks that hold real fascination for visiting twitchers are travelling, mostly from

Scandinavia and Russia, to Continental Europe and Africa, and the absence of south-easterlies to blow the poor creatures hundreds of kilometres off course and onto Fair Isle has cut rare sightings back to nearly zero.

III: A roomful of bad beards

Quite how seriously bird watching is taken in these parts escapes me until the bank robbers take me to the Bird Observatory for the evening 'Log' meeting.

The 'Obs', as they call it, is a functional, if unsightly collection of concrete boxes, and its rooms and dormitories draw dedicated twitchers of all ages from the U.K., Europe, and beyond. As well as a canteen and the island's only bar, it features a distinction that is somehow apropos of dormitories attracting hundreds of members of a single-interest club. It has its own Tuck Shop.

It is often fully-booked — especially during spring and autumn migrating seasons — and its website attracts a half million hits annually. And it is, after all, *the* major tourist draw on an island with only seventy inhabitants.

Observatory visitors pace the hillsides, fields, beaches and clifftops by day, binoculars to the fore and notebooks forever at the ready. And in the evening, after dinner is taken and the dishes packed away, they sit around low tables in the bar, and compare notes in anticipation of the all-important daily Log meeting.

To reach the bar we have to first pause in a cloakroom and observe a pragmatic rule that protects the building's interior from an ever-thickening patina of sheep shit. Cloakroom hooks sag under the weight of mouldering rainwear and the floor swarms with boots and Wellingtons undergoing thick, odorous sock eruptions. The robbers lead the way along a convoluted route of narrow corridors until at last we emerge in a neat room full of bad beards.

Not *everyone* in the room has wispy, patchy facial fuzz. There are four or five females with no facial hair whatsoever — not counting one or two shadowy upper lips — and several men who may actually have taken razor to lower face in the last week or so. But then there are the fashionably unfashionable birder blokes who foster the academic hobo look, untrimmed growth running amok over wind burned cheekbones. At a big table in the library corner, two long sets of whiskers brush the backs of grimy fingernails that dance over computer keyboards. But the unofficial Bad Beard Award goes to a man in his forties who somehow contrives to look completely alone in the crowded room, and who sports a straggly excuse for a full set that no naval rating would get away with, and no self-respecting student half his age would entertain.

Disregarding a lingering whiff of the cloakroom that is explained by a plenitude of bare feet and stocking soles, we manage to get drinks from a wood-lined bar just before it is taken over by a warden toting a dog-eared file folder and a clutch of sharp pencils. The nightly Log commences, and the atmosphere, although perfectly cordial, switches from casual and carefree to academic, competitive and, dare I think it, just a little bit obsessive.

The warden has an urbane self-confidence about him. Change his well-worn khakis for overpriced designer duds, and he could warrant a swivel chair in a fevered London dealing room, but up here he is in control of a very different set of numbers. From what is an exhaustively detailed list of avian species and sub-species, he reads out category after category, pausing after each to listen to reports from the assembled throng on numbers spotted over the course of the day.

Proceedings get off to a telling start when the straggly-bearded loner claims that he saw thirty-one pink footed geese. All around him, eyes roll, but if he notices, he doesn't let it show. From then on, whenever another twitcher says a figure, straggly-beard casually ups it like a bidder playing to the crowd at an antiques auction. When someone reports seeing one hundred and five grey lags, he thinks better of raising the stakes, but provides us with the precise flight plans for twenty of the ones *he* tracked, and the locations to within a few centimetres of two corpses. Cue more rolling of eyes and one or two openly contemptuous sneers.

A woman in a buff-coloured down vest registers twenty-seven red shanks; a man clad head to foot in grey cotton says he saw twenty-eight — and just as the warden's pencil descends towards file page, straggly-beard delivers a withering declaration of thirty-nine. As triumphs go, it is short-lived, because a full second later, he is trumped by a shout of fifty-seven from a clean-shaven chap who floods the entire room with a beaming expression that says *got him!* Straggly-beard looks disgusted by the underhand tactics, while others all around him can barely hide their glee.

I realise belatedly that the warden is paying little heed to the braggart's claims. The man's credibility among his peers is palpably non-existent, and he is the only person in the room who fails to realise it.

I am surprised to find myself quite at ease with the whole scene, as its allure begins to open up to me. Bird watching as a pastime can surely be thrilling (albeit usually only fleetingly), and demand patience and endurance and resourcefulness and outdoor skills as well as other qualities that are at the very least harmless, and perhaps even admirable.

Yet there is something about the fevered nature of the pastime that makes me a little uncomfortable. I cannot help feeling that even here, among its most ardent practitioners, it seems to be mainly about a dispassionate obsession with ticking birds off in a personal log book.

Sure, to mention something so rare or desirable as, say, a lanceolated warbler — only twice ever spotted on Fair Isle — is to instantly watch drool encrust bearded chins. The arrival on Fair Isle of a British 'first', or a bird never before seen anywhere in Britain, soon sees the island airstrip crowded with light aircraft full of birders. At a cost of several hundred pounds per person, enthusiasts as far away as the south of England drop everything, charter a plane, fly to Fair Isle and sprint to wherever the rare animal was most recently seen. There, they peer at it through binoculars, perhaps take a few photographs and (surely the real goal of the exercise) add it to their lists. Then they run back to the airstrip and leave the island.

I wonder too at what might even be a lack of concern for the wellbeing of birds sighted, however briefly, however far away from the bird's native habitat.

For a 'first' sighting to occur on Fair Isle, it requires that a poor creature be blown off course by unseasonal winds, forced to fly hundreds of kilometres from its instinctual migration route until it drops onto the only visible spot of earth, completely exhausted and doubtless bewildered, in an alien, never before visited land. Where, within a few hours, it can find itself incessantly harried by binoculars wearing bad beards.

If the bird ever manages to take off again, it almost certainly perishes at sea, never having regained its intended course.

In the midst of the revered Log session, I am certain that I am the only person in the room who would rather that bird never set eyes on Fair Isle, never mind if that meant I could never set eyes on it.

Months later, I call bank robber Peter on his mobile phone to ask about this, and by pure chance, I catch him when he is back tramping the fields of Fair Isle.

'People don't realise that there is a very competitive element to bird watching,' he says. 'There are about 275 to 280 species commonly sighted in Britain, but very serious British bird watchers, the so-called 'high listers', can have lists of over five hundred. These guys hate to have one put over on them by a fellow-bird watcher, and will drop everything to see a new bird.

'But it's not fair to say we only care about our lists. Even when we do track down a "first", we are always careful to give it space, and not to disturb it too much.'

When I counter that it still sounds to me as if his beloved pastime is surely more about the bird watcher than the bird, he only laughs.

IV: Knitting lessons

When I see the bank robbers in the morning, a black cloud of depression follows Peter around the living room as he complains of a sleepless night caused by an ulcer. Kathy whispers that he might well have an ulcer, but he is always like this on departure day because he hates leaving so much, a theory lent credence by the complete absence of concern on the part of his fellow robbers. For a moment I wonder if he has ever thought of moving to Fair Isle, until I remember Peter has a family and that he makes a good living in faraway Cornwall as a driving instructor. Even if he might be able to convince his family to decamp to an underpopulated island a thousand kilometres north (and that surely qualifies as a big IF), at any given time, Fair Isle might present a pool of potential learner drivers in the region of roughly nobody.

Phil is in methodical mode, making sure he has everything packed; and Mel is his usual chatty self, a man who could talk for England without ever making an enemy.

I am invited to the airstrip to see off the robbers, which is the least I can do, and anyway, they need me to drive one of the two cars back to the croft. Pragmatism is the *only* way in a place like Fair Isle.

Still in pragmatic mode, Kathy first telephones Dave Wheeler, the island meteorologist and airport manager, who confirms that the incoming flight from Mainland will be more or less on time, with the proviso that time on Fair Isle is a lot more fluid than at most locations you find on an airline schedule. The bank robbers set off in the Peugeot, and Kathy and I follow in her rust-ridden VW, for which the Peugeot getaway car will very soon be a welcome replacement. As the VW clears the edge of high ground in the middle of the island, the piercing lights of an incoming plane pop out of the murk before it bumps to earth on the dirt airstrip and rumbles towards the neat building not much bigger than a double garage that provides all the shelter required of a tiny island airfield.

As we approach the handful of cars that sit nose-in to the plain wooden barrier at the edge of the apron area, out reverses the Peugeot. Mel waves cheerily and speeds off in the direction of the croft.

He has forgotten his binoculars, but will be back in a few minutes, and of course the pilot will wait for him; such is the refreshing lack of formality at island airstrips.

The few rules enforced here have nothing to do with interfering jobsworths in shiny synthetic uniforms, and everything to do with safety. Before any landing takes place and until the aircraft departs, a full-sized fire truck sits at the apron's edge, engine warmed and crew of trained part-timers kitted up and ready to roll.

With many visiting aircraft piloted by first-time arrivals, the skeleton crew who run the airstrip have to handle situations in any way they can. I hear about one pilot who tried to ignore repeated warnings from the ground that conditions were unsafe for landing. The pilot, who quite possibly operated out of an airport that sees more traffic in a weekend than Fair Isle does in a month, insisted that of course he was going to fuckingwell land. At which point, the person in charge on the ground declared the airfield officially closed. The would-be incomer had no option but to turn away, doubtless without the slightest inclination that he may well have been saved from himself by islanders with an intimate knowledge of their airstrip's peculiar perils.

The Britten Norman Islander shudders to a standstill only twenty paces from where we lean on parked cars, and nobody moves until its twin propellors splutter to a complete halt. Ever since a fatal accident involving a pedestrian and a propellor — many years ago and not even in Shetland — staff and locals alike have been rightly paranoid about safety.

But the moment propellor blades stop spinning, all formality dissolves, and a miniature swarm of bodies embrace the aircraft with, I imagine, much the same familiarity as they have for generations embraced ferries pulling into North Haven. Hatches open, three passengers disembark, a small luggage hold is emptied and re-filled, and just as soon as Mel skids the Peugeot to a halt in the car park and emerges holding his binoculars up in good-natured apology, doors and hatches close, and onlookers retreat dutifully behind the barrier. The Islander coughs to life, taxis across the bumpy gravel, engines scream and the plane is off, farewells waving from the gloom of the tiny passenger compartment.

I am sorry to see off the nicest bank robbers I ever met, but my day is going to be busy meeting with three generations of one island family.

Play the word-association game with 'Fair Isle', and the most common response will surely be 'sweaters'. I first encountered the island's name in the early seventies, in those all but forgotten mini temples of consumerism past, High Street menswear stores. Town centre shops then were stacked high with seriously desirable 'Fair Isles', crew-necked sweaters in a fine soft wool. The body and sleeves were in one colour — I recall coveting a particular shade of sky blue that I was convinced would go just fine with my eyes — and had a complex, Celtic-looking yoke that encircled the neck front and back.

Although I never owned one, I clearly recollect a couple of things about Fair Isle sweaters. One, they were expensive (but they came from an exotic northern island, right?), and two, they suffered spectacular shrinkage when unsuspecting urban Mums, more used to industrial-strength acrylics, put them through the wash. The streets of Scottish towns were thick with sullen kids desperately trying to look cool in woollen straitjackets that barely covered their belly buttons and suffered three-quarter-length sleeves. And I *still* wanted one.

Thirty-odd years later, I have a chance to talk with Anne Sinclair, Fair Isle's museum curator and an expert on the world-renowned Fair Isle knitting industry. Two minutes into our chat, she tells me to forget about any connection between her beloved Fair Isle and the sweaters deemed so fashionable by 1970s mainland teenagers.

'No yoke pattern ever existed in Fair Isle knitwear,' she tells me. 'Fair Isle patterns always were, and still are, an "all over" design.' Fashion makers in the seventies didn't source the design, let alone the sweaters themselves, from Fair Isle; they simply appropriated its good name.

All of which makes me very glad that I was never taken in by *that* particular passing adolescent fad.

We talk in a little building in the middle of fertile croft country in the southern part of the island. Now the island museum, it was originally constructed as a school in 1860, and later served as the community hall. Today, a modern complex a kilometre to the north doubles as primary school and island hall; secondary students (like Kathy's daughter Charlotte) board at Anderson High in Lerwick.

Organised education came to the island as early as 1732, when a school was established by the Scottish Society for Promoting Christian Knowledge, an organisation set up to provide learning institutions 'where religion and virtue might be taught to young and old'. In Fair Isle, it notched up significant successes on both counts. In the first Statistical Accounts of Scotland, conducted in the last decade of the 18th century on the orders of Sir John Sinclair, a Scottish politician credited with the dubious honour of the first ever use of the word 'statistics', it was reported that the majority of Fair Islanders were competent readers, and that 'many' of them could write. Nearly three centuries on, the SSPCK's aims, not least the one to counter 'a serious landslide to Rome' being achieved by 18th Century Roman Catholic missionaries, continue to bear fruit. Fair Isle's population of seventy remains profoundly Christian, dividing its time between a Church of Scotland Kirk, and a Methodist Church.

But even a half-century before the SSPCK got involved, Fair Isle was already deeply marked by Christianity and of admirable social order, as was noted in *Description of Ye Countrey of Zetland* by Mr James Kay, c. 1680:

> 'There is a little Church here, more formally plenished, & orderly frequented, than will be easily believed. They have always a Reader, who every Sabbath reads ye sacred Scriptures, & (in the Minister's absence) catecizeth them. And it is worth the marking, that Fornication & other such escapes (frequent in other places) are very rare here.'

The building that is now the George Waterston Memorial Centre and Museum, and which Anne Sinclair curates, devotes a large share of its displays to a cottage industry whose international reputation goes back hundreds of years. As far back as the early 1700s, Fair Isle knitters were exporting 'barrels of socks', and although the earliest known existing piece of Fair Isle knitting was only gifted to the Edinburgh Museum in 1856, a century before that, passing foreign vessels — and they were plentiful, as Fair Isle was a landmark well-known to sea captains working the major trade routes — were met by local vessels that rowed out to intercept and trade with them.

The barter trade with passing ships was a bonus to passing ships' crews, but to the islanders it represented vital access to goods from outside the island. The locals' existences were subject to a harsh rental system that saw them pay the land-owning Laird in kind — mostly with meats, eggs and feathers. Curiously enough, under the so-called 'Truck System', knitwear was never covered by the Lairds' rules. The Truck System was banned by law in the 1830s, but dragged on in Fair Isle for decades afterwards, and so for more than a century, income from knitwear was 'untaxed' and highly-prized.

In these waters, intercepting passing ships was a dangerous game, and in 1897 disaster struck when four Fair Isle rowing boats, at sea on a barter mission, were caught up in a gale. Only two of them found their way back to the island. One other was recovered the following day, with four of its seven crew members dead. Four more crewmen on the last boat were never seen again. The disaster left four widows and twenty-seven dependents without a male breadwinner.

Designs from outside Shetland, among them patterns thought to have been passed on over the centuries by sailors from the Baltic and other distant nations, may even have helped Fair Isle stay decades ahead of the competition. Islander knitters — almost exclusively women whose husbands farmed the land and fished the surrounding waters — produced work in several colours at least fifty years before even two-colour knitting patterns reached the rest of Shetland in the early 20th Century. Before passing trading vessels introduced indigo and 'madder red' plant-based dyes from abroad, Fair Isle knitters added colour to their yarn using local plants and some of the many strains of lichen that prosper in its pristine environment.

Dewy-eyed romantics hoping to spot islanders going about their humble lives wrapped in distinctive Fair Isle-patterned sweaters and hats and with thick Fair Isle socks peeking out from the tops of their workboots have forever been disappointed, and for one simple reason. For over three hundred years, knitwear production on the island has had only one motive: to generate much-needed income. Fair Isle knitwear has always been far too precious a commodity for cash-strapped locals to wear. Even now, premium prices paid by upmarket Edinburgh haberdasheries and occasional cruise ship visitors are a significant supplement to crofters' incomes.

In 1902, island order books received a major boost when the thread magnate James Coats ordered 'one hundred of everything' — plus fifty tobacco pouches — for the thirty-three man crew of the S.Y. *Scotia*, a research vessel led by William Spiers Bruce on a twenty-month, 53,000-kilometre voyage to explore the Antarctic. A photograph from a Royal Scottish Geographical Society exhibition held to mark the voyage's centenary shows three scientists in the laboratory of the *Scotia*, all wearing tightly-patterned Fair Isle sweaters. *Real* Fair Isle sweaters, not in the least like the aberrations that borrowed the name seventy years later. Accompanying the photograph is the caption:

> *'Long before London had heard of them, the brilliant hues of Fair Isle were fashionable in the Antarctic.'*

Fair Islanders would take issue with this, since the value and quality of their knitwear was well known not only to Londoners, but to consumers far further afield, long before the beginning of the twentieth century.

During the two World Wars, most of the island men were away fighting, so as well as tending to the crofts, the women produced knitwear that they sold to military stationed on the island, generating funds that literally put food on Fair Isle tables.

Cottage industry production by individual knitters with their own interpretation of designs handed down for generations has continued unbroken. Museum curator Anne was a student in Edinburgh in the 1960s, and remembers seeing a customer in a tea shop wearing a Fair Isle sweater, and being able to correctly identify its creator by name, simply by looking at the pattern.

V: Spinning wheels and butchered lambs

Anne Sinclair's parents Annie and Stewart Thomson are two of the island's most respected elders. A short walk across neat croft land takes me to their storybook cottage next to what looks like a farm outhouse, but was Annie's workplace for nearly thirty years — the old Post Office and telephone exchange, through which every island call was routed manually until an automated system was finally installed in the 1970s. Annie is a native of Fair Isle (the most southerly island in Shetland), while husband Stewart is originally from the isle of Unst — Shetland's most northerly island. They married during World War II, when Stewart was a lighthouse keeper whose work took him all around Scotland's coastline. Annie travelled and lived with (or near) him in an era when lighthouse keepers received a mere twenty-one days' annual leave. This does not sound *too* bad, until you learn that for the rest of the year, they worked four hours on, four hours off. That is, four hours on, four hours off — for more than three-hundred-and-forty days a year.

When he left the lighthouse service in 1957, he and Annie and their three young children came to Fair Isle to live, and have been here ever since.

Only three years before they arrived, Bird Observatory founder George Waterston handed the island's ownership over to the

National Trust for Scotland, so when Stewart and Annie came back, the Trust's management of Fair Isle was in its infancy. Stewart took on the part-time job of Trust Officer, and for the next thirty years organised National Trust and International Voluntary Service annual work camps. Work camps still go on today, with groups of young volunteers from all over Europe spending a few weeks assisting on crofts and performing vital roles in the upkeep of island infrastructure. Everything from drystone dyke building and maintenance to clearing ditches and setting up and mending cables, roads and fences has had help from work camp volunteers. In Stewart's eyes, the roles played by the Trust and by annual work camps have not been so much beneficial to the island's prosperity as vital to its very survival.

'Without the Trust and the work camps, Fair Isle would have been finished long ago,' he says with certainty.

The 1950s were something of a nadir for Fair Isle, a period when its population dropped so low that the island's sustainability fell into serious doubt, never mind that the downward slide was far from a new development. Population decline stretches back another hundred-plus years, to when nearly four hundred souls eked out below-subsistence existences. The limited croft land simply could not feed so many mouths, compelling islanders to be ever-more dependent upon the seas. The realities of the landlord-controlled Truck System only made things worse. Then, in 1845 the 'runrig' agricultural system that had the island's croft land divided into tiny 'runs' separated by parallel 'rigs', or ridges, was abandoned by the landlord, and the land 'planked', or summarily turned into a much smaller number of larger crofts. Overnight, there were not nearly enough farms to go around; twelve families found themselves with no land whatsoever, and several others were left with plots too small with which to sustain themselves. In 1862, after crop failures and a bad fishing season, more than one hundred and thirty out of an island population of three hundred and sixty left forever. The emigrants ranged in age from seven weeks to seventy-two years old and departed aboard an overloaded sloop bound for Kirkwall, Orkney. From there they sailed on for Canada by way of the Scottish mainland. The name of the sloop that took them from their homeland was the *No Joke*.

A half century has passed since Stewart and Annie came to Fair Isle to bring up their three kids, all of whom are resident on the island, as are several grandchildren and some of their twelve great-grandchildren. I know because Annie proudly shows me her 'bragging book', a pocket portrait album of twelve happy faces. The great-grandparents' pride in their family shows in their own smiles. Discussion turns to their marriage of over sixty years, and makes the near-inevitable transition to talk of how few marriages nowadays last nearly so long.

'They don't know what they're missing,' says Annie, sadly. I initially misinterpret this as being judgemental, but she is actually expressing sympathy for folk who will never experience the joys of such an extended family. Stewart apportions a lot of credit for that happiness to the quality of island life that gives islanders as strong a sense of home as any I have ever encountered.

'Kids here have a tremendous sense of home life, an anchor they know they can come back to,' he says.

I tell them how much of a pleasure it has been to talk with them, to get a brief glimpse of island life through their eyes. Stewart waves the compliment aside.

'Some folk come all the way here for an afternoon and see nothing; it's an awful shame.'

He explains: many visitors wander the island without ever managing to talk to locals, and in doing so fail to learn anything about life on the island. This sad observation gets me thinking about Papa Stour all over again.

Before I leave, he shows me his workshop in the outhouse that used to be Annie's Post Office and telephone exchange, and where he builds intricately beautiful traditional spinning wheels. He turns the wood components on a foot-powered lathe that he made with his own hands, its treadle/crank mechanism fashioned from the innards of an old truck engine — crankshaft, connecting rod, piston and all. He hand-crafts every single spinning wheel component, wooden and metal, even perfectly-formed tiny stainless steel springs, and the finished items are things of great beauty.

He tells me he started out many years ago repairing and rebuilding broken spinning wheels from 'bundles of firewood' brought to him by neighbours. Now he tells me he is working on wheels number ninety-two and ninety-three, and some of the first ninety-one now grace homes in Japan, the USA and Scandinavia.

Ian Best and Lise Sinclair represent a young and hopeful generation of Fair Islanders, and a third generation of the Thomson/Sinclair/Best family line. Lise is the daughter of Anne the museum curator/historian (so a grand-daughter of Stewart and Annie), and Ian's mother came to Fair Isle from England over thirty years ago to perform a one-year contract as island nurse. She is still here, as are her husband, son Ian and daughter Fiona — who runs the island shop and is deputy manager of the airport.

Ian works a croft with wife Lise, does part-time crew work on the ferry *Good Shepherd IV* (as do many of the island men), and can be seen at the airport wearing full Fire Crew kit whenever aircraft come and go. Outside of Fair Isle, he is known for the traditional wooden boats he fashions over the winter in the workshop beside the family croft at Kenabee. As a young man fresh out of secondary school, Ian's next move was as unusual as it was bold: he took on a boat-building apprenticeship in Hardanger Fiord, Norway. This meant that not only did he have to acquire all of the same woodworking and boatbuilding skills as his fellow students, but in order to do so, he first had to pick up a solid command of the Fiord's regional Norwegian dialect.

What followed was three years' intensive learning about sailing boats whose design lineage goes back many centuries; and for the last fifteen years, over the course of each winter, Ian has built between two and six boats. Over that time, his work and his reputation have reached far-ranging boat circles, not least because he has built boats abroad, and in public, during single-handed boat-building displays, one at Edinburgh Museum, the other on The Mall outside the Smithsonian Institution in Washington D.C.

His most common creation is a seven-metre (twenty-three-foot) Ness Yoal, built from Scottish larch. Documented evidence of the yoal's design origins go all the way back to 98 AD and the book *The Germania* by the famed Roman historian Tacitus. He reported seeing tribes of *Suiones* in Scandinavia, strong well-armed men with pointed helmets who sailed in fleets of boats with a prow at each end that were propelled by paddles. Although the *Suiones* were from what became Sweden in eastern Scandinavia, Tacitus may actually have documented Vikings seven hundred years before they made a name for themselves. Vikings who sailed boats whose lineage reaches down through the centuries to Ian Best's workshop on Fair Isle.

More than a thousand years after Tacitus noted the double-ended design, similar craft were imported to Shetland from Norway in what set an unwitting precedent for the world-conquering flat-pack furniture makers IKEA. The boats were sent to Shetland disassembled down to their component parts, to be put together on arrival in Shetland, where they could not possibly be built any other way, for the simple reason that the islands were long-bare of the primary raw material of trees.

Only in the early 19th Century, when a trade dispute with Norway prompted a ban on all imports from Shetland's closest neighbour, did Shetlanders take to building their own, with imported timber from mainland Scotland.

I arrive to speak to Ian and Lise just as cynicism about the Press reaches yet another island low. Media interest in Fair Isle has peaked with reports on how the National Trust recently advertised two crofts for rent to families who feel suited to life on the island; Lise's mother Anne was interviewed on the topic by National Public Radio in the United States, which prompted a flood of applications, more than a hundred of them from the United States. When I sit down in the kitchen of Ian and Lise's croft house, the latest edition of a Scottish Sunday broadsheet is spread out over the table. It is open to a full-page story with the header:

You don't have to be mad to live here...

It is bad enough that this is a feature about the rush of interest in properties on Fair Isle and illustrated with a large Fair Isle graphic. But by employing sloppy journalistic sleight of hand, the story leads with the dogshit-dumping shenanigans on Papa Stour — fifty nautical miles and a sociological world away from prosperous, stable Fair Isle.

Lise, very much like her Mum, offers up strongly-held and eloquent views on things relevant to Fair Isle, such as the perception of life in the islands taking place at a slow and gentle pace.

'Folk talking about that never take into account all the dead time in the cities, all the time spent stuck in traffic jams or on trains or waiting for appointments. Here, if you want to do something, you just do it, and now.'

Ian has a caveat: 'Aye, but an infinite flexitime exists on Fair Isle, too.'

They tell me that life here is certainly no idyll, nor is it only about isolation, even if it is affected by the twin forces of geography and climate. What goes on here, they argue, is more about economic pragmatism — hence the holding down of multiple jobs.

'Folk here are not doing six jobs because they think they're really good at six different things,' says Lise.

They do them, she tells me, because this is a small society with next to no full-time opportunities, they have to make ends meet, and because the needs of the community dictate that somebody has to do them.

I am reminded of this later in the day when I talk with Clare Scott. Clare is a slim, attractive, textiles graduate and part-time artist with a studio in the former staff quarters of the South Lighthouse. She hand-crafts exquisite jewellery from silver and gold in designs inspired by Fair Isle textiles, and which she sells to visiting cruise passengers and over the Internet. But income from her art is so sporadic in nature that, as well as performing home social care work for elderly islanders, she also, like most folk on the island, runs a croft.

When our chat runs a little longer than expected, Clare puts immaculately tended fingernails to neat woollen cuff, glances at a tiny stylish watch worthy of a custom jeweller — and says she really must run, because she has lambs to butcher.

VI: The weatherman and the Armada

I leave Kenabee to take advantage of wide open skies and sharp autumnal light. A few minutes' weaving through drystone-walled fields takes me to a point on the coast where Fair Isle became entwined on the periphery of one of the major historic events of the 16th Century. The waters that caress the shore at Stroms Hellier are flat calm, because today's weather comes from the south-west, leaving this eastern shore in the deceptively placid lee of the island.

Within a week of today's date — a little over four centuries ago, and when the weather was also coming from the south-west — a sailing ship carrying more than three hundred men was wrecked within metres of this cliff-lined shore. It was 1588, and weeks earlier Philip II's Spanish Armada had been seen off by the English, and what remained of its 130-ship fleet forced to flee northwards in a desperate attempt to reach Spain the long way — around the northern tip of Scotland. It was a tactic born of desperation along routes never before navigated, and against the prevailing westerly winds. They successfully rounded the north of Scotland and reached a latitude with northern Ireland, where they sailed straight into a hurricane. More than twenty ships were driven onto the Irish coastline, and among three vessels forced by the storm to backtrack north was *El Gran Grifon*, the 38-gun flagship of the Armada's supply squad.

The ship was not even Spanish, but a Baltic 'hulk', or supply vessel hired from the great sea-trading City of Rostock on the north German Baltic coast, and almost certainly crewed by German sailors. This was four-plus centuries ago, and the leader of a great military power wanted to flex his muscle and spread his faith across distant lands of unbelievers. Being short of hardware and manpower, he hired what he needed from compliant states, and sent foreigners into deadly conflict to serve his own selfish ends.

Aren't we just thankful that world leaders can't get away with *that* sort of messianic nonsense nowadays?

Two months after suffering severe damage in the first skirmishes in the English Channel, followed by weeks at sea in sometimes appalling conditions, *El Gran Grifon* was weighed down with extra men plucked from a sinking sister ship, and taking in more water than the weary crew could deal with. Its captain had to get her ashore before she foundered, and sought shelter where there was none, among the cliff faces of Fair Isle's east coast. He anchored in the relative calm of the narrow cliff inlet of Swartz Geo, only for shifting tides to drive the ship onto rocks off Stroms Hellier.

As a child, I always imagined men of war of the Armada era to be forbiddingly huge; *El Gran Grifon*, carrying over three hundred crew and soldiers, measured only about thirty-seven metres at deck level; to put that into perspective, the ferry *Snolda* that brought me to Fair Isle is just under twenty-five metres long, and has a crew of five.

The only measurement on *El Gran Grifon* that could possibly have saved those aboard came to the rescue. The ship came to rest canted at an angle with its towering masts leaning against the cliffs. Nearly three hundred men made it safely to the cliff tops by climbing the rigging before the ship disappeared. Its sunken carcass lay undisturbed for almost four hundred years, until scuba divers discovered it in 1970.

During nearly two months on the island, fifty men died from existing wounds or starvation or exposure. Uglier theories that persist even today — especially among Orkney folk — that many of the fifty were hurled to their deaths from cliffs by locals, is likely no more than malicious rumour. The notion, too, that world-renowned Fair Isle knitting patterns may have been introduced by exhausted mercenary veterans of deadly sea conflict is almost certainly fanciful.

The dead from *El Gran Grifon* are buried in the Spaniards Grave in the south of the island. Of the remaining survivors, fewer than half were to see Spain, despite reaching first Orkney and then Edinburgh safely. Queen Elizabeth declared that no English ship would molest armada vessels returning homewards, but in an act of semantic treachery, the English Navy informed Dutch warships of Spanish vessels' positions. The ship carrying the survivors from *El Gran Grifon* was driven aground by Dutch gunboats, killing many of the Fair Isle veterans.

A short walk north from Stroms Hellier gets me to the croft of Dave and Jane Wheeler which, being the only home on the island with its own weather tower, is not difficult to spot.

If he has one, Dave's CV must be a cracker. The 'Current Employment' section would have any Human Resources specialist reaching for the shredder, as it might read something like this:

Registrar of Births, Deaths and Marriages
Airport manager
Airport fireman
Met Office meteorologist

Crofter
Professional photographer
Freelance weather forecaster
Auxiliary coastguard
Cliff rescue team member
Primary school IT instructor
Web designer

Unlike most CVs, it would not contain a word of a lie, even if these days Dave is spoiled for free time, now that he is retired from posts as relief lighthouse keeper and member of the island fire crew, and has cut his employment list down to a mere eleven jobs.

He and Jane have lived in their croft since they came to Fair Isle in 1974. Both from England, their transition to life on an underpopulated island was eased by having already spent time on the island of South Georgia, Antarctica, almost as far south of the equator as Fair Isle is north. Dave met Jane in 1963, after he had already been accepted for a post as a meteorologist on South Georgia. During a two-year tour, he proposed to Jane by telegram, and she accepted the same way. If that was today, it would be by computer chat room video link which, call me old-fashioned, would not be nearly so romantic. After they married in 1965, they lived in South Georgia for two years. The whaling community there numbered fourteen souls, after which Fair Isle must have felt crowded.

We talk in an office in their croft house. It is a small room with three walls obscured by state-of-the-art computers and computerised meteorological equipment. It is as impressive a home office as I have ever set eyes upon, and despite its geographical isolation, is hooked up to a high-speed broadband connection. Fair Isle, thanks to a pilot scheme implemented by a major telecommunications company, was one of the first communities in Britain to enjoy broadband coverage.

From this little techno-hub, as well as running the weather station and a ten-day regional forecasting service with its own dedicated website, Dave operates his photography business. It is digital nowadays, but draws from thousands of slides and negatives shot over the decades spent in the disparate island remoteness of South Georgia and Fair Isle.

In thirty-odd years on the island, Dave has seen many changes in his lifestyle. Back in the early 1970s, he tells me, crofting accounted for eighty percent of his income. Now, it is more like fifteen percent.

The one constant in his and Jane's lives here has been meteorology. Since he set up the Fair Isle meteorological station in 1974, Dave, with considerable assistance from his wife, has until recently filed fifteen reports a day to the Met Office. Thirteen 'synoptic reports' (their posh title) went out hourly from 06:00 to 18:00, and two further 'obs', as meteorologists call them, were filed at 21:00 and 01:00.

Only very recently were they able to drop the 01:00 obs, but in any case, as Dave describes, they always did 'take it easy' on Sundays, filing a mere six reports at three-hourly intervals from 06:00 to 21:00.

For over twenty-six years, from 1974 until 2001, Dave and Jane never once left Fair Isle together, because one of them always had to stay behind to file the reports. Dave laughs it off:

'Remember that married life here is not like on the mainland; we don't go our separate ways every day to pursue a nine-to-five job — we have each other's company 24 hours a day. So when one of us got the chance to go away for a few days, it was a welcome break for us both.'

Nowadays, relief officers can be drafted in, but Dave recalls how, in the early days of the Fair Isle Weather Station, finding a suitable candidate would have been a challenge.

'Weather observer required, must be able to milk cows!'

Now in his early sixties, he has a powerful stocky presence that belies his compact size and speaks of decades of outdoor pursuits as a rock climber, hillwalker and cross-country skier. He has equally extensive, tight mops of thick grey curls on top of his head as he has on his chin. With eyebrows as thick as ropes and a dense moustache, the only way you could tell if a portrait was the right way up would be by spectacle lenses as thick as beer tankard bottoms. His expression is forever on the verge of creasing up with laughter, and his speech, (like his writing, I later learn), is peppered with the multiple exclamation marks of a man with boundless enthusiasm for everything he undertakes.

His second-most time consuming job is as manager of the nearby airfield. Arrive at the Fair Isle airstrip half an hour before a flight is due, and there is Dave, prowling the ridge where the windsock tries to pull its pole from the ground. (The typical Shetland windsock seems permanently fixed at ninety degrees to the pole, with the only change being to the direction it points.) As island meteorologist *and* airport manager, Dave is uniquely qualified to advise pilots on the conditions now, and the likely conditions minutes or hours from now, when a landing or take-off is scheduled. He is in constant contact with Air Traffic Control at Sumburgh Airport, and in regular radio dialogue with pilots.

That the job of airport manager is vital to the island's communications is only more remarkable when you consider that it is only one of many tasks that Dave manages to juggle. Lise Sinclair is adamant that islanders take on multiple jobs because they have to, not because they are especially qualified to do them. In the case of at least one of her fellow islanders, she is clearly, blessedly, wrong.

VII: One less windshield to wash

When I come down to breakfast, Kathy is worried about her daughter Charlotte's imminent arrival by plane from Tingwall, near Lerwick, and one glance to the south is all it takes to understand her concern. Gale-force winds are driving swollen seas crashing over the jagged skerries out beyond the bay of South Harbour and against the southern headlands of Meoness and Skaddan. Where yesterday there was an indigo blue seascape capped with adorable white horses, there is a maelstrom of foaming breakers and flying spray. Charlotte's flight is due to land in three hours, and Kathy is doubtful that it will get through. What's more, having heard the weather bulletin on the radio and spoken to Dave Wheeler, she is certain that my flight off the island, scheduled for this afternoon, has no chance of avoiding cancellation.

Yet the skies are empty and visibility is almost painfully sharp, so I wrap up and walk for a few bone-numbing minutes south to Meoness headland. Beyond the cliffs at my feet, South Harbour, because of an absence of natural shelter and an assortment of wicked-looking rocks protruding from surging seas, was never a harbour for anything bigger than clinker-built (constructed of overlapping wooden strakes) yoals like the ones Ian Best builds every winter. The working yoals were pulled out of the water to sheltered dug-out slots in the shore called 'noosts' that are still visible, decades after they were last occupied. The word noost, however, occupies a special place in Shetland consciousness, and survives throughout the islands on signs above the entrances to valued locations of shelter and refuge, most of which are bars.

I take refuge in a drystone-walled enclosure at the inner end of the Harbour. Its neat walls on three sides, crusted with desiccated limpets of moss and a thin skein of orangey lichen, are near air-tight, the work of long-gone crofter craftsmen intent on providing a noost for their flocks. The view across the bay is of surging cobalt waters patched with gleaming white pools of foam that swarm around scraggy rocks jutting from below like rotten black teeth.

Unlike the modest structure that occupies soaring clifftops at the island's North End, the South Light, set on low-lying land next to South Harbour, is a twenty-six-metre design classic buttressed on the shore side by the original keepers' compound. Completed in 1892 by David A. Stevenson, it was a manned lighthouse until March 1998, when it became the last light in Scotland to be fully automated.

It stands immaculately whitewashed, with bands of ochre wrapping around vertical window slits and separating the dazzling white of the main tower and the matte black of the light room.

A better angle to photograph the bay with the lighthouse in the background draws me onto a thin promontory that extends from the coastline. Only when I am half way out does it dawn on me just how hazardous this might be. The promontory is pitted with ankle-breaker rabbit holes, and only metres away on either side of me, 30-metre cliffs drop into the crashing surf. Seabirds hover effortlessly in the rushing gale and eye me with what may be curiosity or contempt. I move falteringly forwards, hunched over in a vain attempt to escape some of the weather's power until I flop to ground a few paces from the promontory's end. The washed-out turf is still pock-marked with rabbit holes, but instead of rabbits, from the mouth of each outlet peers an empty bottle. I have stumbled upon an informal drinking venue, probably one favoured by youngsters from the summer work camps. Aside from the omnipresent perils of the cliff edges, it must be a memorable place to perch among good friends and sink a few jars on a mid-summer's night; but right now it is perishing cold, blowing a gale, and no place to be caught hanging around.

My return to the croft is just in time to meet Kathy coming out to the car. Her daughter's incoming flight is officially on, and Kathy is on her way to the airstrip. Acting on impulse, I go along with her. It is a decision I will very soon wish I had never made.

When Kathy pulls the bank robbers' Peugeot into the airport car park, I proceed with great care. Gale force conditions mean that, if I don't want the car door to end up halfway down the airfield, opening it demands the utmost caution.

Dave Wheeler talks animatedly into a radio handset from the ridge near the windsock that sends shudders down its pole, and among the waiting parents, already buzzing with anticipation of seeing their kids for the first time in weeks, there is a conspicuous air of unease. Conditions are so bad that a landing may not even be possible.

Tension rises when word filters through that the plane is a few minutes out, and that the pilot will try to land. The gusting windstorm makes standing outdoors miserable, but everyone gives up the shelter of their car for the chance of catching an early glimpse of the aircraft emerging from the murky northern skies. We hear engines buzzing insistently long before it looms suddenly into sight. The noise from twin propellors dips and rises alarmingly as the pilot uses horsepower to counteract fierce wind gusts and keep her on track for the airstrip that runs from north-east to south-west across the middle of the island. Because the gale is blowing directly from the south, the pilot has to make the approach in a 'crabbed' position. To any experienced pilot, crabbing is the stuff of routine, but today, the degree of crabbing required is extreme, and it makes for terrifying viewing. We stand just south of the midway point of the runway, with the lower half of the airstrip laid out to our left. The plane's nose is pointing directly at us, or about forty degrees from the angle of the airstrip. I know that the pilot is fighting to keep the Islander flying as close as possible to the direction of landing, and due to the intense side wind, he achieves that by flying sideways. As the undercarriage creeps ever nearer to the rocky airstrip, still pointing the wrong way, not a sound comes from the waiting onlookers. At the last possible second and in one slick movement, the pilot applies opposite rudder to swing the nose hard to the right and eliminate the crab, and puts the wheels firmly to earth. The suspension strains and the Islander bounces a metre or more back into the air, but on the second attempt it grips the airstrip and very soon the din of reverse thrust begins to slow her down. The plane, the pilot, and the island's entire population of teenagers are safe, and the car park crowd heaves a collective sigh of relief inspired by as remarkable a piece of flying as I have ever witnessed.

The adult swarm that rushes towards the parked plane bubbles with emotion and adrenalin, and ashen-faced kids step out to hug parents with a lot less self-consciousness than they would normally display. The pilot murmurs reassuring words to each passenger individually, the way parents try to avert hysteria in kids on the verge of going into shock. I hear him say that he was only going to make the one approach, and up until the moment the Islander's wheels touched down, he was debating whether or not to pull out and head straight back to where they set out from.

Teenagers and parents filter towards the cars, and I walk ahead to help Kathy's daughter Charlotte with her suitcase. It is big enough to need to go into the Peugeot's boot, so I put one hand above the boot lid, and with the other, thumb the release button.

In an instant too brief to register, the southerly gale gets under the boot lid, blows it past the hand that was intended to hold it down, strains its hinges w-a-y beyond their operational limits — and detonates the rear windscreen into thousands of glass cubes that ricochet around the Peugeot's interior like fake snowflakes in a Christmas ornament.

Glass is still tinkling while I am still trying to catch a boot lid that now rests on the rear parcel shelf. I bow my head and wish for the power, if not to turn the clock back, then at least to render myself invisible. A car park full of people avert their gazes, and Kathy takes control.

'Never mind. These things happen when you live on an island. Jump in, and we'll get down to the house for a coffee.'

Which is exactly what we do, me sitting in the back with an arseful of safety glass, Charlotte quietly dealing with the emotional fall-out from a horrifying landing followed by the partial destruction of the new family car, and Kathy listening to two or three apologies before telling me to give it a rest. You live on an island with extreme weather, things happen, and you deal with them. Draw a line under it, Ron.

But calling out the roadside repairman is hardly an option on one of Britain's most remote communities, so the car will have to go to Mainland. To make matters even worse, it is not even Kathy's car. In modern Fair Isle folklore, I am destined to be forever associated with the near-destruction of the borrowed robbers' getaway car. On a cock-up scale of one to ten, this is an easy thirteen.

The last time I spent a full hour struggling with a vacuum cleaner does not spring readily to mind, but it takes easily that long to try and trace every last shard of safety glass that has found its way into parts of the car I did not even know existed. Kathy arrives with a few square metres of croft-strength polythene sheeting and several rolls of powerful gaffer tape, and we take the Peugeot to the shelter of the island schoolyard, where we fashion a temporary replacement. I say 'we' because I do cut the tape to size several times *and* hand things to Kathy whenever she issues instructions in the clearest of terms.

The end result would not win many prizes, but it does, I learn much later, function perfectly throughout the entire Fair Isle winter before the car finally makes it to Mainland. There, it undergoes repairs that cost about as much as the old Peugeot is worth on the second-hand market, but a whole lot less than a reliable getaway car is worth to a bank robber or a crofter on a remote island with no public transport.

After the horrors of the landing, the pilot is not about to take on the conditions for the afternoon flight, which is cancelled, and when he leaves without passengers, it comes as no surprise. Forecasts predict the storm blowing itself out by tomorrow morning, so I should get off the island then.

In a land where weather patterns can stay in the extreme zone for days or weeks at a time, minor gradations of change are welcomed for the opportunities they present, and by mid-afternoon things are brightening up. The wind drops a fraction and the skies clear, so I stuff the bad weather gear into a small pack and set out for Malcolm's Head.

I zig-zag through the fields to use climbing stiles set into fences to protect them from the heavy footfalls of birdwatchers. Most fields are cropped short, and have hay roughly stacked in asymmetrical blocks, soon to be packed up and stored for winter feed. Malcolm's Head is a steep headland reaching out from the west of the island towards sea and sky, and soon I face the brief but exhausting uphill slog through damp moorland trimmed by generations of foraging sheep. The highest point on the headland is only 107 metres above sea level, but it offers a birds-eye outlook over the south end of the island and beyond to the thirty-kilometre channel between Fair Isle and the Orkney Islands, for centuries a busy trade route known as 'The Hole'. This is a viewpoint manned by islanders going back to the Napoleonic Wars of the late 1700s and early 1800s, when look-outs were posted to hilltops, eyes peeled for French invaders who never arrived.

One hundred and fifty years later came the very real possibility that Fair Isle might become Hitler's first foothold on British soil, and Malcolm's Head remains littered with the imperishable concrete remnants of a World War II look-out post whose sentries must have watched in helpless horror during the winter of 1941-42 when the South Light twice came under Luftwaffe fire, killing three lighthouse keepers' family members.

The horizons are draped in a dense haze that obscures Orkney, but agrarian southern Fair Isle is laid out like a cartographer's rendering. The entire island occupies under 570 hectares, and from here, more than half of it sits in plain view. From the South Light to the Feely Dyke, a man-made barrier that, like Hill Dyke on Papa Stour, separates northern hill grazing territory from the 'in-bye' farmland in the southern third of the island, it sits like a meticulously detailed three-dimensional model. With binoculars, I can pick out individual houses including Kathy's croft, the museum curated by Anne Sinclair, and the homes of most of the islanders I have visited in the last couple of days. Three kilometres away Sheep Rock is almost unrecognisable, its outline strikingly different from this angle and its ski-slope upper reaches hidden from view.

But the real source of awe is the island's west coast, a vaulted line of vertical cliffs a hundred metres or higher marching unbroken into the distance, their faces deeply indented by narrow geos. Fair Isle is carved from Devonian age sandstone, and cross-sectioned cliff faces break the scene down to its basic elements. Gigantic layers of 370-

million-year-old stone were originally laid down in horizontal beds by rivers and streams. Since then, millions of years and colossal tectonic forces have tilted the beds until they now stand at seventy degrees from horizontal, separated by identifiable lines of 'bedding planes' that highlight the distinct layers. Off the coast, the geometric theme continues, with tall offshore skerries shaped like cones and pyramids, their angles precisely matching parallel lines built into neighbouring cliffs.

I take all of this in from a seated position. The land on the north side of Malcolm's Head slopes sharply towards a point of no return and a one-hundred-metre precipice. The southerly gale has receded since this morning's airstrip drama, but it still has moments that arrive in fierce, salt-laden blasts, and that make a retreat to a safer viewpoint the sensible option.

This is a farming community with a five-thousand-year history, one that in recent centuries has swung between famine-causing overcrowding and near-terminal underpopulation.

As recently as the early 1970s, Fair Isle faced the spectre of unsustainability, the looming possibility of forced abandonment, but once again it has bounced back.

George Waterston and the National Trust between them gave the islanders the means to survive, and today as a community it almost prospers, even if its childbearing population remains too small to sustain resident numbers from within. The sporadic, inevitable need to seek, from the UK and further afield, fresh blood, fresh skill sets and fresh-faced kids to keep the school functioning is itself a sign that Fair Isle, despite being a world apart from the problems that beset Papa Stour, may not be quite holding its own.

And yet, things could be far, far worse. In 1972, the permanent population was an ominously low forty-two inhabitants; the rise in head count to the present day register of around seventy has saved the island, at least for the present. As elder statesman Stewart Thomson says, if it weren't for the National Trust and the volunteer summer work camps, Fair Isle might not still be adding to its five millennia of continuous habitation.

Almost worse, it could have ended up like Papa Stour, sustainable only with the forbearance of the Islands' Council — and bereft of the native element that protected its heritage and culture and the once-fundamental reason for its very existence as a miniature island society.

VIII: Flight paths

When I stir from sleep the next morning, the first thing to attract my attention is the absence of noise. For the last thirty-six hours, incessant gales have maintained an unbroken soundtrack of howling and mewling, so to wake up to absolute silence is a treat, not least because I hope to fly out later this morning. Today is Saturday, and tonight I have a date in Lerwick with fourteen accordion bands, a prospect that would normally excite me as much as the thought of eight hours in a dentist's chair *sans* anaesthetic, but which up here is something to look forward to.

Unlike yesterday, the airstrip is without the gale or the fearful air of uncertainty — and yes, without the Peugeot's rear windscreen.

Only two Loganair pilots fly to Fair Isle, so the islanders are on first-name terms with both of them. Today's pilot is the same one who faced yesterday's awful conditions, and Kathy has a word with him to confirm that I can ride up front.

I make my way to the plane, memories of the previous day's embarrassment all too fresh and high dudgeon at the ready should anyone dare make capital out of it. That I am unable to detect any sidelong smirks is of little consolation, since it is probably because I am unable to look anyone in the eye.

Up close, the Britten Norman Islander has the air of a relic from a bygone era, but it is, after all, precisely that. Built in the eighties to a 1960s design, this is an aircraft design that first turned up for work when Prime Minister Harold Wilson wore a Gannex raincoat and the first coat of paint was still wet on Coronation Street. But when the daily remit is multiple short hops between tiny bumpy strips in a climate that flickers between the blustery and the apocalyptic, this sturdy little craft is hard to beat.

The first time I got up close to an Islander was a few years ago at Kirkwall in the Orkney Islands, and when the pilot invited me to fly up front with him, he didn't have to ask me twice. He showed me aboard the cockpit, and I revelled in what were surely jealous glowers from passengers in the cramped compartment behind me.

There were two seats, twin sets of controls, metal-rimmed analogue dials by the dozen and silvery toggle switches and pedals and lever things straight from a Biggles book. I tried but failed to shroud my growing excitement as I buckled up, impatient for the pilot to clamber in the other side and get this adorable, big kid's dream of an aircraft off the ground. After a minute, the pilot opened my door again, and said, reasonably,

'Mind if I sit there?'

Too late, the penny dropped. There was no other door. I was strapped securely into his seat. Cue barely suppressed twitters from the commuters in the back, and cue a McMillan blushing fit to rival an Orkney sunset.

But mortal humiliation makes for lessons learned, so when I meet pilot Eddie Watt and he ushers me aboard, I duly slide over to the co-pilot's seat, thinking to myself, 'embarrassment free, for once'.

Then Eddie jumps aboard and does a double-take that Oliver Hardy would have been proud of.

'You're the guy who had the accident with Kathy's car yesterday!'

He didn't even do the decent thing and wait until the engines were roaring before he said it.

In Orkney, I flew a half dozen times in an Islander, but again, I am amazed at the leisurely manner in which this little plane gets off the ground. One second we are bumping along towards the flinty airstrip's blind summit, propellor tips roaring only an arm's length from the cabin's side windows, and the next we are in the air. If pointed into a strong enough wind, the Islander can take off at only thirty kilometres per hour. A competitive hundred-metres sprinter runs faster than that.

A few seconds later we fly over the *Good Shepherd IV* sitting high and dry in its ramped North Haven enclosure, then skirt the line of cliffs and offshore skerries that jink and twist all the way to the island's North End, until we reach open sea. Eddie takes the Islander up to about one-hundred-and-fifty metres and levels off.

Forty-ish and fit-looking, Eddie Watt has a natural charm about him, and a strong sense of self-confidence that is both impressive and endearing. He has flown Islanders in Shetland for the last nine years, but before that he spent five years flying all over Africa for

Mission Aviation Fellowship, a Christian charity that operates light aircraft in support of aid agencies from bases in thirty countries worldwide.

The early nineties were scary times to be in Africa. Eddie flew in Rwanda shortly after eight hundred thousand Tutsis were massacred by the Hutu Militia at a rate of ten thousand a day. He flew aircraft carrying refugees, some of whom were almost certainly perpetrators, rather than victims, of the atrocities. His work took him to the Sudan, Zaire and the Congo, the mere mention of which has him pursing his lips and shaking his head at the memories of how rough things could get there.

I bring things closer to home, and ask about yesterday's landing with the school kids aboard.

'That was durrty, durrty wedder,' he says, 'I pride myself in no' frightening the bairns,' (in his Shetland dialect it sounds like *berrns*), 'And yesterday I didn't manage that. I felt awful for the bairns.'

Flying around Shetland, Eddie tells me, even in this age of satellite navigation systems and never mind the high-tech assistance of Air Traffic Control at Sumburgh Airport, is all about line of sight.

'Local knowledge is everything,' he says, pointing out the massif that is Fitful Head in south Mainland, a three-kilometre-long face of perpendicular clay slate, where Sir Walter Scott placed the fictional home of the prophetess Norna in his classic *Pirate*. At three hundred metres tall, the cliffs loom at twice our current altitude.

As the Islander's shadow vaults wave crests below, we fly over Clift Sound, a narrow North Atlantic corridor that cuts north-south between Burra Island and south Mainland. Eddie points east at a clefted valley called Quarff that runs straight across Mainland, and that pilots seek out during treacherous conditions for sheltered passage from one side of Mainland to the other. He tells me it can get a little scary when you meet the coastguard helicopter, known as 'Oscar Charlie' for its registration index, coming the other way.

'But Sumburgh usually keeps us right,' he smiles broadly, as he casually dips a wing to show me a house on the shore of the island of Trondra. It is his family home, which from this altitude, is not only easily identifiable, I can distinguish the make and model of the car parked in his driveway.

Tingwall airport emerges from the misty haze, and after a few words with a traffic controller, Eddie puts the Islander into a long banked turn that incorporates in one fluid movement a smooth descent and final approach rounded off with a textbook landing so gentle that the tyres don't even chirp.

'Right on the numbers,' he says as the wheels come down precisely on the huge white digits at the beginning of the runway. I have never even wondered where that metaphor originated. He taxis to a cluster of small buildings, parks the Islander in front of a hangar and when the propellors splutter to a halt, instructs us to wait at the miniature terminal for our luggage to be brought over. From the terminal doorway, I watch Eddie himself transfer the bags into the back of a pickup, drive it the fifty metres to where we stand, get out and personally hand over each item of luggage to its owner. In Shetland at least, the service industry is alive and well.

LERWICK AND VOE

I: Divided loyalties

A fellow passenger volunteers a lift into Lerwick, and drops me at the Clickimin Complex, a £16 million (more than $30 million) health and leisure centre that would be the pride of towns ten times the size of Lerwick, and which is just one vivid illustration of the benefits derived by the islands from the North Sea oil industry. Thirty years ago, when the excitement over oil revenue was at fever pitch and Shetland Islands Council agreed to host a crucial supply and distribution terminal at Sullom Voe, oil companies found themselves agreeing to a levy imposed on every barrel of oil to land in Shetland. Local Councils are seldom credited with much in the way of long-term planning savvy, but Shetland Islands Council's hard-nosed stance reaped rewards that today are self-evident throughout the islands; in a road network that would be the envy of any county in the U.K., and in omnipresent leisure complexes that grace even small hamlets, of which 'the Clickimin' is the crown jewel.

The Clickimin Complex also hosts Lerwick's only campsite. I have lugged a tent everywhere for the last ten days without once taking it from its waterproof packaging, and now that the weather forecast looks truly awful, its day has arrived.

Any tent in fine weather is fun, but a quality tent in hellish weather is unbeatable. The joys of sleeping separated from raging elements by only a couple of microns of high-tech fabric are a mystery to the uninitiated, but try it once, and prepare yourself for a long love affair with the near-outdoors.

After I pitch temporary digs in the shelter of a shower block, I take myself off to the pub to catch the second half of a football match.

The Douglas Arms is heaving with your average Scottish football bar crowd. Ninety-eight percent men, many of them visibly drunk, and in the main good-natured, albeit with the customary profanity that goes with the drunkenness. On a big screen suspended from the ceiling, Scotland, one of the world's oldest footballing nations, is receiving a lesson in the game from Belarus, one of the youngest. I look around the crowd and wonder how many of them could find Belarus on a map. I certainly couldn't.

It is near the end of a World Cup qualifying campaign in which Scotland's performances have precisely matched the entire nation's secretly-held expectations by being woeful. True to the long-established script, however, an upturn in form in the final stages of the drama presents the team with a mathematical possibility of qualifying for next year's World Cup Finals. The possibility is wafer-thin, but that was never enough to crush this nation's hopes, a task that, as ever, befalls the team themselves, who play their role with depressing predictability, and lose to Belarus by one goal to nil.

Shetlanders make a big deal of being Shetlanders first, and Scottish second. Many go one step further, and claim to be more Norse than Scots, and none that I meet ever mentions anything about being British.

This makes the fervour on display in the crowded pub all the more bemusing. The atmosphere is as ardently pro-Scotland as it would be in any mainland Scottish pub, even if the passion is partly rationalised by the legion of non-Shetland Scots dialects being spoken around the bar. Next to me is a Sullom Voe oil worker from Inverness, who tells me he works ten days on, four days off. By the looks of him, he's three-and-a-half days into a four day drunk. The man on my other side joins in the conversation, but he is so blootered that what he obviously considers to be speech emerges as a monologue of random consonants; I nod frequently, wink at what are hopefully appropriate moments, and insert the odd friendly chuckle to break up the silences.

When the Scots' misery ends, the bar population halves. A woman wearing an England football top and enough jewellery to fill a pawnshop window steps up to the bar and pleads with the barmaid to switch to the remaining minutes of an England match on another channel.

Sadly, a change of channel offers nothing in the way of consolation, as England command a deserving lead over Austria. Then England captain David Beckham gets yellow carded twice in as many minutes, and as he takes the long walk towards an early shower the stunned silence in the Manchester stadium is so complete that I wonder if he might be able to hear the rumbling chorus of well-oiled jeers hailing all the way from a smoky pub in Shetland. Nationalism is a terrible thing, so of course I remain aloof, proud to be above the mindless jeering. Or maybe I don't.

A drink-heavy arm drapes itself over my shoulder, and the Inverness oil worker breathes ninety-proof alcohol in my face.

'Bluidy Shetlanders try to let on they're no' Scottish,' he says. 'But listen tae them. They're as Scots as the rest o' us — an' jist as full o' pish.'

II: Fourteen accordion bands

There is a glaring chink in the thin armour of the argument that Shetlanders are more Norse than Scottish, and that is the thriving Shetland Fiddle and Accordion Festival, held annually since 1988. The festival does exactly what its title suggests: it celebrates fiddle and accordion music. *Scottish* fiddle and accordion music.

The festival is evidence of Shetland's fantastic success at nurturing traditional music to the extent that youngsters in the islands grow up *wanting to play the accordion.* In much of urban Scotland, no musical instrument has less street cred among kids, who associate it with old duffers murdering songs that they only ever hear sung when Grannie has dipped a little too deeply into the sherry reserves. In Shetland, there are pre-teen accordion virtuosos in every school.

The same goes for the violin, since in Shetland, the fiddle remains central to local musical culture and entertainment.

How central? Consider this: the most popular instrument brought to regular musical jam sessions in Shetland pubs is not a guitar or bass or even a harmonica. That honour goes to the fiddle. Shetland's greatest living hero is traditional violinist Aly Bain, and its two best-known and longest-running bands are Da Fustra and Hom Bru, who for decades have played variations on acoustic folk and dance music, violins included.

All of which goes to explain why the Grand Ball at the Clickimin is the highlight of the Accordion and Fiddle Festival, and each October, the hottest ticket in town.

I complete the hundred-metre trek from my one-man accommodation suite to arrive a little before nine o'clock, and to find the festivities in full fling. The well-stuffed 'cloakroom' is a few rows of pegs on wheeled frames in an otherwise unoccupied bar area, nominally watched over by a Buddha-like pensioner who introduces himself as Charlie Johnson, but tells me he is known as Chaz Jazz for his many years' hosting a jazz program on Radio Shetland. Like every DJ I ever met, he is inordinately proud of his enormous record collection, and we compare notes on the albums of Ella Fitzgerald, our shared favourite singer. As we chat, new arrivals come in to hang up their coats, but not without exchanging greetings with Charlie, who apparently knows everyone by name.

In the main hall, at least four hundred people swarm the dance area, packed tight like seabirds on a coastal swell, undulating in time to music from bands who occupy a long platform at one end of the room. A few hundred more watch from tables that sag under the burden of elbows poking from rolled-up shirt sleeves and best party dresses, and hundreds of plastic tumblers that brim with alcohol and soft drinks.

The crowd is a complete cross-section of the community. Kids as young as five play erratic games of tag, ducking under trays laden with drink toted by wiry old guys seventy years their senior. On the dance floor, multiple generations of families spin and twirl, their steps sending rhythmic vibrations through a sprung floor criss-crossed with the multi-coloured markings of a dozen different indoor sports.

Usually when Scots dance, the floor features multiple pairs of women keeping each other company while their men get down to the serious business of drinking their legs out from under themselves. Here, almost every couple features a living, breathing and dancing male, and only a very few pairings consist of two females, often obviously related, and sometimes separated by generations. Grandmothers twirl contentedly in the company of their daughters or grand-daughters.

Over the course of the next few hours, I watch one pixie-like figure with a tightly permed cloud of blue-white hair dance continuously, without so much as a break. My guess is she is in her eighties, and she grins endlessly while she wears out partner after partner from a long table of family members, most of them decades her junior.

Two compères in tight tartan slacks and funny shrunken blazers with big silvery badge-button decorations lining the vent seams and lapels, introduce the ever-rotating array of musicians. Almost every troupe is called The (Insert Male Name Here) Scottish Dance Band, and though each band is met with loud applause, by far the most enthusiastic cheers erupt whenever a Shetlander's name features in the intro.

Robert Lovie from Aberdeenshire is one of the compères. He tells me that this year the festival has drawn bands from Norway, Canada, the USA, the Scottish Borders, Northumberland and Ireland.

Nicol McLaren is a leader of his own dance band in Perthshire, though at the festival he too functions as a compère, as he has done for the last ten years. Nicol and Robert seldom get a moment to themselves. If they are not introducing the latest band or the next dance with all the pomp and some of the confused diction that I associate with Masters of Ceremonies at professional boxing matches, they are being dragged by the hand to the dance floor by women of all ages, where they clearly relish the dancing as much as they do the attention. It occurs to me that if I got myself a suit just like theirs, it might pay for itself in free dance lessons.

Nicol introduces me to one of the musicians. Shetlander Margaret Scollay is a fiddle and piano player and teacher who is well-known in traditional music circles, and she explains that one determined Shetlander was responsible for almost single-handedly rescuing traditional music skills in Shetland.

The late Dr Tommy Anderson's name is one I encounter often in Shetland, and each time he is spoken of in terms bordering upon reverence. Shortly after World War II, Tommy Anderson was so dismayed by the decline in traditional music in Shetland that he set himself the task of getting it back onto the local schools curriculum. Margaret tells me that she was a direct beneficiary when in 1974, one visit from Dr Tommy to her school on the island of Yell inspired forty-four kids out of a school roll of one-hundred-and-ten to take up the fiddle. Thirty years on, Margaret herself is a peripatetic music instructor, teaching fiddle in the local school system, and is known around Scotland for her work with traditional bands.

As she speaks, the floor behind overflows with dancers at ease with a range of dances whose names are entirely new to me. Announcements for the Virginia Reel, the Mississippi Dip, the Southern Rose Waltz and the Circassian Circle are received with whooping enthusiasm. Margaret explains that country dance clubs have become hugely popular all over Shetland in recent years, and because of them, most people are familiar with the dances being introduced with bubbly gusto by Nicol — and by Robert, who comes over to introduce me to someone else I really ought to talk to.

Andy Ross was a compère at the first ever festival in 1988, has attended almost every festival since, and, like Chaz Jazz, appears to be on first name terms with every one of the eight hundred people in the hall.

He has hardly let go of my handshake before I get a recital of his country dance music broadcasting CV. From north-east Scotland, Andy presented a Scottish dance music show on Moray Firth Radio for twenty-two-and-a-half years. (Something tells me that I had better not forget the 'half.') But even the cosy world of dance music broadcasting has room for controversy, and Andy was sacked for criticising, live on air, the station's policy on Scottish music. Before I have the chance to feel sorry for him, he informs me that he now has his own show on an Internet radio station. This allows him to reach a whole new global audience, and it is with considerable pride that he tells me of a new Andy Ross fan club in Dallas, Texas.

A lady stops to chat, and eavesdropping is like hearing two halves of unconnected conversations. Andy speaks in easily understood Moray Scots; the woman communicates in notched strings of alien syllables out of which I catch maybe one word out of twelve. Andy laughs when I tell him I didn't understand anything she said.

'She's from Whalsay,' he says, as if telling me the island she hails from explains everything.

I watch a middle-aged couple take to the only quiet spot in the building, a corner at the side of the stage, so that the woman can teach her faltering partner the dance being performed so enthusiastically by several hundred people only metres away. Their lack of self-consciousness is appealing, their enjoyment in the teaching process self-evident, and it soon captures the attention of others. Two elderly sisters fall in behind them, learning from the learners.

Cecil Hughson owns the main camera store in town, is a professional wedding photographer, and his band Da Fustra, as well as being the longest-running band in Shetland, was the BBC Traditional Dance Band of the Year for 2004. Da Fustra was formed in 1969, when Cecil and other Shetlanders were students in Edinburgh at a time when the Edinburgh Shetland Association had over five hundred members. Da Fustra (named after a low-lying rock off the island of Unst) found itself with no end of professional engagements, many of them weddings. Shortly after that, the discovery of oil in the North Sea dramatically changed employment prospects in Shetland, and many Shetlanders returned home, Cecil among them. Now, while Da Fustra still attend festivals in mainland Britain, the majority of their engagements are in Shetland, and the Edinburgh Shetland Association's membership roster has shrunk to under two hundred.

I am pleased to look around the crowd and see so few men wearing kilts. Mel Gibson has a lot to answer for, but even apart from the dire revisionist fantasy that was Braveheart, the movie committed what are, in my (albeit unpopular) view, heinous crimes against fashion and Scottish national identity. In a little over a decade since Braveheart, the kilt has made a huge comeback in Scotland, and is now *the* fashionable menswear element at special occasions. My inability to comprehend its appeal puts me in a tiny minority among Scots; at a recent wedding I was the only family male not wearing a kilt — and I am frequently the target of incredulous derision for not conforming to what is now a universally-accepted national costume.

The kilt of today is a derivative of the *feileadh beag*, or 'little wrap', in Gaelic, and seems nowadays to be inseparable from accepted notions of Scottish identity.

And yet the kilt as it is today came about by being passionately endorsed by that great Scot, Queen Victoria, (born in Kensington, London, of a Buckingham-palace-born father of almost completely German lineage) whose mother was a Saxe-Coburg from Germany, and whose beloved husband Albert was not only a Saxe-Coburg, but was her mother's nephew — Victoria's own first cousin.

The Royal Couple's oft-noted fondness was for the 'little wrap', itself quite possibly an invention by an 18th Century English industrialist called Thomas Rawlinson. Rawlinson is believed by many (and disavowed by just as many others) to have been concerned for the fire safety of Highlanders who came to work at his ironworks in the Scottish Highlands wearing the genuinely traditional *feileadh mór*, or 'big wrap'. He is said to have advocated the removal of the upper part of the garment, making it less susceptible to the fire dangers of the iron works, and in doing so might well have been responsible for the invention — or at the very least the 'improvement' — of the kilt to the form in which it is recognised today. However it came about, more than a century after Rawlinson's day, the abbreviated little wrap was rendered fashionable overnight when it was so wholeheartedly embraced by Victoria and Albert.

Textile makers with an eye on demand rushed in to summarily conjure up previously non-existent tartan designs to exploit every available clan market. And so we have the modern kilt. Probably 'invented' by an Englishman, granted regal imprimatur by Anglo-German Royals, shamelessly embellished by the Victorian English garment trade, and now seemingly an indelible symbol of our proud Scottishness.

When I notice how few kilts there are at the Grand Ball, I ask two young Shetland stewards about it. I call them stewards, but there is clearly no need for bouncers on a night like this, despite the oceans of alcohol disappearing down revellers' throats.

They tell me that the kilts on show tonight will almost all be worn by Scottish mainlanders. Shetlanders, they concede, *might* wear a kilt to a wedding, but hardly ever to any other occasion. They concede that this may well be another manifestation of the 'we are Shetlanders first, and Scots second' syndrome. Never mind that tonight, the hall is filled with Shetlanders savouring country dance music of the highest order of Scottishness.

As if to turn attention back to Shetland, one of the stewards says he has recently started the process by which he may one day be the Guizer Jarl, the leading figure at Up Helly Aa, a process that will take at least fifteen years' heavy involvement in the annual fire festival and celebration of all things Norse. For about the tenth time in the space of a few days, I am implored to make the effort to get back to Shetland for Up Helly Aa, which takes place in the last week in January. Against my better judgement, I begin to think he may be right, since this is no more out of character than, say, if I was to consider getting measured up for a kilt. Even if I know which one is the more likely to happen.

III: *boom*/clump-*chirp*

When I looked forward to bad weather I should have been careful what I wished for. Most of my next day is spent hiding in the restricted exile of my tented preserve, reading and poring over maps.

Tomorrow I head north to explore the upper half of Mainland, and though there is plenty in the maps to look forward to, cabin fever comes on quickly in a one-man tent with a bare metre of headroom, so by mid-evening I am ready to brave the worsening elements. It is the last night of the Fiddle and Accordion Festival, and there is live music in a popular Lerwick bar called The Lounge, so I wrap up and head for da toon.

The points of the compass hold little relevance and command even less awareness in my daily life, but here in Shetland I recognise a growing consciousness of a hitherto alien concept. The streets of Lerwick's Hillhead are laid out with an almost American attention to grid patterns, main roads running north-south intersected with uniform perpendicularity by east-west side roads.

Creeping up on the town centre while a strong southerly wind fires horizontal rain at me, I soon seek shelter from garden walls on the south side of the cross streets, and dread having to make right-angled turns into north-south wind tunnels filled with hurtling, freezing rain. What should be a leisurely stroll turns into a soggy feat of endurance, and when at last I trudge up the steep stairs into The Lounge, water is running off my jacket and soaking through my trousers.

In a corner of the room, three fiddlers are sawing away with equal parts vigour and skill. Their accompaniment is simplicity itself — bass guitar and piano. A pony-tailed woman of about thirty hammers spiritedly at an upright piano whose inner workings leap and jive, the front panel removed and the top lid folded back in the time-honoured manner of pub singalongs. I watch closely as she unknowingly gives me a lesson on the crucial significance of the piano as a percussion instrument.

Her striding left hand plays the role of a bass drum, hammering out octaves in a percussive 'on the beat' rhythm by which all the other musicians march.

clump
clump
clump
clump

With her right hand, she complements this in an off-the-beat counterpoint, with chirping three- or four-finger chords on the second half of every beat.

clump-*chirp*
clump-*chirp*
clump-*chirp*
clump-*chirp*

This is pushed along in relentless 4/4 time by the bass guitar booming all four beats in the bar.

boom/clump-*chirp*
boom/clump-*chirp*
boom/clump-*chirp*
boom/clump-*chirp*

All of which leaves the violinists free to drive a melody above the background rhythms in tight *da-dum-tee-dum, da-dum-tee-dum* unison through taut eight-bar sequences of comforting predictability.

I watch drinkers all around the crowded lounge raise glasses at the end of eight-bar phrases in subconscious synchronicity.

boom/clump-*chirp da-dum-tee-dum,* **DUMM DUMM** *(slurrrp)*

Fiddlers change seats regularly, new arrivals extricating instruments from rain-spattered cases; there are no stars and no egos to pander to, just a refreshing willingness to play and as basic a readiness to allow all comers to be heard.

What I am enjoying so much is the undisputed acceptance of the need to celebrate and cultivate the cultural fabric that is centuries-old indigenous music.

Music of this genre can be quite difficult to find elsewhere in Scotland, yet tunes whose origins share the same deep roots play today in clubs and theatres and in homes across the world. Early-20th-century Appalachian Old-Time, a wildly popular American dance discipline, was rooted in Scottish and Irish folk music not at all unlike what keeps toes tapping in The Lounge tonight. Out of Old-Time grew Bluegrass during the Second World War, and which today enjoys a resurgence that remains imbued with Celtic strains. Even Country & Western, twanging guitars and glutinous sentimentality and all, can trace its influences back to Scots-Irish origins.

Tonight's weather conditions started out bad but fell away, and they manage to deteriorate even further as I retreat towards my tent. Huge dollops of rain fly parallel to the ground in front of a southerly gale that has grown in intensity since I tracked the route in the opposite direction. As I zig-zag through the street grid, north-bound sections see the backs of my legs stung from behind. The only upside is that, with a gale behind me, I float forwards effortlessly, feet hardly skimming the rain-swept pavement.

Forty-eight hours ago, wary of the southerly gales that had been battering Fair Isle, I pitched the spindly tent in the northern lee of a solid brick building. Last night, the southerly failed to show, but tonight it is here in force, and with it comes vindication. I crawl into my shelter, spread wet clothes across what little area there is that I am not about to lie in, and coory up in my warm sleeping bag. Then I lie on hard ground for hours, listen to the gale strain every seam and string and peg of the tiny tent — and say repeated thanks for the instinct that made me park it so close to the building. Never mind that I am in a high tech foul-weather tent devised to withstand storm conditions, for if it was pitched in the open, I might well wake up in a different place from where I go to sleep. Not that I actually get to sleep until after dawn breaks, when the gale at last subsides.

I awake in mid-morning to a clearing sky and a break in the rain long enough to strike camp and get my weary bones on the road north.

IV: In a young man's footsteps

In 1830, sixteen-year-old Thomas Mountford Adie walked the eighteen miles (twenty-nine kilometres) from Lerwick to Voe with a heavy sack of flour on his back. More than one-hundred-and-seventy years later, I cover the same ground with my heavy rucksack, except I take the bus. The ongoing threat of rain and a belatedly-acquired knowledge of how ridiculously cheap public transport is in Shetland (a nod of thanks once more to the oil levy), sees hitch-hiking dispensed with for the day.

The enterprising Adie lugged his sack from door to door around the homes at the inner reaches of the fiord-like Olna Firth and sold his flour to crofters and fisher folk in the little coastal community of Voe. The profit he generated inspired him to set up as a General Merchant in the area, and what was to become T.M. Adie & Sons, one of Shetland's best-known and most influential trading houses, was born. For one-hundred-and-sixty years, the company operated out of this tiny village, employing hundreds of people around Shetland. The business finally closed in 1991, but almost every building in quiet Voe lives on in testament to what was a manufacturing and trading empire of international significance.

In 1952, the London outfitters to the Royal Geographic Society-supported assault on Everest that led to its first ascent by Edmund Hillary and Tensing Norgay the following year, ordered twenty-four sweaters. Adie & Sons' weavers developed a two-ply Shetland yarn from the finest wool plucked only from around the neck of the fleece. Fine yarn and finer spinning resulted in sweaters that weighed under 200 grams (less than eight ounces).

In 1981 I stood in the check-in line for a flight from Kathmandu to Bangkok, when the man in front of me took a half step backwards and turned day into night. From deep within his shadow, he looked closer to seven feet than six feet tall and almost as broad in the shoulders. I glanced down at his bag, a beaten hold-all with a name embroidered in mustard letters along the zipper. *Ed Hillary*. Over fifty years ago, woollen sweaters that covered this colossus of a man and helped keep him alive at the highest point on the planet, weighed less than a decent-sized chocolate bar. T. M. Adie & Sons traded on their Everest connection for decades, and supplied woollens to a later expedition, when Chris Bonington led the first successful assault on Everest's south-west face in 1975.

A century before Hillary and Tensing's historic moment, T.M. Adie was building a business with the same determination that as a young man saw him take that eighteen-mile hike with a sack of flour across his shoulders. His general merchant business in Voe soon expanded into buying, curing and selling the catches of local fishermen, then into operating its own fleet of sailing vessels that worked the waters as far away as Faroe and Iceland.

T.M. died in 1884, having outlived six of thirteen children fathered with his wife Wilhelmina. For much of the latter part of the century, sailing smacks belonging to Adie & Sons continued to work the northern oceans. They ranged from twenty to sixty tons, were between forty and sixty feet long (roughly twelve to twenty metres), and harvested their catches of ling and cod using only hand lines. They also earned a well-deserved reputation for smuggling duty-free

Faroese brandy into Shetland, a task made more onerous but no less rewarding by the attentions of fast Revenue Cutters.

Fishing voyages were long, gruelling, and broken up by turnaround periods in Olna Firth lasting only a few days — time enough, maybe, to recover from a few too many Faroese brandies.

During the season of 1897, the 65-ton ketch *Granville* made three trips. The first departed Voe on 19th March for the Faroe Banks, returning in mid-May with 4,500 cod. Trip two left Voe on 21st May, and re-appeared in Voe on 27th July with 6,100 cod. Then on 2nd August, she set out for a thirteen-day sail to Iceland, followed by thirty days' line-fishing in strong wind, fog and snow, before sailing back to base in only six days to land 15,000 cod. This means that every one of more than 25,000 fish was caught on lines that were hand set and hand baited, and hauled aboard without the use of mechanised winches. Even after fish were freed from hooks, the work was not nearly done. Crewmen had to split and gut the cod, then salt every individual fish while deep in the hold of a sailing smack suffering the worst the North Atlantic could throw at it.

In the late 1800s the company set up fish curing stations, including the one that brought short-lived security to the people of Papa Stour.

As general traders, the company bartered tea, flour, salt and other staples for locally-produced woollen wear and knitwear; later, they set up commercial weaving and machine-woven knitwear workshops, promoting and selling Shetland woollen wear and textiles at the luxury end of the market. All of this took place from the tight cluster of erratically-placed buildings that is Voe, and which opens up in front of me as I walk downhill from the bus stop. My destination is the pierside sail loft that Shetland Amenity Trust have converted into the flagship of their camping böd network. The böd occupies the upstairs floor of a restored mid-19th century harbour building that for many years held Adie's ships' sailing gear, and later served as a knitwear workshop.

It now plays host to about thirty bunks in a commodious lay-out with an outlook over the end of the firth that would have architects and interior designers falling over themselves to convert it into a jewel of a private apartment. But thankfully, Shetland Amenity Trust and North Sea oil money have prevented such a fate befalling this key piece of Voe's social and economic history.

I am to share the böd with an eccentric Englishman called Clive. Now *there* is a name you don't come across very often any more. The only Clive I can remember was in my primary school class in the sixties, a lad whose friendship I valued implicitly, if only for the most pragmatic of reasons. He stood easily a head taller than any other kid in the class, while I occupied the opposite end of the height spectrum. The best way I ever found to disappear from the radar of predators was to ally myself to someone far too big to tangle with, and Clive was the perfect protective foil. Wherever you may be now, Clive, I thank you for untold beatings and bully sessions averted solely by virtue of you standing by me, elbow to shoulder.

When I arrive at the böd, today's Clive is very much at home. Like the bolder kid who has already staked his claim to the best seat in the classroom, his worldly belongings — including a beaten-up mountain bicycle and trailer — are dispersed throughout the smaller of the böd's two rooms, the one with the pot-belly stove to keep the northern chill out of the air. If Clive seems almost embedded in the böd, it is because he has been here for weeks and is likely to remain in residence until next spring. Clive is retired, wears his still-blonde hair unfashionably long, and from the look of him, either his ears occupy notably different heights on either side of his head, or he is in the habit of sitting on his spectacles.

At first I guess he may be about sixty, but he soon tells me he is seventy-one, and since retiring from a job in the chemical industry six years ago, has been travelling non-stop throughout Britain and Ireland by bicycle. He has an array of tattered maps marked with routes and dates and a bottomless pit of stories about waking up in bus shelters to find himself being pointedly ignored by commuters on the way to work.

Clive has a voice that rattles window panes in faraway buildings, but it is delivered with infectious good cheer, and he soon makes me feel almost at home, even if I do opt to set up camp in the far corner of the other room. With a voice like that, if he even murmurs in his sleep, I do not need to be only a couple of bunks away, tempting pot belly stove or not.

I take over a distant corner bunk with a window looking directly onto an ageing fishing boat perched on its barnacled keel on the concrete quayside. The Donna Rose is about fourteen metres long and currently undergoing repairs; later, Clive bellows helpfully in my ear to say that the one man I can see is doing all the renovation himself, working from a selection of spindly home-made ladders nailed to its hull timbers. Areas around its waterline are tidily reinforced with neatly-tacked copper plate, but below that the sandstone-red protective paint is encrusted with shellfish that might have come all the way from the English Channel or beyond, as the Donna Rose still wears a Penzance registration.

Above the waterline the hull is painted a pleasing powder blue that contrasts sharply with the rust-streaked rigging above it. The boat's decks support a confusion of metal booms and poles and masts and pulleys and cables that brings to mind an indoor trapeze act I saw in North Korea. The only differences being that the rigging on the boat looks infinitely safer, and the repairman isn't wearing stage make-up that would have embarrassed Groucho Marx.

The whole thing balances on its keel, held vertical only by stout lengths of timber jammed between the quayside and the underside of the boat's deck edges. She is so close to the böd window that if the wrong piece of timber slipped out of place, the trapeze rigging could end up sharing my bunk.

V: Mussels and membranes

My sleep in an otherwise unoccupied and frigid room the size of a tennis court goes thankfully undisturbed by boat rigging intrusions, and the next morning finds me wrapped up in every item of clothing I own, duck-waddling past the Donna Rose towards where Keith Robertson's little workboat bobs against the floating marina. Keith is the part-time böd warden, and full-time proprietor of a mussel farming operation whose production lines form neat patterns a couple of kilometres out in the firth.

After I gingerly lower myself into the slippery workboat, Keith fires her up, reverses us away from the marina and immediately points back at the wash from the twin outboards' propellors.

'Looks more like coffee than water,' he says, and he is right. The hillsides above Voe are so heavy with peat that run-off from the thousands of streams and burns that feed the firth runs peaty brown. Since fresh water is lighter than salt water, the run-off forms a thick browny blanket that stretches across the surface of the firth. Factor in the higher freezing temperature of fresh water compared to salt water, and boats that moor in the Voe marina have to be tough enough to handle ice three centimetres thick in mid-winter; this explains why the Donna Rose wears a new protective belt of shiny copper plate around its waterline.

Keith has been farming Olna Firth for just over twenty years; for fourteen of those he endured the boom-to-bust-cycles of the salmon farming business, but for the last seven years he has been farming mussels.

The conditions this morning are freezer-room cool with frigid rain falling like oil drops so that the moment I allow bare hands to creep from the protection of sleeve ends, my fingers go numb, and after a few minutes clinging protectively to chilled aluminium, I say goodbye to all sensation in my digits. Behind us, the bubbling brown mix makes me think of iced coffee before you add the cream and watch it clot and swirl.

I ask Keith if he has to rent his sea-space, and learn for the first time that an entity called the Crown Estate owns all the waters around the entire British coastline to a point twelve nautical miles (just over twenty-two kilometres) offshore. The same Crown Estate holds one of the biggest real estate portfolios in Britain, worth nearly £6 billion, including entire historic neighbourhoods in downtown London; then there is the fifty-five percent of Britain's foreshore, the land between the mean high and mean low tide marks, and approximately half of the nation's estuary beds and tidal river beds.

The name of the estate provides a clue as to where all this goes. From the time of William the Conqueror (he of 1066 fame) until the accession to the throne of George III in 1760, the entire portfolio was the absolute property of the ruling monarch. George III gave it up in 1760 in return for the creation of the Civil List, a schedule of payments from the state to a (some would say none-too select) extended group of Royal family members.

The properties of the Crown Estate are managed independently, and all profits derived from its operations are paid directly into the Treasury.

None of which stops mussel farmers and other aquaculture businessmen from resenting having to rent stretches of unoccupied waters.

Keith pulls us up to what looks like rows of black plastic barrels held evenly spaced by thick seaweedy ropes and with heavy weights reaching down into the coffee mix. Which, it soon turns out, is exactly what they are. As Keith employs a long boat hook to draw us towards one float, a cormorant stands like a statue on a neighbouring one, perhaps wondering if he should simply ignore us. He eventually thinks better of it and flies off, wing-tips splashing ever-gentler parallel trails across the surface of the firth.

I stand dripping iced rainwater while Keith trawls the brown-black firth with bare hands that must surely be blessed by total detachment from his central nervous system. Fingers like callused bananas come up gripping a fat rope encrusted with sea life. The only problem is that most of the life hanging to his carefully-arranged web of ropes is as unwelcome as it is uninvited. He calls them 'sea squirts', an ugly name that flatters the beings in question.

Weighing down his floats and threatening his crop of mussels are clustered legions of what look like tightly packed translucent penises.

To cleanse the rope framework of thousands of ugly engorged membranes means hauling each individual strand aboard the boat to laboriously dip its every stretch in a lime solution. This somehow gives all sea squirts the go-forth-and-detumesce message without harming nascent mussels, which at this point in their development are microscopic grains clinging to the ropes.

From setting the ropes in early summer, when the water is full of the plankton-like life form that develop into mussels, it takes three-and-a-half years before the mature shellfish can be harvested, during which time any number of uncontrollable factors might come into play. Even mere days prior to harvest, when the rope lattice is thick with perfectly formed mussels, a strong gale from the wrong quarter can see a soul-destroying percentage of a crop nurtured for more than three years disappear to the bottom of the Firth.

Every year, Scotland produces three thousand tonnes of mussels; of that, Shetland is responsible for a little more than half. The vast majority are exported elsewhere in Europe, where they are sought-after delicacies. Another huge plus in the mussel's prospects is that demand for it in the UK is so low that that the sales curve has nowhere to go but upwards. The flip-side to this is that any significant rise in home market demand would require a sea-change in British culinary and dietary habits that is at best unlikely.

Keith pushes us off from the mussel farm, but when he turns the key to re-start the engines, only one fires. As the boat continues slowly forwards, he abandons the controls and moves sure-footedly to the rear of the boat to tend to the fuel tanks. I watch with great interest, never taking my eyes away for a second; whatever he has to do takes time while he fiddles with lines and connections. He nods at me once or twice, and I smile back with encouragement that I am sure he doesn't need but that I hope he might in any case appreciate. He looks at me again, this time his head nodding more animatedly, and I nod back, enjoying the cosy feeling of men-at-work bonding. Then he walks quickly forward to brush politely past me and rescue the boat before it runs onto a rocky shoreline that was creeping up behind me while I concentrated on nodding congenially.

The firth as a workplace is something to be in awe of. We are about five kilometres from the wilds of the open North Atlantic, and good fortune and Ice Age glaciers have set out overlapping islands and headlands that protect the inner waters almost completely. The firth here never experiences ocean-driven swells, and even minor surface roughness arises only when gales roar in from the west.

The surrounding hillsides, after days of non-stop rain, are zig-zagged by so many streaks of fast-running brown water that four or five streams can hit the coast within metres of one another. Even a long way out on the firth, the streams continue to turn its waters into that inky black-brown of cold coffee that changes to a latté machine browny-white foam in the wash of the boat propellors.

Houses are sparse on the landscape here, and even the main road connecting Lerwick to Brae, Shetland's second-largest community, can be empty of traffic for minutes at a time. Keith's boat is the only watercraft moving, and right now there is a profound sense of calm at rest around his lovely workplace, the Olna Firth.

WHALSAY AND FETHALAND

I: Bonnie Island

I set off the next morning with a new island in my sights. On the other side of the main highway to Lerwick a side road points towards the district of Lunnasting and the ferry port of Laxo. I begin my trail on foot in a chill wind that makes me thankful for a tight-knit woollen hat picked up in a Lerwick charity shop, and right now a nominee for the best fifty pence I ever spent.

My newly-emergent faith in Shetland as one of *the* best places in the world for hitch-hiking is lent yet further support when the first car to appear pulls over. It is a new Mercedes with a fresh-smelling interior so eye-dazzlingly clean that I worry about the threat I may pose to its upholstery — until the couple in the front say that of course they can take me to the Laxo ferry pier. They are locals on the way to the village of Vidlin, and when I tell them that I am staying in the Sail Loft at Voe, the woman is curious about the camping böd. I love the inflected dialectic in how she asks about it:

'Whit lak is da camping böd?' she says.

Five minutes later they detour from the main road to drop me at the waiting room for the ferry to Whalsay. And ten seconds after I wave them off, the chill around my ears tells me my precious woolly hat has departed with them.

The loss hangs heavy during the wait for the next boat to Symbister, a modern ro-ro car ferry with plush cinema-style seating, the best vending machine coffee I have ever tasted, and wonderful views over the choppy strait that separates Mainland from the island of Whalsay.

Mention Whalsay to Shetlanders from elsewhere, and the inevitable corollary is *money*. Whalsay folk have made the fishing industry their own in recent decades, so much so that not even the oil-employment-blessed communities of Brae and Lerwick can hold a candle to the purchasing power of a Whalsay fishing family.

The name Whalsay comes, like most Shetland place names, from Old Norse, from 'Hvals-oy', which might be translated as 'Whale Island' or 'Island of Whales'. Depending upon whom you ask, the name derives either from regular sightings of whales from the island, or due to the island's resemblance to a whale when viewed from at sea. The common thread is the sea, and in the case of Whalsay, nothing could be more apt.

Sail into Symbister harbour with a map to hand, and it doesn't require a deep understanding of the oceans to glean why seafarers have operated out of here for hundreds of years. As well as being sheltered from most of what the North Sea can throw at it by the embrace of a natural harbour in the south-west corner of the island, Symbister gets further protection from Mainland to the west; even the narrow sea channel north is cut into two separate Sounds (Linga and Lunnin) by the almost plug-like qualities of Linga Island. Add two giant dog-leg-shaped breakwaters, and the harbour looks as if the wildest tempest from any point of the compass would barely ruffle its waters.

Inside the sanctum, upwards of fifty pleasure craft crowd nose-first against both edges of the smallest, innermost jetty, while two other elongated quays bustle with activity around a variety of working fishing vessels. Further out, hugging the inside of the harbour breakwater, sit two of the giant trawlers that make this little harbour on this little island one of the most important deep-sea fishing ports in all of Britain.

As I walk around the harbour's edge, something about it piques my curiosity. In all the ports and harbours I have ever explored, built-up settlements have *always* swarmed to the shore to meet the boats. The symbiosis between vessels that work the waters and buildings that profit from them dictates cheek-by-jowl existences. Yet on this natural curving coastline there are more sheep than buildings. Fenced-in pasture lands reach all the way to the inner harbour, and the few nearby homes perch further up the hillside. Save for a couple of fishing industry warehouses which have the look of recent decades about them, there are hardly any structures, and virtually no private dwellings, anywhere near the water's edge.

Months later, I look into this. I read everything about Whalsay I can track down, but find no clues as to why a harbour central to the island's prosperity for hundreds of years remains so undeveloped. The quest is about to be dismissed as a lost cause when, on the back of a tourism pamphlet for the island, I spy a few telephone contacts. Since it may be improper to bother the island physician with such a self-serving enquiry, I call the local police station, but the sole island copper is not at his desk. Which leaves one last Whalsay number, that of the impressive Leisure Centre on the hill above the harbour.

The phone hardly has a chance to ring before it is picked up by a young man.

'Whalsay Leisure Centre.'

'Hello, I visited Whalsay a few months ago, and I have one or two questions and I don't know where to get the answers.'

'Oh.'

'I wonder if you know somebody I could talk to, someone who knows a bit about the island's history—'

'—Ye'll be wahntin to tak tae ma Granny. She's wi' the Whalsay History Group. Her number is 01806. . .'

And so a cheerfully helpful young man whom I have never set eyes upon puts a stranger in touch with his Granny Marina, treasurer of the twenty-strong Whalsay History Group, and who is no more put out than her grandson at the oddness of the enquiry. The lack of development around the shore of Symbister harbour, she explains, is all down to the Bruces.

From the 17th Century to the middle of the 20th Century, a succession of Bruces were the all-powerful Lairds, or landlord/owners of Whalsay, and the iron rule with which the Bruces controlled Whalsay was enough to give landowners a bad name. In one documented case, when two Whalsay men eager to put bread on their families' tables had the temerity to join a whaling vessel without first asking the Laird's permission, he banned them from returning to the island. Yes, you read that correctly — he exiled people from their own home island.

On the hillside above Symbister Harbour is the symbol of one of the Bruces' profligacy, the mansion home whose views of the harbour, as I am told months later by the helpful Marina, were cosseted by Lairdly diktat — by forbidding any islanders from building on the land between it and the harbour shoreline. Completed in 1823 by the sixth Robert Bruce of Symbister, and built of granite shipped over from Mainland, Symbister House remains one of the largest mansions in all of Shetland. Despite the use of forced labour (for the Laird was able to add what amounted to slavery to the list of grievances against him), the building cost the astonishing sum of £30,000 in 1823 money, which translates to more than twenty million pounds, or forty million dollars in today's funds.

The sixth Robert Bruce's fiscal madness crippled the estate, and the last Laird to remain on Whalsay, a gentle man whose modest nature undid a lot of the damage done to the Bruce name over preceding centuries, died in 1941. Today, the grand folly that is Symbister House is part of the island's school.

One of the few buildings that hugs the harbour shoreline is the restored Hanseatic Booth, a historic totem of trading days whose involvement in Whalsay's economy long preceded even the Bruces'.

The Hanseatic League (from *Hanse*, medieval German for 'guild' or 'association') was the European Union of its day, a tight network of trading posts throughout Northern Europe and the Baltic. Having grown from a loose, 12th Century agglomeration of North German trading cities set up to protect their mutual commercial interests, the League came to dominate Northern European trade for over three centuries. More an economic entity than a political one, it nevertheless exerted huge powers. When a Hansa vessel was attacked by Norwegians in 1284, the League responded by enforcing a trade blockade that quickly brought the whole of Norway to heel.

Symbister's Hanseatic Booth, with its own tiny rock pier, was the League's Whalsay outpost, from which resident German traders did business through ships from Hamburg, Bremen and Lubeck that arrived every summer laden with goods otherwise unavailable to Shetlanders. Food and drinks (including beer and liquor), fishing equipment, household goods, seeds, cloth and iron tools reached Whalsay this way. Hansa ships departed weighed down with butter, textiles and fish oil. Every year, five hundred tons of salted ling fish left Whalsay for Germany, and Shetland's importance to the Hanse's fish markets was noted in 1539, when fully one-fifth of Bremen's imported 'stockfish' — fish air-dried naturally without added salt — was from Shetland.

Consumers today tempted by that leatherette sofa with the pop-up leg breaker footrests, or maybe an authentic mock Victorian garden gazebo, and who are taken in by the 'buy now, pay later' credit trap, might be surprised to know that in Shetland; the same trick was alive and well five centuries ago. Whalsay folk drawn to luxuries otherwise beyond their means were given a year's credit for purchases bought from the German traders, with the proviso that they guaranteed the sales of their own goods to the traders the following year. So as well as being in permanent debt to their Laird, the locals soon found themselves in a never-ending credit squeeze from their German trading partners.

All of this is explained in superb fashion in the atmospheric little two-storey Booth which the less well-informed may mistakenly confuse for a museum, when of course these days the correct term is an 'Interpretive Centre'.

I eventually return the Booth keys to the general store across the street that itself is worthy of a tour. As the only shop on an island with a thousand inhabitants, the diversity of its stock lines have to be seen to be believed.

I first saw reference to it on the Undiscovered Scotland website, where it is described, with only the merest hint of hyperbolic licence:

'... while the island's one shop is extremely well stocked, on some days of the week you are likely to find a wider choice of peat digging implements than sandwiches.'

It sells petrol and diesel from a miniature forecourt outside the building; on the ground floor is a general store of the old ilk, with power tools, building and DIY materials, step ladders and all manner of ironmongery hardware right down to a selection of chains by the metre and buckets of nails and wood screws for sale by the kilo; through a doorway are clothes and toys; and upstairs a well-stocked supermarket serves up most needs in the way of food, drink and household supplies.

From the store I take the uphill trail along what is still known to islanders as Bremen Strasse.

I pass a few identical semi-detached houses that would not be out of place anywhere else in urban Britain. On one hangs a Police Station sign, which has me thinking that the local cop shop is a three-up two-down semi, until I realise the house is the policeman's quarters — and the caravan in the back garden must serve as his police station. I speculate that its 'detention centre' may be a garden shed complete with lawnmowers, strimmers and broken bicycles.

Island architecture varies from council house dull to millionaire conspicuous splendour. One glaring monstrosity boasts a driveway so extravagant that it might actually appear on Whalsay road maps. Aesthetically-impaired creations that reek of new money compete side by side for attention. The people of Whalsay have suffered financial penury over the ages, so perhaps it is understandable that fishing families who have made their fortunes the hard way, by dragging them up from the depths of the Atlantic and the North Sea, choose to flaunt their wealth.

Not that this can entirely mitigate the sequence of visual assaults committed against the visitor's eyes. If the wives and girlfriends of the entire Manchester United first team were to design their own street, it might look a bit like this.

It takes only a few minutes to leave behind most of the housing, but hopes of gaining sight of the island's far shore from the top of the first rise are dashed when all it presents are views of a fresh water lochan overlooked from the far side by a development of new homes. It takes another couple of kilometres of trudging into a freezing north wind before I reach the next crest and achieve, at last, enough elevation to cast my eyes upon the island's east coast, which stands firm against serries of white-tops driven hard and fast by the powerful wind. I clamber across a roadside stream and up a small rise of gnarled heather, and the view broadens to take in surf-battered holms and skerries to the north-east.

Not for the first time in Shetland I am struck by the sensation that the scenery up here is the stuff of poetry. On Whalsay this is especially apposite, because for nine years until 1942, the island was the home of the most important Scottish poet of the 20th Century, Hugh MacDiarmid. Born Christopher Murray Grieve in Langholm near the English border, MacDiarmid (1892 – 1978) lived here with his second wife and their son in a cottage called Sodom (from the Norse, *Sud-heim*, 'southern house'). This was during the Great Depression, and their existence here would have been a hard one; even today, after renovation by the Shetland Amenity Trust to serve as a camping böd, Sodom still does not have electricity.

MacDiarmid's earliest poems, which many see as his most beautiful, were singing Scots-language lyrics. Later, he completed the monumental and intricate *A Drunk Man Looks at the Thistle* which is still recognized as one of the great achievements of the Scottish Renaissance. With this success behind him he took an editorial post in London, and he and his first wife, Peggy, moved south with their two children — but there both his marriage and his working life fell apart.

During an ensuing period of great difficulty and stress, he met a young Cornishwoman, Valda Trevlyn, who as well as loving and supporting him for the rest of his life, carried his flame for the remainder of her own after his death in 1978.

Almost a lifetime earlier, poverty brought them to Whalsay; here, MacDiarmid's reaction to the landscape that stands before me now brought on a new life-view of 'scientific materialism' and a return to writing in English. Despite — or perhaps because of — the straits they found themselves in, it was during his time on Whalsay that he achieved the pinnacle of his poetic output, the collection *Stony Limits*.

While writing poems that were to place him in the upper pantheon of Scots poetry forever, MacDiarmid kept up a prodigious level of correspondence with friends and rivals on the British mainland. A controversialist who thrived on confrontation, MacDiarmid altered Scotland's view of itself in ways that continue to reverberate today. Credited with founder-member status in the National Party of Scotland (set up in 1928, it was the precursor to the present-day Scottish National Party), he was both an ardent Nationalist and an avowed Communist, and earned the peculiar honour of being thrown out of both parties because of his membership of the other.

West coast, Foula island
Whether brought about by geophysical cataclysm or by millions of years of North Atlantic erosion, the west coast of Foula is a stunning five-kilometre-long cliff face that soars for hundreds of metres above the wave-thrashed shoreline.

New Advance ferry, Ham Voe, Foula island
Little more than a gash in Foula's brutal cliff-lined coastal landscape, Ham Voe is the only viable port on the island.
The New Advance ferry sits high in its concrete berth, protected from storms that can close down ferry services for
weeks at a time.

Maun's Hill, Papa Stour
Despite offering only sixty metres of elevation, Maun's Hill gives up superlative views over the deceptively calm inner
waters of Hamnavoe, and beyond to Mainland.

South Harbour, Fair Isle
Despite the name, the island's South Harbour was only ever home to rowing boats, as the bay is wide open to southerly gales. In the background, the 1892 Stevenson South Light was the last lighthouse in Scotland to be automated, in 1998.

Lerwick Harbour
A century-old fishing smack lords over the inner boat harbour at Lerwick, while in the distance, Victorian architecture climbs the Shetland capital's hillside.

North-east Foula island

Viewed from the headland of Strem Ness, the northern third of Foula is a dramatic canvas, with the pinched-dough-nut Gaada Stack standing tall in the face of everything the North Atlantic throws its way, and Soberlie Hill pointing towards the mighty North Bank cliffs.

The Altaire at Collafirth pier

The Altaire is the largest vessel in the British fishing fleet, and the only one of Shetland's eight pelagic trawlers not based on the island of Whalsay. The benefits it brings to the 300-strong community of Ollaberry and North Roe are vital.

Stewart Thomson, Fair Isle
Stewart Thomson married into Fair Isle society more than sixty years ago. Today, four generations of his and his wife
Annie's family still call Fair Isle home.

Voe Sail Loft camping böd
The restored 19th Century harbour building that is today a Shetland Amenity Trust camping böd was once part of a business empire set up in the mid-1800s by Thomas Mountford Adie. T.M. Adie & Sons were general traders, operated fishing fleets and ran spinning and weaving operations out of the tiny village of Voe for more than 60 years.

Coastal tombolo and St Ninian's Isle
Apart from during exceptional storm tides, St Ninian's Isle remains connected to south Mainland by its soft sand tombolo. The island is famed for a treasure trove of 9th-Century artefacts turned up by schoolboy Douglas Coutts during archaeological excavations in 1958.

Wester Wick, Fethaland
The Gloup Disaster of July 1881 killed fifty-eight fishermen in ten *sixareens*, and was the beginning of the end for *Haaf* fishing. Fethaland onlookers watched one *sixareen* reach Wester Wick atop a wave as high as conical Busky rock seen on the left of the photo.

Fair Isle airstrip
Charlotte Coull, second from right, follows her mum Kathy after a hellish gale-rocked landing aboard the flight from Mainland. A few seconds later, she sees the same gale destroy the rear windshield of the new family car – thanks entirely to my negligence.

Flying towards West Mainland
The twin-propellor Britten Norman Islander is the perfect inter-island Shetland workhorse, able to operate from often rudimentary airstrips even in foul weather. Loganair pilot Marshall Wishart points the Islander towards West Mainland.

Coastguard helicopter over Sumburgh Head
Known to every Shetlander by its registration index Oscar Charlie, the coastguard helicopter is as familiar to islanders as the village policeman of old – and just as important to the welfare of locals and visitors. Here it flies over Sumburgh Head on the way to its base at nearby Sumburgh Airport.

Kids at play, Walls, West Mainland
Like a scene out of the 1950s or 1960s elsewhere in the country, kids in the small community of Walls make their own fun.

Geologist Allen Fraser at Eshaness, North Mavine

Geologist, meteorologist, tour guide and raconteur Allen Fraser describes Eshaness as 'the best cross-section of the anatomy of a volcano to be found anywhere in the British Isles'.

Up Helly Aa Guizer Jarl's squad
Early in the evening of the annual Up Helly Aa fire festival, the squad of the ceremonial leader 'Guizer Jarl' warm up
They have another twelve hours to go before the singing and chanting are over for another year.

The Snolda departs West Burrafirth
Flanked on either side by the low-lying coastline and the North Atlantic, Burra Firth in west Mainland is wide open to the elements. How Vikings and other sailors of long-gone times survived such waters in flimsy, oar-powered vessels, is impossible to imagine.

As I overlook Whalsay's eastern shore, I rue all the coffee consumed earlier, and realise that if only I can protect tender extremities from the icy wind, I may have to resort to what country folk call a 'green fielder'.

From where I stand, there is an unrestricted line of sight along three kilometres of road that reaches towards the island's lightly populated north-east. Behind me the view stretches only to the brow of the hill I just cleared, and the road comes to within about fifteen metres, but since not a single vehicle has passed me yet, there is no great gamble in taking a leak right here. And anyway, having mulled it over for a minute too long, waiting until later is no longer an option. After a quick glance in both directions, it is time, as they say so lyrically on the Indian sub-continent, to *do the needful*.

Except the needful zone is enclosed behind multiple layers of clothing, and an exercise that should take a few seconds now takes an age. At long last, hands protectively cupped against the wicked wind, I finally get to savour an urgently-anticipated moment. Then a glance to the north-east reveals not one, but two vehicles coming south at speed. Because of the huge wage packets commanded by its young fishermen, Whalsay has the reputation of being the 'boy racer' capital of Shetland, and right now two boy racermobiles are screaming across the landscape at speeds so far in excess of the legal limit that they will be upon me long before my present mission can possibly be accomplished. I have no option but to turn my back on the onrushing cars, remove one hand from protective detail, raise binoculars to eyes, and feign interest in the near-featureless grey soup that is the North Sea. As two highly-tuned cars roar past only metres away, I carefully pivot northwards to keep my back to them — then, as quickly as is humanly possible given an impending state of frostbite, I return one chilled appendage to where the north wind doesn't blow. Only the Doppler wail of two sets of air horns suggests that my impromptu charade fools nobody. Maybe the cloud of steam performing a northwards arc over the heather gave the game away.

Back in Symbister, there is time to wander the harbour quays before catching the ferry to Mainland. Whalsay may be famous now for the mightiest of British trawlers, but the island's fishing history embraces much more than the top end of the market. A couple or more centuries ago, the *Haaf* was central to Whalsay's early

117

involvement in commercial fishing, back in days when fishermen were bit-part players in a Laird's hard-fought commercial game, and disasters that wiped out male breadwinners blackened Whalsay history with depressing frequency. If the depredations of nature were brutal, almost as arbitrarily evil were the machinations of navy Press Gangs, who plucked men from *sixareens* in mid-ocean to press them into naval service, never to return to Whalsay, their families never to learn why they were gone nor even if they were alive or dead.

After all those long centuries of suffering at the hands of a triumvirate of Lairds, Press Gangs and continental credit providers, the fishermen of Whalsay are finally having the last laugh. In the last seventy-five years, almost every outlying Shetland island has seen a sharp decline in its resident population. Some, like Papa Stour and Foula, have suffered drops of seventy-five percent or greater; the three large northern isles of Yell, Unst and Fetlar have all seen populations halved in the same period. Whalsay is the only island to buck the trend, its population rising from around nine hundred in 1931, to just over a thousand today, something that could never have happened were it not for the economic powerhouse that is the fishing industry.

In the evening I sit at a long table in the Sail Loft camping böd when the door opens and in wanders a vaguely familiar face that I take a few seconds to identify. It is the man who drove the gleaming new Mercedes that took me to the Laxo ferry pier this morning, and he carries in his hand my woollen hat. Despite protestations about 'just passing', he has obviously driven far out of his way, and I am humbled by the generosity of spirit that inspires him to make such a kind gesture to a stranger.

Over the coming weeks, as I criss-cross Shetland, my ear lobes are frequently and earnestly indebted to this kind man. I would take my hat off to him, if I wasn't so scared of losing it.

II: The fridge, the soapstone and the walrus

British artists through the ages have been prominent in the upper ranks of watercolourists and landscape painters and photographers, something that surely comes from the nation's ever-changing quality of light. Shetland in autumn is a watercolourist's joy, and this morning the briefest of glances through the rusted rigging of the Donna Rose shows me how beautifully the light has at last changed. After a week spent looking at island life through the filters of a badly-faded 1920s black-and-white movie, I wake up to bright sunshine, blushing blue skies, cotton candy clouds and sharp blue-black shadows. Even the coffee-coloured Olna Firth wears an all new sparkling sheen.

David Murray calls to say he cannot pick me up as promised, but that his nephew Brydon will be down to get me. Soon, I am heading north in a sturdy four-wheel-drive pick-up of the sort of dimensions so beloved of urban Mums intent on safely navigating the perils of ten-centimetre-tall speed bumps while pre-teens Farquar and Tamsin struggle with the alphabet in the back. Beside me is a soft-spoken young man with hands like shovels. Brydon is a stockman for the family crofts in North Roe, the northernmost peninsula on Mainland, and instead of brats in the back seat, he carries the standard crofter's issue of two working dogs in the covered pick-up bed. The only time I don't have to strain to hear what Brydon says is when he lets go with a rebuke at the dogs in a roar that sends ripples through the black floats in Keith's mussel farm hundreds of metres out on Olna Firth.

He talks softly of the year-round duties of a stockman, and points out the hill areas where sheep from many crofts are free to roam for several months of the year, and can only be brought back by the combined efforts of the Brydons from all over the region. This is the land around Collafirth Hill, a lump on the landscape which stands severe and expansive and stony. It is yet another stretch of glacial landscape, one where surely even the toughest of sheep must struggle to eke out enough nourishment to survive. Brydon speaks of his life and his work with a deep understanding of where he comes from, and perhaps just a hint of curiosity, or even yearning, for what else might be out there in the wider world.

Below Collafirth Hill is a deep sheltered coastal inlet that gives the hill its name, and which is the home base of another gleaming pelagic trawler, a near duplicate of the two I saw yesterday on

Whalsay. The *Altaire* is moored at a jetty not much longer than itself, and sits high in the water, its holds empty. We sweep past, the dogs behind us barking at something that bothers their heightened senses, but which eludes me completely.

With driving skills far beyond his years, Brydon takes the four of us along tight weaving tarmac barely wider than the pick-up, until the road crests a modest hill that presents a whole new landscape. Flowing ahead is verdant farm land with the waters of Yell Sound to the east, and brown-hued hill country to the west. Prosperous crofting terrain occupies a lush coastal plain dotted with signs of light habitation. I see it at its most beautiful, its richness of colours drawn out by crisp autumnal morning light. Even the homes of North Roe have their own appeal, from the bigger stone manses with the look of the 19th Century about them, to neat modern bungalows with kids' swings and slides in the gardens and fat sheep greedily eyeing tidy lawns from just over the fence.

Brydon pulls up at one such bungalow and introduces me to his Uncle David. David is a lean character in his late thirties who spent some years in New Zealand before returning to the family land and to marry a Lerwick lass and father three daughters. A farmer to the core, David is passionate about the history of his homeland, and works part-time to promote it as a tourist destination, based upon both its beauty *and* its history.

I transfer myself to a different four-wheel-drive pick-up with a different pair of working dogs in the back, and David drives us north. We skirt the sheltered bay of Burra Voe and climb the long gentle slope through fertile farmland to Isbister, the northernmost croft on Mainland, and farmed by David's father, Douglas. We weave between farm buildings to a gate with a sternly-worded sign telling visitors not to drive beyond this point. According to David, the sign might as well not be there, so often do cars push on through, frequently to end up stuck and have their drivers come back knocking on the farm door to plead for help.

I shake my head at such tales of tourist sloth and smirk with relief as I hold the big gate open while David drives through.

Everything north of here is Isbister farmland — and at its northern tip is the focus of David's tourism marketing efforts, the Fethaland peninsula. As the dirt road exits the farmyard, it climbs steadily with the promise of fine vistas ahead.

The reward is worth the short wait. Instead of an outlook over the extreme north end of Mainland, a bowl-like depression scoops the land towards another crest, beyond which remains the promise of Fethaland proper. The bowl is lined with a tan vegetation carpet stippled by bubbling eruptions of rock. Spread out like a new blue tarpaulin lies a glistening lochan backed by a small hill where three sheep point towards its miniature peak with geometric perfection.

The road rides down the bowl and back up the other side, and tall wooden posts march beside it holding up thick power cables before they vanish over the crest and into the dip beyond, only to reappear on the final rise in the distance, climbing to the tip of the headland to a squat lighthouse that offers the only dash of white upon the landscape of greens and blues.

I take that back. There is another tiny dash of white on an off lying island, one more remote lighthouse to safeguard shipping, crucial in a stretch of water travelled daily by island-sized tankers feeling their way to and from the oil terminal at Sullom Voe. As if on cue, between the two lights and the hazy blue ocean horizon, a gigantic, slow-moving black and red stripe of an oil tanker makes steady progress southwards.

The next crest at last reveals the sheltered double sided crescent of rocks and grass that is Fethaland, a narrow neck of land that attaches the peninsula's tip to North Roe.

On a sunny autumnal day, it is a scene soaked in natural beauty that exudes a deep sense of isolation and tranquillity. And yet for decades this was a centre of back-breaking labour, untold hardship and occasional, community-wrecking tragedy. For here was Mainland's most northerly and most heavily worked centre of *the Haaf*, a makeshift village that popped up each summer for the *Haaf* fishing season, and played home to as many as a hundred *sixareen* row-boats, their crews, their families, the host of workers required to service them and their catches, and even the Lairds who helped lock the fisher folk into this life. For at least three months of every year, several hundred hardy souls, Shetlanders from elsewhere in the islands who fitted the *Haaf* into a calendar of cyclical crofting and fishing seasons, called this tiny sheltered cove home. Today it lies barren of residents, and has been since the last crofter family moved out in 1944. David is more than familiar with the tale of the last crofter family because among them was his father Douglas, who was born here in Fethaland in 1936, and departed its lonely shores along with his parents when he was eight years old. Douglas, who as an infant lived in the most northerly home on Mainland, now resides at Isbister farm, only about three kilometres south of here, and still Mainland's most northerly occupied home.

The ruins of the croft house where Douglas was born remain standing, and the first thing I notice is how small it is. Frills were unheard of in Fethaland in the 1930s; Douglas's family had one room for living in, well water, a peat or driftwood fire for heat and cooking, and candles and paraffin lamps for light. The front windows — square holes in the drystone construction — face towards Yell Sound, and Douglas's father kept a paraffin lamp burning on one window ledge all night as a navigation beacon to Whalsay fishermen rounding the point of Fethaland as they entered the Sound on the way home. In return, the fishermen supplied him with enough paraffin to light the house year-round. It was a most pragmatic arrangement; fishermen could navigate the point after dark without fear of running aground and drowning, and Douglas's family were able to navigate their one-room house without falling over the furniture.

In another ruined croft, David shows me a feature that has survived a century of abandonment. A built-in cupboard space incorporated into a gable wall made of thousands of pieces of gneiss rock has a smooth slab of white quartz set into its bottom edge. Following David's instructions, I put the palm of my hand on the lichen-mottled rock wall next to the quartz, then transfer it to the white quartz shelf. The difference in temperature is remarkable. The stones that make up the inside of the house wall may have a little stored heat in them — but the quartz shelf in the 'refrigerator', because that is the role the quartz shelf once served, feels many degrees cooler.

Much later, my scientist friend Jay enlightens me. This is down to something called 'thermal conductivity', or how a material conducts heat away from any other matter, in this case my hand. Quartz is a highly efficient thermal conductor, meaning it draws heat out of my hand so quickly that it feels cool to the touch. Since it would have precisely the same effect on, say, a slab of butter or a hunk of fresh fish, then it had a refrigerative effect on food stored upon it more than a hundred years ago.

The ancient Greeks believed quartz was water frozen by the Gods, and called it *Krystallos*, or 'ice'. And the Romans, while they busied themselves expanding an Empire across hot and sweaty foreign lands, were known to carry pieces of quartz with which to keep their hands cool.

The Fethaland village site is on a thin waistline of land that runs roughly north-south between opposing curves of stony beaches, each forming a bay — Wester Wick and Easter Wick. Shetland is full of Norse place-names that end in 'Wick', which is an old word for a bay, usually populated, and is the origin of the term 'Viking'. As one Shetlander told me, the word Viking is not so much a statement of nationality as it is a job description. Wicks, being coastal bay communities, were preyed upon by marauding Norse invaders, who went 'wicking', or plundering.

For more than a century until around 1900, Fethaland was a fishing station occupied throughout the summer *Haaf* by, depending upon who you talk to, anywhere from a few hundred to as many as a thousand fisher folk. The structures that played homes to the families and provided shelter for their *sixareen* row-boats remain, crumbling under the incessant onslaught of the elements, untouched and unrestored, even unexplored by experts who could make sense of Shetland's last and most complete set of remains pertaining to the historic *Haaf*. This is an archaeologist's dreamscape, a restricted area with a documented history of habitation and industry. Seemingly the only thing preventing archaeological investigation is the lack of momentum on the part of the academic powers and the governing body that maintains titular and legal hold over this 'Scheduled Ancient Monument'.

Not only do some of the *Haaf* homes and the *Haaf* boat noosts remain in situ, but there are also signs here of a prehistoric homestead, and fifty metres north on the 'Isle of Fethaland' that is not (at least not any more) an island but a headland attached to the rest of the peninsula by the beach, are indications that Vikings indeed did some wicking here more than a thousand years ago. Yet nowhere is there so much as an information board, let alone protection from unsupervised visitors. A curmudgeonly surge of moral outrage on my part is balanced by the realisation that I get to savour this fascinating site without the interference (alright, protective measures) of any controlling authority. When I was a kid, this was normal, and we have the family pictures of us wandering undisturbed around Stonehenge to prove it. Maybe, rather than worrying about the lack of investment and control over this stunning setting, I should just tread carefully and enjoy it.

I see Fethaland at its prettiest and most accommodating, under blue skies, in warm temperatures, with not a hint of rain or wind. But the poor souls who worked the *Haaf* from here would often have seen it in an altogether different light. David points at a cone-like rock jutting out of the waters of Wester Wick. The rock has for centuries been known around here as 'Busky', a name that David never knew the origins of until recently, when he was showing a party of Norwegians around Fethaland, and they laughed out loud as soon as he mentioned it. Busky, they explained, means 'lump' in Norwegian, and what a lump it is, nearly twenty-five metres of solid rock drawing its own exaggerated doughnut of castor-sugar froth in the swirling waters around it.

Busky plays a central role in one of the most dramatic stories of Fethaland, and in an event that is seen by historians as the beginning of the end for the *Haaf* fishing industry. The Gloup Disaster of 21st July 1881, so named because most of the *Haaf* fishermen who died that day were aboard *sixareens* from Gloup in north Yell, happened when a raging summer storm caught entire fishing fleets at sea. In all, ten boats were lost and fifty-eight fishermen died, including an unknown number from Fethaland. In Gloup, the disaster wiped out almost every male in the local population.

The majority of the deaths were among crews who chose to try and reach land, and who perished when their boats were driven ashore by the storm. Yet in Fethaland the story goes that one boat made it to safety in the most spectacular of conditions. Its skipper brought his *sixareen* into Wester Wick soaring on a cresting wave that eye-witnesses swore was as tall as Busky rock. Standing on the shore where the wave would have broken and looking out at Busky towering over the placid bay, it makes for a terrifying mental image.

David leads the way up the lush green hillside that is Isle of Fethaland, points casually at a few rocks on the hill that he assures me mark a prehistoric settlement, and leads me to a cliffside viewpoint on the east side of the headland. From where we sit perched atop a small cliff (small only by Shetland standards; a tumble over it would certainly be fatal), Yell Sound is a six-kilometre-wide sea corridor separating us from the Yell coastline that stands like an undulating rock curtain. A few kilometres south, the giant tanker slips through the ever-narrowing strait towards the terminal at Sullom Voe; from there, it will soon retrace its course, laden down with North Sea crude.

Within a stone's throw of our clifftop vantage point, a tall stack stands as a monument to the memory of a woman known only by her name: Maggie Clark. Nobody remembers who the eponymous Maggie was, and David fails to convince me that at the top of the stack is the shape of a seated woman wearing a shawl. At the foot of the cliff beneath us, a happy looking seal bobs around in water so crystalline that it could be cut from a Caribbean tourist brochure. Closer to the cliff, a large rock takes a deep breath, flaps its tail and becomes an honest-to-goodness sea lion.

David points out a cliff face so smooth to the touch that the rock's common name of 'soapstone' is instantly understandable. More correctly known as 'steatite' (but known in Shetland dialect as 'kleber' or 'clebber' — from 'kleberg', Norse for steatite), it consists entirely of a mineral called talc, which, as well as being at the softest end of the standard scale of mineral hardness, is what talcum powder is made from. In rock form it is solid and translucent, and for centuries was valued as an easily-worked source material for dishes or pots. The wall face beside us is pocked with shallow circular indentations, one-millennia-old evidence of Vikings done a-wicking for the day, cutting out bowls and pots from the hillside. All around the indentations are pieces of hand carved graffiti; names, initials and dates going back to the 19th Century, when just over the neighbouring crest, the harsh way of life that was the *Haaf* remained an ongoing reality.

A pre-historic homestead, hands-on evidence of Viking activity, a completely unrestricted visual museum of the *Haaf* fishing of the 18th and 19th Centuries — and even the occasional sea lion. Fethaland has it all, plus a complete dearth of tourists that only further cements its appeal.

III: Hinterland economics

David's two dogs stand side by side in the truck bed, tails doing synchronised windscreen wiper impressions. We have been away for more than an hour, mostly within sight of the dogs, and for all that time they have been free to come or go, the gate at the back of the pick-up bed wide open. But being working dogs — as opposed to anthropomorphised pets lavished with praise and store-bought cookies whenever they achieve major behavioural milestones like shaking paws and sitting on command — and since their master never gave them permission to leave the truck, they remain inside, eagerly but patiently awaiting his return. These, if I could ever muster the patience to train them to this level, are my kind of dogs.

David offers to show me them at work, and drives us along the track towards Isbister until he spots three woolly animals loitering like teenagers outside a liquor store. He pulls over, lets one of the dogs out (she is the mother of the much younger second dog and which is only partly trained), and with the help of a little plastic whistle gadget that he places between his teeth, sends her off to work.

The innocent targets are about two hundred metres up an uneven hillside, but the collie covers terrain so rapidly and with such sure-footedness that she becomes a black-and-white superdog streak, paws barely skimming the turf, her gaze never wavering from the animals. David switches wheep-wheeeeep instructions to control her arc around behind the sheep, who by now are well aware of the canine charge and showing signs of heading for the hills. In less time than it takes to convince a determined Labrador to stop ingesting the contents of a fridge, three jittery animals find themselves escorted down the hillside at speed to a point on the road only a few metres from the pick-up. David calls the dog off and she trots forwards, eyes locked on him as if seeking praise for a job well done; meanwhile, the sheep slink away, looking almost indignant at the unseemly intrusion. But there I go on my own anthropomorphic exercise, since the sheep could just as easily be wondering why the dog decided not to eat them.

'I often stop up here and do this for visiting tourist groups,' says David. 'They love it.'

While crofting and, to a far lesser extent, tourism are central to the local economy, the peninsula's realists know that the sustainability of the area is dependent upon the giant tangerine-coloured trawler tied up at Collafirth Pier. The *Altaire* is Britain's largest fishing boat, and the economic benefits of having it based locally are vital to over three hundred residents in Ollaberry and North Roe. Even at the most basic level, the general store at Collafirth would not survive if it was not for the custom it enjoys from the *Altaire's* owners, who directly subsidise shopping for the whole community by sourcing their supplies, not in Lerwick where prices are lower, but in Collafirth, where the locals would be lost without the shop. When the community's medical practice needed a new defibrillator, the ship's owners paid for one. On top of this, there are highly-paid crew jobs for local men, and the money that filters through them into the local economy.

I learn this while we drive to Collafirth Pier, where the ship is tied up. The small pier occupies the former site of a Norwegian-operated whaling station, and lies deep within a north-south bay that itself nestles far within east-west-facing Colla Firth. Sheltered, however improbably, by land on all four sides, it is a supreme natural haven. The *Altaire* is just over 76 metres long, and when it entered service in 2004, it cost its shareholders £16 million. David parks the pick-up on the pier and we walk straight aboard. I don't suppose the keys are in the ignition, but she does sit unmanned and unguarded.

I am still feeling like an uneasy trespasser when urgent footsteps pound the gangway behind us. David introduces me to the Chief Engineer, who has just been alerted at home by an onboard alarm. Not, as I first imagine, a security alarm tripped by us, but a technical alert that requires the Engineer's attentions. Concerned with engineering issues and unperturbed by David giving a stranger a guided tour, he scurries off to investigate.

I have spent time in hospitals that were less sanitary than this trawler, which is so spotlessly clean that it somehow manages not to smell of fish.

The second impression I get is of top-grade components of a quality that would not be out of place on a brand new military installation. Everywhere I see exotic high-grade metals sewn together with welds so exquisite that they would reduce any craftsman welder to tears of admiration. As we walk the decks, David throws nuggets of information my way. The three-kilometre-long trawl nets are so heavy when full, that hauling them aboard would be impossible. Instead, the ship performs a U-turn and sails back alongside the full net, which is emptied using an immensely powerful vacuum pump that sucks the catch aboard through a 24-inch (60 centimetre) alloy nozzle at a rate of eighteen tonnes of fish per minute.

The *Altaire* is powered by a V-16 monster motor putting out 8,000 kW (10,700 BHP), and which at maximum output burns 1,400 litres of diesel per hour from its 650,000-litre tanks. I quickly do the mathematics; a casual 'fill her up' instruction at the fuel pump could cost her owners *half a million pounds*.

Through cabin windows I get a glimpse of the living quarters. The ship has twelve single-berth cabins and one four-berth, each with its own private bathroom. One single cabin is like a modern hotel room, except better-equipped, complete with Sony Playstation bolted to the desktop. The galley would not shame a five-star hotel, and the crew lounge boasts a giant flat-screen television and DVD library. Between long hard shifts in tough conditions, the men of the *Altaire* live in as much comfort as money can buy.

The word 'pelagic' refers to mid-ocean, as the ships trawl at medium depths, and neither scour the surface waters nor scrape the ocean floor. There are only twenty-eight pelagic trawlers in the British fleet, and Shetland is home to eight of them, seven on Whalsay, and the *Altaire* here in Collafirth. What makes it worthwhile to invest such huge sums are the fishing quotas acquired over the years by vessel owners. Even if you had a spare £20 million and fancied the life of a pelagic trawler skipper, without a quota, or entitlement to catch a specific tonnage of certain types of fish, your shiny new boat could do nothing to generate a return. At the time when David gives me a tour of the *Altaire*, its owners have the rights to annual quotas of 9,800 tonnes of mackerel and about 2,000 tonnes of herring. At 2005 prices, fulfillment of the quotas would generate over £11 million in a single season.

When David voiced fear for the region if there was no *Altaire*, he had good reason to be concerned. The skipper of the *Altaire* had been caught selling 'black' fish — fish caught in excess of permitted quotas — in Denmark. The authorities take a necessarily dim view of such conduct (never mind that it is almost certainly widespread), and when David showed me around his friends' trawler, court verdicts had yet to be delivered. The possibility of a fine so huge as to close down the *Altaire* altogether was very real.

In two separate rulings in October and November 2005, the punishments were handed down. For pleading guilty to landing 7,600 tonnes of illegally caught herring and mackerel, the skipper and the ship's mate were ordered to cough up a total of just over £1 million. The future of the *Altaire*, incarnations of which have operated from Collafirth since the 1970s, is secure, and the people of Collafirth and North Roe can sleep easy.

David takes me to the top of Collafirth hill for one last view over the lovely land that he calls home. From amidst the Ice Age glacial detritus of crumbled boulders like oversized packing cases, the coastal scenery of Collafirth and beyond is dazzling. Below us, the *Altaire* sits at peace in its sheltered bay; across the narrow Sound, the isle of Yell stretches across the horizon like one giant rock deposit; and to the north, snatches of coastal inlets hint at the crofting prosperity of North Roe and Fethaland. From here, I sense the powerful attraction of a place of great beauty and history that pulled David Murray homewards, all the way from New Zealand. The Kiwis call New Zealand 'God Zone' — short for God's Own Country; but if there *is* a land of the Gods, it might just as well be found up here as anywhere else in the world I ever travelled, New Zealand included.

THE ISLAND OF YELL

I: Peat country

To Yell and back. Come Yell or high water. For whom the Yell tolls.

And they only get worse as I stride north out of Upper Voe and try to concentrate on tabloid-esque puns. I am using the name of Yell, one of Shetland's biggest islands, the one I savoured so many fine views of yesterday from the other side of Yell Sound, and the target of today's thumb-powered travels. The brisk pace and the concentration are vain attempts to ignore the deathly cold wind that hits me bang on the nose. *When Yell freezes over* becomes the new favourite.

The road is completely empty of traffic, so for the better part of an hour, I keep the pace up and the blood circulating. When at last a car stops, I am once more surprised to see a single middle-aged lady stopping for a stranger, but since she too is headed for Yell and can take me to Toft to meet the ferry, the notion of delivering a lecture on personal security is quickly dismissed.

I barely put cold bum to warm seat before she reads my mind.

'I don't normally pick up folk,' she says, 'But you looked respectable.'

She is a crofter who lives on Mainland, but her husband has family land on Yell, so she is on her way to help him with the sheep. We drive the deserted highway past the long naked peninsula of Gardaness Hill next to the narrow seawater inlet that is Dales Voe; my map tells me that the voe on the far side of Gardaness is called Colla Firth, the same as the deep inlet inhabited by the *Altaire* trawler.

Postmen must have a hard time in Shetland. The same place names crop up all over the islands, relics of days when Norse invaders affixed titles to wherever they swarmed ashore, names that were often based on geographical settings. In an archipelago full of fiord-like inlets, the same names crop up time and again. Hamna Voe (or Hamnavoe) appears all over Shetland, because 'Ham' in Norse means 'harbour', and 'voe' means 'bay'. In a coastal landscape full of merciless cliff-lined inlets, a safe boat haven was worth remembering.

We soon reach the cheerless coastal community of Toft, and my kind driver lady has timed her trip to meet the next north-bound ferry, which already sits against the modern pier.

The trip across four kilometres of sheltered strait takes long enough to delight in the warmth and comfort of a ferry that feels like it just rolled down a shipbuilders' launch ramp, one doubtless situated anywhere but Scotland. The tiny country that for over a century built a vast percentage of the world's commercial marine fleet is nowadays unable to construct anything bigger than a row-boat if it doesn't come wrapped up in a government subsidy. Shipyards from Norway to Turkey can do it, but we cannot. Figure that out if you can.

The ferry port on the southern tip of Yell is a miniature community called Ulsta, but before I leave the ferry, and since the nice crofter lady is cutting off to the east, I am back to hitch-hiking, which is about to prove problematic. For safety reasons, I am made to wait until all vehicles leave the car deck, and only when strolling through deserted Ulsta does it dawn upon me that I just stood back while my only chances of a lift disappeared.

Ulsta is a pier with a car park, a sell-everything-known-to-mankind General Store which will not be selling much right now as it is closed, a light dusting of houses and the requisite dumb-as-manure canine that barks incessantly at the merest sign of movement. It unleashes foaming rage at each of the passing vehicles, then quietens down to recapture its breath in time for me to approach. He must be a big favourite among the neighbours.

I spent most of the 1990s in Hongkong, where problem dogs were nothing unusual. Friends whose flat was mere metres from one animal that did its best to keep an entire village awake all night, every night called the local police station so often that, the moment they gave their name, they received nothing more than empty assurances. One night, when their newborn baby had not slept properly for days, they made the usual call to the police station, and ten minutes later, the only British policeman assigned to the village arrived. He wore a slightly crumpled dinner suit, and by his own admission had just returned from a 'bloody good night out'. After they walked him out to where the dog frothed and roared, he first expressed sympathy and understanding. Then, from beneath his cummerbund he pulled a police revolver and shot the animal dead. To my friends, committed pacifists and avowed vegetarians though they were, it came as the most welcome of surprises.

As I leave behind Ulsta's own four-legged noise abatement argument, the season changes like a page flipped on a calendar; the wind dies and the sun makes a welcome appearance amidst a newly floodlit sky that threatens to take a mad turn and go all blue on us. The temperature rises, and as I unzip my jacket and pocket the woolly hat, I begin to savour a solitary walk.

The road climbs steadily until it assumes a course high up on the west side of the island, and walking pace allows me time to relish the views over Yell Sound. Keeping one hopeful ear open for signs of traffic from behind (there is none), I make use of my binoculars. I can pick out Colla Firth, where the trawler *Altaire* lies snug beyond a protective headland; on the other side of the firth squats the dome-like lump that is Ronas Hill. A little to the north, like a twee illustration in Readers' Digest, circa 1965, the farming community of North Roe glows in the mid-morning sun; and in the distance, its landscape alive with dancing shadows cast by fast-moving cloud cover, the peninsula of Fethaland points towards severe offshore skerries and beyond to waters that lie empty all the way to not-so-distant Arctic ice floes.

A little more than an hour out of Ulsta, I look down at the Ness of Sound, a cranium-like bump of lush croftland that would be an island if it were not for a shaley neck connecting it to Yell. On a summer day, it would be a dreamy picnic spot, with views over Yell Sound to small uninhabited mid-Sound islands and North Roe and Fethaland beyond.

While I scan the sights I sense a distant rumble, like a herd of beasts thundering across the plain. Except there is no plain, and of course there are no beasts, and the binoculars bring to focus a tightly-packed necklace string of vehicles rushing out of the south. The latest ferry-load of cars has arrived, and now streaks north to catch the ferry to Unst, the last island in the Shetland chain.

I count the string. Seven vehicles, close together and travelling at speed. I stand next to a field dotted with somnolent sheep, my thumb raised high. The cars are upon me even before my arm begins to tire, and as the first six scream past without slowing I face the possibility of at least another hour of walking. Then the very last car slows rapidly, tyres squealing against wind-dried tarmac. A couple from Lerwick, out to make the most of the good weather, are heading for Unst, and of course they can take me to Gutcher at the top of the island.

'People find Yell monotonous', the lady crofter told me earlier, and I understand what she meant as I take in the sights from the back seat of a speeding hatchback.

Monotonous is a little unfair, but mono-tonal is close to the mark, at least at this time of the year and as we move inland, where the landscape is draped in the russet brown of pre-winter.

After the lush croftland of the west coast, inland Yell's landscape is notable for a lack of things to take note of. Except, that is, for ample evidence of centuries of peat cutting. Peat is found all over Shetland, and nowhere is it more ubiquitous than on Yell, where it forms a carpet across the island that sometimes reaches several metres in depth.

Ever since the passing of the last Ice Age glaciers about ten thousand years ago, peat has formed from sphagnum mosses on waterlogged terrain where plant decay is inhibited by acidic soil conditions. As well as being a growing asset, albeit at the glacial rate of one millimetre per year — or about four inches a century in old money — peat performs the same vital task as the world's forests. It stores huge reserves of carbon that would otherwise find its way into the atmosphere, adding to the 'greenhouse effect'.

In an archipelago bereft of trees for fuel, for thousands of years, peat's high carbon element has held a key role in heating and feeding Shetlanders. So central is it to Shetland lives that even nowadays, some Shetlanders abide by the superstition that the peat fire in the home hearth should never be allowed to go out; it is not unknown for more traditional Shetland families, when they move to a new house, to take with them the burning fire from their old one, smouldering in a metal bucket.

On one wind-blown Yell moor, peat gathering is going on *right now*, three hardy men wrestling a wheelbarrow across rugged terrain. They have been 'casting peats', and now face the tough slog of getting the fuel off the moor and onto the back of a farm truck.

The hatchback driver attacks the roads with confidence, slowing only when we scythe through the cluster of buildings in the middle of the island that is prosaically named Mid Yell. As soon as we leave the homes behind, he picks up the pace again. He drives with skill, treating the road like an empty race track, neatly clipping the apex of every bend, wrong side of the road or not. Thanks to the absence of traffic and unbroken views that stretch far into the distance, I am not unduly scared by the pace, and as it is, only the suspension of the little car is complaining.

He regains his earlier position at the rear of the north-bound convoy, which we follow all the way to the ferry pier at Gutcher, and where the couple join the line for the ferry to Unst, while I head for the comforts of the Wind Dog Café.

Gutcher consists of about four buildings and a ferry pier. Next to the small queue of vehicles awaiting the next boat to Unst is a long, single-storey building that reminds me of temporary classrooms that popped up around Scottish schools during the baby-boomer years. From within this modest structure, the famous Wind Dog Café manages to serve multiple functions.

As the name suggests, it is indeed a café (by day), but one which in summer evenings transforms into a respected à la carte restaurant. It also plays the crucial role of warm shelter bolt-hole and source of food and refreshments to ferry-goers. To call it an Internet café might be to over-inflate the importance of the solitary PC on a desk at the far end of the room, not that that stops me from using it to catch up with my email. The computer sits amidst shelf units packed with neatly-labelled books in well-fingered plastic covers. If the sturdy metal shelves filled with systematically-filed titles look like a segment

THE ISLAND OF YELL

plucked intact from your local library, it is because the Wind Dog gives up a slice of its floor space to the Shetland public library network. I settle in for lunch, and later, while I soak up excellent fresh-brewed coffee, I browse the many books on Shetland. Notch up one more informal role for the Wind Dog: tourist information research hub.

II: The otter, the crofter and the cynic

The ferry for the isle of Unst works out of a modern hydraulic pier, but across a short stretch of glassy water squats the old stone jetty that performed the same role for decades. As I look towards it, the harbour surface is broken by the arc of a creature too small to be a porpoise, yet sleek and fast-moving. Shetland boasts the highest density of otters in Europe, but this is my first opportunity to see one at close quarters. Its sinewy frame sweeps parabolic curves through the sparkling water's surface, and the hunter's head soon breaks the waterline. Held fast in the otter's jaws, the death throes of a fat fish fire glistening droplets that speckle the gleaming bay. The otter goes back below, and when it reappears only seconds later, the fish is duly despatched.

Wary of the twenty-four kilometres of lightly-travelled road that stretch between me and the ferry back to Mainland, I set off southwards on foot, and for a while, in the absence of motorised traffic, the sky provides the entertainment. It is fat with clouds of teased cotton candy that thicken and turn slatey grey until the sun is swallowed whole, only for it to break boldly through for a few seconds at a time when fleeting gaps in the cover appear.

In Japan there is a fascination for such shafts of sunlight that throw a downward beam through a break in the heavy cloud, and they are known as 'goko', or 'light shining from behind Buddha'.

I watch a Shetland goko sweep across northern Yell, its beam curving over the landscape like a theatre spotlight flashing over actors and props on a carefully darkened stage, in a beautiful illustration of colour temperature. The temperature of the backdrop is cool, a muted grey-blue that is sliced apart by the orangey-warm glow of the goko beam.

I am so intent on watching the sun play with the scenery that I almost miss the man leaning against a fence, and in the end it is only the sharpness of pipe tobacco smoke that alerts me to his presence.

He is a big old guy who was once a lot bigger than he stands today in thick tweed clothes bought when there was a lot more to him than leans over a fence now. Even his dog-tooth tweed cap sits like it was made for his big brother. There is a welcoming gleam in his eye and when I pause to speak to him he looks as if he had expected nothing else. This is a country man with time for a word with the few folk who pass his way. He tells me he is a crofter, with sheep to tend to, somewhere over there — he waves an arm in no particular direction — and as he speaks, he habitually fingers the right front edge of his cap, as if the action helps him concentrate. I know it is a habit because it is the only part of his hat darkened by farmer's finger grime.

He volunteers that he has been all over, all over the world in his days as a merchant seaman, but when I ask how long ago he was at sea, he is unsure. A big arthritic finger taps at a temple and he says,

'The old mind's no' sae good any more.'

Then he goes back to saying that he was all over. All over the world. But not Norway, he tells me, something we share the funny side of, Norway being Shetland's closest neighbour.

Perhaps it is a while since he had a chat, because he soon tells me how much he enjoyed his travels to exciting places, and shares with me his regret that he failed to make the most of the opportunities he had. He winks and mimes the glass-in-hand-tipped-to-lips gesture. Precious time ashore in a mad rush to take in more of the sauce than the sights.

'All the places ah went, ah saw nuthin', no' a thing,' he says, regret written in his big sad eyes. Then his face brightens at another thought. "Cept mebbe twa whoors!'

He tells me he gave up drinking 'twenty or thirty years back. And ah havna hud a drop since.'

I am at least six kilometres out of Gutcher before the first vehicle appears from behind, but the merest wave of a thumb is enough to bring the van to a halt. Its driver is a tradesman with two kids up front, and he tells me to get in the back. From a perch on the floor of a noisy van full of sharp implements swinging wildly from nails and hooks, I learn that, like me, he makes a point of picking up hitch-hikers whenever possible. It is a payback thing that only experienced hitch-hikers understand, and this guy tells me of travels that took him all the way across Canada, which rather puts the remaining few kilometres to Ulsta in the shade. He nonetheless goes out of his way to take me all the way to the pier for the Mainland ferry.

The view to Mainland from the ridge of a stout breakwater, across the choppy channel where the ferry cuts a frothing furrow towards me, is bleak. Dark rainclouds cast a wearying gloom across the southern horizon, where many more kilometres of hitching await me if I am to get back to the comfort of the camping böd at Voe.

Six vehicles sit between painted stripes in the queue for the ferry, and I opt for the car with one solitary occupant, a young man. He lowers his window, and agrees to help without so much as a flicker of indecision. Only then do my eyes move to a passenger seat piled high with boxes; the footwell in front of it, too, is crammed tight. He is a student heading back to the Scottish mainland after a break, and with the small car fit to burst with his belongings, there is surely not enough space remaining for even a small Scotsman. But with the optimism of youth and a seemingly near-total disregard for his own property, he rapidly performs the feat of three-dimensional jig-saw required to free up the passenger seat.

Stuart welcomes me aboard and almost immediately takes control of a rambling discourse so free of circumspection that it feels like a chat with an old friend. He is neither short on opinions nor remotely reticent about expressing them. Many Shetlanders I meet are critical of the SIC, or Shetland Islands Council, the local governing body politic, but where others shake heads and express the odd grouch, Stuart is scathing. He brings up the subject himself, and launches into a withering tirade.

'A bunch of corrupt arseholes,' he says. When I say that, from what I have seen, they seem to be doing a decent job, only good manners prevent him from sneering at my foolish ways.

'One week you'll see a picture in the Shetland Times of the SIC, and then the next week you'll see a photo of the big-knobs of the Masonic Lodge at a function in Lerwick, and guess what?' He almost spits it out. 'It's like looking at the same picture twice, except in one shot they're squashed into bad suits, and in the other, they're wrapped up in all that daft Mason shite.'

When we leave the ferry at Toft, he shows another, more understanding side of his young character, telling me that Toft has its share of problems. At 27 miles (about 43 kilometres) from Lerwick, the little community is about as far from da toon as you can get without leaving Mainland, and it feels like it.

The old village of Toft was expanded overnight in the mid-seventies to house incomers who arrived to construct the Sullom Voe oil terminal, only a few kilometres to the south. Two camps were built for the influx, and at the height of the construction period, when they housed five thousand workers, Toft on a Saturday night must have been like Dodge City. The remains of the camps still endure, twin eyesore landmarks to the boom times and testimony to the Council's naïve, if well-intended hopes of attracting business to Toft.

In the decades since the oil terminal's completion, the isolated little community has suffered. The Shetland Times runs sporadic stories about unemployment, vandalism and drug problems, issues at once loudly denounced and vehemently denied by differing resident factions. But surely the very fact that Toft is the focus of such attention says something appealing about Shetland. The island group's population is so small that a large percentage of Shetlanders will not only be concerned for the way of life in Toft and for its residents, they will themselves be personally acquainted with some of them. And this, never mind that the village is home to only about twenty people.

The Australians have a down-to-earth way with language that sees their day to day speech peppered with classic snippets of linguistic adaptability. One of my favourites is 'morish', as in, *oi tell ya myte, that cake is a bit fackin morish*. When Stuart drops me at the Sail Loft, I have been gone for about nine hours, more than four of which were spent walking deserted rural roads through atmospheric scenery that dripped with history. Going by my experiences so far, this Shetland place is proving just a little bit *morish*.

NORTHMAVINE AND BRAE

I: NATO raiders and Johnnie Notions

Mavis Grind may sound like a Yorkshire child who drew two short straws at a pre-christening party, but is in fact an isthmus only a few metres wider than the curving two-lane road that it supports. This slender arc of land is all that connects the district of Northmavine to the rest of Mainland, and all that separates the innermost reaches of opposing voes that probe inwards from the Atlantic and the North Sea.

Not even Shetlanders can agree on how to say Mavis Grind. While the second word is usually pronounced 'grinned', the first is spoken by some to rhyme with 'Travis', but by others to sound just like the woman's name Mavis. What they do agree upon is that it comes from Norse and means, 'gateway of the narrow isthmus'.

My ankles are lapped by thick wet grass on a hillside overlooking the gateway. Beside me stands Allen Fraser, a retired meteorologist (I go forty-odd years without once crossing paths with a meteorologist, then in Shetland I meet two in the space of a week; I theorise that this may be because Shetland has more weather than anywhere else I ever visited). Allen is also a respected geologist and one-man operator of *Geotours*, a bespoke tour company that specialises in guiding visitors to Shetland's geological highlights. He fills me in on the long-held theory that Mavis Grind was a point of portage for Viking longboats en route from Scandinavia to Iceland, and seeking a short-cut to the Atlantic. A television company recently explored the theory by successfully lugging a replica boat over the isthmus, but Allen remains skeptical.

'It's not just the boats you have to consider,' he says. 'They were unwieldy enough, but they held six tonnes of ballast and anything up to twenty tonnes of cargo or supplies. All of that would have had to be stripped out, ported up and over the isthmus, then re-positioned after the boat itself was carted over. I just don't see it being worthwhile.'

Not that Mavis Grind has been a stranger to the act of portage. For hundreds of years and until as recently as the 1950s, local four-oared fishing boats, or 'fourareens' were routinely hauled between North Sea and Atlantic Ocean.

Even as he puts paid to one link with ancient Shetland, Allen points me to historic evidence, not from a thousand, but from four thousand years ago. Scattered around our feet are weathered stone blocks that I would never have given a second glance. Allen explains that they are remains of a Neolithic farmstead from circa 2000 B.C. Four thousand years after they were laid down, two stones continue to stand taller than the others. Known as *orthostats*, they mark the entrance to the farmstead.

Historians estimate that Neolithic Shetland's population may even have equalled today's, with the key difference that, instead of being clustered mainly in villages and small townships, its agrarian population would have been spread throughout the land they worked.

I take in the view from a tiny postage stamp of flat space overlooking the *gateway of the narrow isthmus* where, four millennia ago, a family of farmers looked over the land they depended upon for survival.

In Neolithic times, sea levels were considerably lower — they are estimated to have risen as much as 120 metres since the last Ice Age — meaning the farmer who once stood here could work fertile coastal land that has since been swallowed by the rising oceans. What is now a narrow gateway may once have been a wide open corridor.

Allen explains that four thousand years ago, temperatures were two or three degrees Celsius warmer than they are today, and that it was the deteriorating climate that caused uncultivable blanket bogs, and resultant peat coverage, to eventually bury huge areas of agrarian land. Add rising sea levels to the equation, and over a period of centuries, Shetland's subsistence farmers were slowly but surely edged off of the land.

A few minutes later we are on the south shore of Ronas Voe, an eleven-kilometre coastal corridor that is one of the narrowest and longest of Shetland's voes.

'It is different from all the other voes you will have seen for one simple reason,' says Allen. 'Ronas Voe is the only truly glacial fiord in Shetland, cut out by an Ice Age glacier maybe fifteen thousand years ago. That is why the coastline on the north shore is so sheer.' He raises a hand in tribute to Ronas Hill, at 450m, the tallest point in Shetland. Viewed from a sand spit on the opposite side of the dog-legged voe, its rust-coloured Feldspar granite sparkles as it plummets into arctic blue waters with a finality that suggests it may continue downwards a long, long way. This is an impression lent credence by Allen, who tells me that this is by far the deepest of Shetland's voes.

It all makes for a spectacularly picturesque spot that for centuries has provided sanctuary from the travails of the North Atlantic.

During World War I, it served as a Royal Navy anchorage. Nearly one-hundred-and-fifty years before that, in December 1773, during the Anglo-Dutch wars, the heavily armed Dutch East Indiaman *Het Wapen van Amsterdam* holed up here, perhaps to wait out unfavourable weather or carry out repairs. Whatever the problem, the delay surely stretched far longer than they might have hoped, for in February 1774, three British frigates slipped into the voe and attacked. Hollanders Graves, on the shore of the voe, marks where Dutch seamen who perished in the assault are interred.

The sand spit where we now stand was, at the turn of the twentieth century, a Norwegian whaling station, and before that, herring from the *Haaf* fishing boats came ashore here. At its landward end sit a few metres of rusting rail tracks and a handful of narrow-gauge bogey axles. Allen sees me examining them, and says, with a grin, 'You can read about these in a book.'

'I can?'

'It's called Railways of Shetland.'

Now I know he is kidding, since Shetland has no railways. Or at least no passenger railways. The joke that is no joke begins to dawn on me, and he explains. In 1997, a railway devotee by the name of

Wilfred F. Simms published a booklet detailing all of Shetland's cargo tracks like the one here on Ronas Voe that used to haul whale meat and herring from fiord side to loading area, a distance of at most fifty metres, yet still faithfully recorded as one of Shetland's 'railways' by Mr Simms.

A narrow twisting back road, immaculately surfaced, empty of traffic and almost completely without nearby dwellings, emerges on the broad bay shore of Ura Firth. Nearly a quarter of a century ago, this lightly populated sea loch was the unlikely focus of conspiracy theorists, inspiration for a festival of head-scratching that obsessed over the resemblance between Ura Firth and San Carlos Water, 13,000 kilometres away in the Falklands Islands.

San Carlos Water, known to British Forces during the Falklands conflict as 'Bomb Alley', was the scene of a May 1982 amphibious night landing by four thousand men of 3 Commando Brigade. The landing received such saturation coverage in the British press that Shetlanders began casting their minds back to September 1978, when a massive NATO amphibious landing swept ashore in sleepy Ura Firth.

Conspiracy theorists speculated that the uncanny resemblance of the coastal topography of the two distant locations surely meant that, as far back as 1978, the British must have had eyes on capturing the Falklands, even though they already ruled over the islands. Like most conspiracy theories, it was so nonsensical that the only real surprise is that it attracted any subscribers whatsoever.

The 1978 NATO landing at Ura Firth was part of a four-yearly exercise that went under the name of Operation Northern Wedding. This gigantic operation, with its cast of forty thousand men, twenty-two submarines and eight hundred aircraft from nine countries, would have been meticulously planned years in advance, making any perceived connection between those plans and, years later, a South Atlantic invasion, spurious at best.

Allen shares with me one much-retold anecdote from Operation Northern Wedding.

'NATO marines slipped ashore in full camouflage, wrapped head to toe in the fake grass stuff that was meant to help them creep, perfectly diguised as a lump of landscape, to within metres of their targets — only to be accosted by little grannies coming out their kitchen doors carrying steaming mugs of tea, bellowing,

'If de midder could only see de noo! I tocht du cood do wi a haet scaar o tay tae tow de oot'.

Translation: *If your mother could only see you now! I thought you could use a hot cup of tea to thaw you out.*

Leaving Ura Firth behind, we crest a coastal rise overlooking St Magnus Bay, and Allen switches from narrator of humorous anecdotes to committed geologist.

St Magnus Bay on the west side of Mainland has been the focus of debate for a very long time, possibly ever since the first geologist opened his atlas and spotted that the bay forms most of the broken, near-circular outline of an eleven-kilometre-wide depression.

The coastline of west Mainland looks like it has had a bite taken out of it. A few kilometres offshore, a crater-like depression in the sea floor plunges to 163 metres, or double the depth of the surrounding seabed. Debate over the crater's origins divides geologists into two mutually-opposed camps.

(Adherents to the Creationist 'theory' that God created the Earth in a week about five thousand years ago might want to look away now.)

The first geological school of thought sees the crater as evidence of a meteor strike of unimaginable power and proportions. This school claims it may be one of the largest meteor strike craters on Earth, and they theorise that the meteor responsible may have struck Earth in the Jurassic or early Cretaceous Periods — or 175 to 70 million years ago.

All those millions of years ago, the land where the depression lies would have been above ground. After which, so the theory goes, rising sea levels filled the meteor crater, and erosion from the oceans — as well as the passage of Ice Age glaciers — gradually obliterated the western edge of the bowl-like landmark.

While he refuses to discount a meteor strike outright — a canny move, considering we *are* talking about events that happened so many millions of years ago — Allen aligns himself with the other camp, the ones who postulate that the crater of St Magnus Bay may have been formed by a mighty volcanic eruption in the Early

Carboniferous Period, or around 350 million years ago.

'I am of the view that, because volcanic rocks make up much of the bedrock around St Magnus Bay, it may well have started life as a collapsed volcano, or *caldera*,' says Allen.

A caldera, from the Spanish for 'cauldron', is created when part of the rim of the crater at the top of a volcano becomes unstable and collapses. Allen tells me that classic examples of caldera are found on the Greek island of Santorini and at Lake Toba on Sumatra, Indonesia — which doesn't make me feel too clever, since I have spent several days at both locales without for a moment wondering how they came about, let alone learning what a caldera was.

We next pause at a little cemetery beside the road that climbs the hill to Eshaness cliffs. We stop because geologist and storyteller Allen has an eye for history, and in particular the history of John Williamson, who was born and lived all his life at yet another place called Hamnavoe, just a handful of kilometres from where he now lies in this cemetery.

Ask Shetlanders about a John Williamson who lived in Northmavine in the second half of the 18th Century, and you will more than likely draw blank expressions. But re-phrase your enquiry to ask about *Johnnie Notions*, and be prepared to be regaled with stories of a remarkable man whose insight into a hellish cyclical disease was nothing short of visionary.

The Mortal Pock was what they called Smallpox, and with good cause. In the 18th Century, the disease swept through the islands with terrifying regularity, routinely wiping out a quarter of all Shetlanders. Shetland's most distant communities, perhaps because of their isolation, often suffered worst of all; once the disease came ashore, there was nowhere to hide. Death rates on the island of Foula were so high that, in a deeply traditional society where funerals were (and indeed, still are) attended only by men, there were not enough surviving males to carry the coffins; instead, the corpses of beloved ones had to be dragged across the island with ropes.

Born in 1740, Williamson could be excused his lack of formal education since, in those days, there was no school in Northmavine. A crofter and weaver by profession, he became known for being clever with his hands, dabbling as a carpenter, clock-repairer and blacksmith.

But it was his capacity for invention that led to his nickname of Johnnie Notions, and by far the most revolutionary of his notions addressed the scourge of smallpox. The science of inoculation was already known to the medical world in the late 1700s, and somehow Johnnie must have learned of this method of preventing disease, because he came up with his own system for inoculating the people of Northmavine against smallpox, one that was as painstaking as it was effective.

He took live pus from smallpox sufferers and dried it in peat smoke before mixing it with camphor and sandwiching it between panes of glass, which he buried underground for seven years.

Somehow, a weaver with little formal education grasped the crucially important theory of *attenuation*, or reduction in virulence, of the virus — more than fifty years before Louis Pasteur achieved worldwide renown by doing the same for anthrax.

None of which would have done much for Johnnie's cause had he not understood the importance of one other critical element in his inoculation process. After the smallpox mix had lain underground for seven years, he introduced it to the body of the patient by raising a thin flap of skin using a scalpel of his own construction, and placing the mix under the flap. In doing so, he successfully applied the inoculation *without drawing blood* and therefore without directly infecting the patient's bloodstream. (Infinitely more qualified medical pioneers of the period routinely killed patients by introducing diseases directly into the bloodstream using a lancet.) He finished the treatment by wrapping the wound in cabbage leaves, which were known for their mildly antiseptic qualities.

It was astonishing enough that Williamson/Notions took it upon himself to inoculate around three thousand of his Northmavine neighbours in this way; but truly astounding was how, among those treated, not one recorded case of smallpox occurred. Only years after Northmavine's own pioneer had 'solved' the smallpox crisis in his part of Shetland did renowned English doctor Edward Jenner devise his own system of inoculation, using the less virulent cowpox strain as the inoculative source. Ironically, even that did not arrive for general use in Shetland until 1804, the year after John Williamson/Johnnie Notions was buried here in Eshaness Cemetery.

Allen draws my attention to a memorial that attracts almost as many curious visitors as Johnnie Notions' does. It is a large flat tombstone, its lettering so faded by the elements that it is all but lost, but which is helpfully replicated on a metal plaque:

> DONALD ROBERTSON BORN 14TH JANUARY 1785,
> DIED 4TH JUNE 1848 AGED 63
> HE WAS A PEACABLE, QUIET MAN AND TO ALL
> APPEARANCES A SINCERE CHRISTIAN

'His death was much regretted which was caused by the stupidity of Lawrence Tulloch in Clothister who sold him nitre instead of Epsom Salts by which he was killed in the space of five hours after taking a dose of it.'

The poor Mr Robertson died as a direct result of an honest, if perilously negligent error on the part of shopkeeper Tulloch, which led to Robertson's church minister instituting the barbed epitaph. Mr Tulloch, you see, belonged to another branch of the Christian faith from Mr Robertson. It might be safe to assume that, in certain Shetland church circles back then, the dictum about 'turning the other cheek' may not have held much sway.

Tulloch stood trial in Lerwick for culpable homicide and the negligent and reckless sale of saltpetre (potassium nitrate; a poisonous ingredient in fertilisers and a key component of gunpowder) instead of epsom salts. A fifteen-man jury found him guilty, but requested that he be shown leniency due to his unblemished character and the absence of intention in the death of Robertson. Sheriff Charles Neaves sentenced Tulloch to eight days' imprisonment in the prison at Fort Charlotte, after which, pressure within the community was the likely reason that Tulloch and his family soon departed Shetland. Now all that remains as evidence of his Shetland days are the faded, bitter words of a disenchanted pastor on a tombstone at Eshaness cemetery.

II: Geology made interesting

Stephen Simpson, my long-suffering primary contact at the Lerwick Tourist Office who is endlessly generous with his time and knowledge, waxes like a broken record about the grandeur of Eshaness. And yet, even though I arrive amply forewarned, no amount of preparation could properly have set the scene.

I walk the cliffs with Allen, trying yet failing to take in what he tells me about the region's geology. I say failing, because no matter how much Allen tells me — and this guy knows his stuff — I can grasp neither the enormity of the tale nor the dizzying time frame in which it is drawn. When an expert points to a rock feature the size of an apartment block and tells me with certainty precisely how it was formed *400 million years ago*, my mind is so completely absent of insightful thoughts that I begin to worry. Worry that in his professional career Allen may never have spoken for so long without once being interrupted by a single intelligent question.

Eshaness owes its forbidding landscape of gigantic, Atlantic breaker-gouged cliffs to 400-million-year-old volcanic activity. Allen explains that the geology of Eshaness and of areas to its south, around the curved maw of St Magnus Bay to the island of Papa Stour, suggests that this large part of western Mainland is what he refers to as a 'volcanic province'. Over a period of millions of years, back when this stretch of land sat in the middle of a desert set close to the equator, a sweeping range of volcanoes and volcanic eruptions cut and carved and blasted the landscape into the dramatic shape that it commands today. Evidence of volcanic activity, so long as you have a guide of Allen's expertise to point things out, is *everywhere* at Eshaness.

'What you have here is the best cross-section of the anatomy of a volcano to be found anywhere in the British Isles,' he says. 'Every stratum in the cliff face, every embedded boulder set in hardened rock tells the story of a volcanic episode, of lava flows cooling and setting to form a new top layer on the landscape, only to be covered up by subsequent eruptions and fresh magma flows.'

If vast cross-sections of coastal cliff look like they are the product of thousands of tons of boulders and rock shards swept together like dried fruit in a cake mix, it is because that is how large swathes of Eshaness were indeed formed, with molten lava and rocks adopting the roles of dough and raisins.

Allen strides purposefully across boggy fields and over slippery stiles set on fences that run straight at the cliff edge, where they curve just far enough towards the abyss to discourage even the most determined of sheep. I keep just far enough behind Allen that the sound of me fighting for breath may be swallowed by the ever-present shrieks of seabirds and the rumbling and crashing of Atlantic breakers.

Our next stop is a feature called The Holes of Scraada, translated as the Devil's Caves, after Old Norse for 'Old Scratch', or the devil. Formed by the partial collapse of the roof over a long cavern that runs directly inland from the cliff shoreline, it makes for a narrow ravine, longer than a soccer field, and thirty metres deep. The open section was naturally roofed in until 1873, when it collapsed only moments after a local lad walked across it. Between the collapsed section and the coastline is another hundred metres of cave tunnel, its roof intact, the temptation to cross its land bridge an easy one to resist. From deep within the cave comes the roar of the sea, which today fails to reach through to the exposed section. Allen assures me that when the wind is coming from the west, water thunders through the tunnel and into the open ravine, and there is no difficulty in imagining how it was named after the Devil himself.

Almost adjoining the Holes of Scraada, and of far greater interest to geologists, is the Grind of the Navir, which Allen describes, without a trace of hyperbole, as 'nature's most dramatic feature on Shetland.' At this point he might detect a hint of scepticism in my expression, for he quickly subjects me to the full geological tour.

Translated as 'Gateway of the Borer', Grind of the Navir refers to twin rock buttresses that stand tall on either side of a coastal notch, like giant teeth straddling the bloodied gap where a molar once lodged. The 'gumline' looms fifteen metres above sea level, and between it and the Atlantic the shore ramps steeply downwards. Under correct storm conditions, explains Allen, the elements come together to create a chute for waves higher than a three-storey building to steamroller through the gateway and onto the small flatland behind the Grind itself. On the plateau, evidence of dauntingly powerful forces lies in plain view.

Allen points to massed ranks of rocks piled around the inland edge of the plateau.

'Those rocks,' he says, 'were all quarried from the land *inside the gateway* by enormous storm waves funnelled through the gateway itself — and piled up in these ridges by the power of the water. Literally tonnes of rock, physically broken out of the shoreline and swept anywhere up to a hundred metres inland.' He points back at the Grind and I can now identify, between the gateway's bastions, areas of the rocky cliff top that have been plucked apart by the incoming force of thundering waves.

I look more closely at the huge boulders around the inland edge of the plateau, and which are almost building-material-like in regularity, many with parallel edges and neat corners, and are stacked carelessly like long curved ridges of discarded library books. Some of them are three metres long, and must weigh half a tonne or more. There are three clear ridges of the stones, with the tallest ridge standing 3.5 metres high.

'Think about pebbled beaches you see on the coast,' says Allen. 'And how, towards the shore side, little ridges of stones form raised lines at the high water mark.'

He points to the piles of enormous boulders.

'These are their Eshaness equivalent.' He swings a hand from faraway sea to the stacked rocks. 'These half-tonne stones sitting well inshore and fifteen metres above sea level are a *storm beach.*'

They are also stark, recordable evidence of what geologists refer to as CTSDs, or Cliff Top Storm Deposits. CTSDs are rocks, from thumbnail-sized pebble shards to five-tonne boulders the size of delivery vans, that extreme weather can deposit inland, even on shorelines ringed by towering cliffs. The extremity of such weather conditions mean that storms of sufficient power to bring about fresh crops of CTSDs only affect very limited areas of any nation's coastline — and even those, perhaps as seldom as once every other decade. Eshaness, Allen tells me with visible pride, is prime CTSD country.

Extreme examples of CTSDs arise something like this: successions of powerful waves driven by ferocious storm conditions batter the cliff surface, dislodging a large rock section which drops loose into the face of yet more onrushing waves, which sweep it upwards, higher than the cliff top edge where, like a tennis ball being thrown up for service, at the top of its arc it is met, not by a tennis racquet but by a gigantic rogue storm wave so powerful that it can fire a five-tonne boulder fifty metres inland.

As we trek back along the boggy clifftops to the car park,

movement at sea catches our attention, a sailing ketch searing south through the never-ending succession of North Atlantic peaks and troughs. It is running before the wind, sails reefed in yet still firing it across the horizon at a rate that will have its skipper running on pure adrenalin. There are no Shetland yacht basins north of here, so our adventurer might have sailed, in the wild mid-October weather, all the way from Faroe or even Iceland, perhaps retracing treacherous routes battled, a millennium or more before, by Viking longboats aiming for faraway Scandinavia and home.

III: Teacher man

I wonder if the schoolteachers I endured in the sixties and seventies have any idea how prominent a place they occupy in former pupils' memories.

The primary and secondary schools I attended had staffrooms riven with despots who merrily wielded power by swinging leather belts with finger-numbing regularity. In much more of a minority were the few teachers blessed with the character and skills to put kids at ease and in a frame of mind to actually learn something. There was the middle-aged chemistry teacher who wore his hair as long as any teenager's and turned up for work every day in a black velvet suit. Only a few doors along the corridor, a physics teacher I admired could silence a roomful of chatter with one raised eyebrow, then reduce us to tears of laughter with a single syllable.

I am on my way to meet a teacher whose reputation more than precedes him. It sweeps around the islands, his name on the lips of Shetlanders of all ages.

On Papa Stour, Martin Strickland loaned me a wonderful little book written by him about the place names of the island.

Two different car drivers who rescued me from the side of roads on different islands picked his name out of the air and urged me to look him up.

The affable barman at the Pierhead Pub next to the Sail Loft camping böd, David Leask, was so certain that I would benefit from a chat with his old English teacher that he dug out a telephone book and stood over me to be sure I noted the number correctly.

When at last I pick up the phone and call George P.S. Peterson, I feel uncomfortable about the brazen attempt to invite myself into a stranger's home, but a short conversation only confirms what everyone has already told me. This is one very sweet man.

I explain that I am in the area, that I enjoyed his book about Papa Stour, and wonder if I might be able to visit him sometime for a chat.

'Of course you can,' he says.

'When would be convenient for you?'

'Just now is fine.'

Then, when I set out to hitch-hike the few miles to Brae, I am almost immediately picked up by a young carpenter who turns out to be yet another former pupil of Mr Peterson, and who is *very* eager that I pass on his fondest regards.

Half an hour after I hang up the telephone, the carpenter drops me at George's house, a cottage set back from the shore of the broad voe that is hugged on three sides by Shetland's second-largest community of Brae. Two minutes after that, I am at rest with a steaming mug of coffee, and already wishing that there were more men like Shetland's favourite teacher. A few of them in Central Scotland in the seventies would not have gone amiss, for a start.

George is a very tall, with a thatch of thick white hair, hands the size of dinner plates and thoughtful eyes that twinkle from behind big-framed spectacles. We sit in the front room of the house he shares with his wife, and which has the mark of grandparents perfectly content to live in a minefield of grandkids' toys. George's chair backs onto the window, as if he has become numbed to the unbroken million-dollar view of the voe, where a solitary windsurfer extracts every ounce of power out of winds so strong they whip the surface around him into cresting breakers. As he cuts white zig-zags across the voe, he leaps through the air from wave top to wave top; he is wrapped from head to toe in a hypothermia-proof wetsuit without which, mere minutes in these waters would be a short struggle to a predictable demise.

Although George Peterson is also well-known for his writings about Papa Stour, he was actually born in Lerwick in 1932, and moved to the island with his mother, a 'Papay' native, when he was five years old.

In the late 1930s, Papa Stour's population numbered about one hundred. All the men, George's father included, were either fishermen or merchant seamen, a function of necessity since farming could never provide tenants with a cash income; worse than that, crofting on Papay was so close to subsistence-level that it could not even meet the rent on the croft land. This left it up to the men of the family to generate much-needed cash, and that meant either fishing or the merchant navy.

George is a surviving bridge to the long-gone days of tenant crofters and *Haaf* fishermen of Victorian Shetland, his sharp mind filled with stories of the 19th Century passed on to him by word of mouth on Papa Stour sixty or more years ago. Men who had worked the *Haaf* before its demise late in the 19th Century shared with young George tales of the harsh existences they eked out as young fishermen working thirty or forty miles (fifty to sixty-five kilometres) out at the edge of the continental shelf in open, six-oared wooden boats.

They were tough times, but George takes issue with the widely-bandied notion that the lives of the people back then amounted to slavery.

'That's a load of nonsense,' he says. 'People worked slowly, at their own pace, but never stopped. There was nobody standin' over them with a whip.'

Nevertheless, he *is* talking about an era when fishermen worked in boats without shelter, hauling lines of hooks literally kilometres long, entirely by hand. And on their return, their contract with the landlord who owned the boats and all the fishing gear meant that all the fisherman got to keep from the catch was the heads and the livers. And woe betide them if they landed without their full complement of fishing equipment.

'When rapid storms came wheelin' in oot o' the Atlantic,' George says, 'Sometimes the men had to cut their lines just to save themselves. And if they came back without the lines, landlords held them responsible for replacing them.'

George remembers how the men, who worked *sixareens* with only rudimentary sails that were near to useless when sailing into the wind, used to say:

"A south-easterly gives ye a sore löf (from Norse — 'palm'), but never a sore heart."

(Meaning: sheltered by Mainland from south-easterlies, they may still have had to toil long and hard to get home to Papa Stour, but at least they were spared the mountainous seas swept in by westerlies roaring in from the open Atlantic.)

Despite all this, they managed to coax an income out of sea and land, and though times were difficult, they were not without their pleasures.

'I remember sayin' tae my Grandmother, "ye musta been killed wi the wark that ye haed tae do,"' he says, recalling her reply:

'It was the funs that we haed that keepit us goin', she told him.

When George was a child the early herring season in May drew boats and itinerant workers from Orkney, as well as from Fraserburgh and Peterhead on the east coast of the Scottish mainland, 'gutting lasses' with their alien dialects (possibly Gaelic, George thinks, but just as likely impenetrable Aberdonian). He holds fond memories of these hardy visitors.

'Ye always knew when the heilan' lasses were tired, because that's when they stertit singin', he says. One year, he remembers, a visiting barrel maker brought his bagpipes, and on Sundays he used to lead all the gutting lasses to church, walking ahead playing his bagpipes like the Pied Piper himself.

'The kirk was so packit, that on warrm days the doors were left wide open, and ye could hear the singin' from a long way off.'

In the 1930s, the entire permanent population of Papa Stour were locals, so the island's traditions and customs and peculiarly inflected dialect remained intact.

In late 2005, things are very different. With only four 'natives' left among a population of about twenty, local culture on Papay is history. George and his family retain a croft on the island and visit regularly to tend their fifty sheep. So despite having lived for more than forty years in Brae, he has seen, up close and first hand, his home's culture and traditions dwindle away to nothing.

'The curtain is jist about down on all that,' he says with audible regret. 'These things are all lost now, and once gone, they are lost forever.'

On the way back to Voe, I drop in to a local store, where the shopkeeper lady, a local woman of around fifty who has never seen me before in her life, cheerfully asks after my day.

'I've been chatting with George Peterson, the retired schoolmaster,' I say.

She almost melts across the shop counter, and could not look more impressed if I had casually mentioned free-climbing the North Face of the Eiger alone, barefoot and under cover of darkness.

'He's a luffly, luffly man,' she says, almost dreamily, in the manner of a pre-teen talking about her latest pop star crush. 'An' oooh, wi' a voice ah could listen to *ahl day long.*'

IV: South Atlantic salad days

I spend the next morning up to my hips in blood. Not stuck listening to the songs at an Old Firm football match, but re-living the four seasons that Gibbie Fraser spent whaling in the South Atlantic. Gibbie is the editor of a book about Shetlanders' experiences in the waning years of South Atlantic whaling. He drops in for a chat about dangerous times in the dying days of an industry that nowadays seems barbaric, but which nearly half a century ago constituted not just an adventure but an economic lifeline to men like young Gibbie.

Shetlanders' affinity for the tough life at sea has been known and understood since long before even Press Gang cutters roamed the islands' coastlines more than two centuries ago. So many Shetlanders crewed on merchant vessels that in the 19th and early 20th Centuries, on islands like Yell and Papa Stour, the *majority* of the Dads and older brothers spent much of the year working at sea.

If the idea of hunting the planet's largest mammals to the point of endangerment is beyond the pale in this era of environmental enlightenment, the nickname given to the thousands of Shetland sailors who crewed merchant vessels the world over was not much better. North Sea Chinamen they called them, a tag that surely was born of Shetlanders' ubiquity in the merchant sailing world — in much the same way that Chinese labour was so prevalent during the construction of the American railroads.

Gibbie is a tall man in his early sixties with a trim figure that would be the envy of men decades his junior. His handshake makes me think of cables wrapping around the take-up drum on a dockside crane, and he looks me in the eye with warmth and curiosity combined. I too am curious, about the life of a whaler working the wild waters of the South Atlantic around the time I was born, and about what made a young man opt for that life.

The motivating factor was simple: money.

'In 1958, long before oil came to Shetland, most of the work was in crofting, but even at best, that only provided an existence. Back then, just about the only year-round work was in the traditional trades like joinery and plumbing, meaning that many Shetlanders had to supplement their incomes by going fishing or whaling,' says Gibbie, who joined his first whaler in October 1958 at the age of sixteen.

'Whaling appealed to Shetlanders because it was winter work. We went away in early autumn when most of the crofting work was done for the year, and came back in the spring in time to pick up jobs on the crofts again.

'Even better, we couldn't spend the wages while we were at sea, simply because there was nothing to spend them on. When I came back from my first season away, I brought home £210 in cash from seven months' work.' In 1958, that was a *serious* wedge of money.

Gibbie worked for three seasons on the same whaler, the Southern Broom from the Salvesen Company's fleet of whale catchers. A Scottish outfit, Salvesen was involved in South Atlantic whaling from its inception in the early 1900s until the trade came to a halt in 1963. Its whaling fleet had the curious distinction of operating out of two ports on opposite sides of the globe, both called Leith. Home base was the Scottish port of Leith near Edinburgh, but operational base during Southern Hemisphere summers (Shetland winters) was Leith Harbour, on the island of South Georgia, more than thirteen thousand kilometres away and so deep in the South Atlantic that the next stop beyond it was Antarctica. For a youngster fresh to the industry, these were exciting times, and Gibbie worked on whale catchers for four seasons out of the next five.

'I started out as a Mess Boy, so I didn't have deck duties, but when my work was done in the Mess, I had the run of the ship; I could go almost anywhere I wanted and do anything I liked. I was on first name terms with everyone except the Gunner.'

Gunners operated and fired the harpoon with the explosive

charge built in that discharged after it hit the whale, a complex and dangerous job. They were almost always Norwegian, and were deferred to by crews whose bonuses were entirely dependent on the Gunner's absence of fear and his skills as a hunter.

Gibbie may not have been allowed to undertake deck duty in his first season, but he soon found himself above decks when the crew got down to their favourite off-duty pastime: cribbage.

'They were cribbage addicts,' he says, 'But because they played for cigarettes and I didn't smoke, whenever a card game got underway, they put me at the wheel. There I was, alone on the bridge of a thousand-tonne, 60-metre whale catcher in Antarctic waters — sometimes even in iceberg fields — and I was sixteen years old.'

The Southern Broom was a former 'Flower Class' Royal Navy corvette that served in World War II under the name of HMS Starwort, and creature comforts on wartime corvettes did not even stretch to an enclosed bridge. So young Gibbie manned the wheel on its 'open bridge' — open to the elements, like an old tub in a Spencer Tracy movie. If he wanted to check the radar for icebergs he had to leave the bridge, slip into a hut-like room in the superstructure, and wait for his night vision to adjust to the interior lighting before repeating the whole sequence in reverse. He soon learned to take all this in his stride, if only to avoid the ire of the cribbage players.

'You didn't interrupt a card game for anything short of a *real* emergency,' he laughs.

In 1904, fifty-four years before Gibbie arrived in the South Atlantic, C. A. Larsen, a Norwegian with experience of whaling in the Arctic, set up the first whaling business in South Georgia. The market for whale oil and other by-products was so profitable that within eight years, there were seven whaling stations on South Georgia, and the virtually unrestricted exploitation of the giants of the sea was under way.

From 1904 to 1965, over 175,000 whales were processed at South Georgia alone, and in the whole region, nearly 1.5 million animals were taken. By the time Gibbie arrived to work in the waning years of the industry, the toll inflicted on whale populations was grave, and even he, in his four seasons, noticed numbers declining.

'During the second-last season, we caught 14 Blue whales in one day; one of them was 96 feet long (about 30m). But we could see the catches declining. In the last season, the majority of the whales caught were Sei whales, which previously we ignored while we went for Fin and Blue whales.'

Today, more than forty years after the industry became uneconomic in the South Atlantic, and despite a 1982 International Whaling Commission moratorium (a relatively toothless ruling that numerous nations have chosen not to subscribe to), Blue, Fin and Sei whales remain classified as endangered.

Although he recalls that 'about fifty percent of animals were killed with one harpoon,' Gibbie admits that he 'couldn't help feeling sorry for them'. Not all whales were taken so easily, and he ruefully remembers Sperm whales taking as many as five killer harpoons before succumbing.

'When blood blew from the blow-hole, then you knew they were finished,' he says.

Animals killed were brought alongside, inflated with air to keep them afloat, then hauled, either to 'factory ships' or to South Georgia for processing. Gibbie remembers with obvious distaste the factory ships, where men called 'flensers' removed the blubber and 'lemmers' butchered the meat.

'The entrance to the main work area was called Hell's Gate,' he says, 'And with good reason.'

Gibbie's adventures in whaling came to an end when Salvesen abandoned the trade after the Southern summer of 1962-1963. He later worked on Aberdeen trawlers for four winters, once spending seventy-two hours on deck without sleep, and since 1966 he has done seasonal creel fishing off Shetland. But nothing in the intervening decades has come close to matching the excitement and camaraderie of his seasons in the South Atlantic.

'It was a way of life,' he says. 'The best years of my life.'

UNST

I: A blether and a bus shelter

The name Baltasound inspires thoughts of remote isolation in chilled northern climes. It somehow makes me think of far-flung fishing stations in isolated Alaskan river valleys where, instead of a bus stop they have a lake and light aircraft rigged with skis in winter and landing floats propped up in a bear-proof shed for use during brief seasonal thaws.

Shetland's Baltasound on the island of Unst might not be quite so remote as parts of Alaska, but getting there without a car from the camping böd at Voe is something akin to crossing the Wild West on the Pony Express. I opt for public transport which, in order to travel twenty-five kilometres as the arctic skua flies, involves a walk-bus-ferry-minibus-ferry-minibus-walk expedition that swallows up the better part of a morning.

The bus to Toft at the top of the island goes by way of Sullom Voe Terminal, the mother lode of oil revenue and employment that has transformed Shetland in the three decades since North Sea crude first came ashore by way of twin undersea pipelines and giant tankers that creep south through Yell Sound.

Gigantic oil storage tanks loom over immense areas of open concrete criss-crossed at speed by logo-emblazoned cars, trucks and jeeps. Vast expanses of shoreline are swallowed whole by colossal tankers hooked up to thrumming umbilical lines.

At the security gate, an electronic ticker-tape sign runs a never-ending loop of don't-even-try-to-ignore-this red letters. Matches or cigarette lighters are strictly prohibited; breach this rule, and say goodbye to your entry pass and your high-paying job. That the sign even exists suggests the scary image of diehard smokers caught sneaking quick puffs on site in the past.

When the bus pulls into Toft, it is met by the gaping maw of the *Dagalien*. Or perhaps that should be *one of the* gaping maws, for the *Dagalien* achieves roll-on-roll-off status, not by having a ramp at the stern and a bow that raises and lowers, but by having two bows. Pointed at both ends, she can criss-cross the strait without ever turning around.

The organisers of Shetland's public transport, unlike their counterparts elsewhere in Britain, have somehow grasped the value of having different vehicles, even different modes of vehicle, arrive at meeting points at around the same time.

The minibus that awaits the *Dagalien* at Ulsta whisks the few foot passengers north towards Gutcher, and the next leg of the transport odyssey. Sitting next to me is a lady who could speak for Shetland. So highly-tuned is her oratory that, within minutes, I have her potted life story so firmly impressed upon me that a written examination would present no challenge.

She tells me what line of work she used to be in before retiring, a snippet that only convinces me that this lady missed her calling, and that the teaching profession was deprived of a born educator. She is from England originally, and she met her husband on Unst, and after they married, there was no question that they would stay, not only in Shetland, but on Shetland's most northerly island.

'There's a Shetland saying about sheep,' she says, seemingly apropos of nothing. 'Sheep, you know, never forget the exact piece of pasture on which they were born. So much so that, at the first opportunity, they will rush back to that very spot as if driven by deep-rooted instinct.

'Shetlanders say that sheep are *'hefted tu the groond'.'*

She is clearly building up to a point with supreme narrative skill, and thankfully there is not too long to wait.

'All the best metaphors,' she says, 'can apply to people, too.' She winks. 'My husband — he's *hefted tu the groond'* of Unst.'

She sticks by my side as we move from the Yell minibus to the ferry for the short hop from Gutcher to Belmont on Unst and transfer to another minibus for the drive up to Baltasound. When we pull up at her home, still as loud and irrepressively good-natured as ever, she bids me a warm cheerio. The driver catches my eye in the rear-view mirror but says nothing. I think I spot a knowing smile but I don't care; my volunteer teacher's zest for life has made my morning.

The name Baltasound — up here it is pronounced 'Baltisoond' — is thought to have come from the Norse name Balti (not uncommon in Norwegian place names), combined with *sound*, for a strait or channel of water. Viewed from the garden of Ordale House, it is not so much a village as a rural community spread around an inner coastal landscape whose waters enjoy near-total protection from the North Sea. That protection comes in the form of Balta Island, a long, low barrier that sits like a jar cap poised to close down the seaward end of the Sound.

There are a couple of clusters of homes with the stamp of mass-production about them, one of which turns out to be Ministry of Defence housing that has a locked-up, abandoned look. The rest of Baltasound is spotted almost arbitrarily around a flat coastal landscape, neighbouring buildings separated by a hundred or more metres of salt-washed rocks or fields cropped bowling-green short by sheep with thick coats that ripple in the wind.

Ordale House has been a guest house since 1948, but long before that was the 19th Century home of an ancestor of the current Laird, and for the last couple of years has been the home and B&B of a pair of peripatetics with faraway roots. Patrick is originally from Dufftown on Scotland's north-east coast, wife Eve is Canadian, and in the last couple of decades, as well as Shetland they have lived in Canada, Ireland and Australia. Patrick is a laconic IT specialist with a serious bent for DIY; over the course of the next 48 hours, I seldom see him without a toolbox or a ladder to hand.

Eve is his perfect foil. A born conversationalist who could strike up a blether in the Gobi Desert and whose heartfelt, raucous laugh is never far from burbling to the surface, she takes genial charge of the B&B and always has time for a chat. Within minutes of arriving, I hear tales of her and Patrick's lives together in different parts of the planet; she bubbles with enthusiasm for everywhere they ever lived.

She kindly grants me the freedom of her kitchen to rustle up my own lunch whenever I am ready. Soon after she says so, I spot Patrick climbing a ladder and out of courtesy, mention it to him. He looks at me from under furrowed brows.

'Have you cleared that with Eve?' he says, face deadpan. 'It's **her** kitchen.'

In early afternoon, dense cloud shows no sign of coming down to smother the landscape, and Eve offers me the loan of a bicycle. I set off around the Sound with one simple goal in mind: to be the northernmost person in all of Britain.

Before I get out of town, I pay my respects at one of the most inspired pieces of installation art I have ever seen. The brainchild of local lad Bobby Macaulay, it is a perspex bus shelter on the northern edge of town that has been decorated and furnished to give it a touch of comfort and class. With sofa, table, microwave oven, 'computer', net curtains and even colouring books and crayons for its younger patrons, Baltasound's bus shelter boasts a Visitors' Book filled with appreciative inscriptions by travellers from as far away as Australia and North America. More than a thousand visitors a year sign the book. In statistical terms, that would be akin to twenty million people signing the visitors' book at the Tower of London, every single year.

It has its own award-winning website (designed by Bobby; search for 'Unst Bus Shelter'), and the shelter itself was bestowed the heady accolade of Best Bus Shelter in Britain by people who should know what they are talking about, the esteemed editors of Buses Magazine.

Today the shelter's décor reflects an African theme, as Bobby is presently studying for his International Baccalaureate in Swaziland.

Continually featured in press articles and discussed on Web forums, the shelter is maintained by family and friends while he is away, and his mother Jane even hosts sewing parties to create new displays. It was first decorated in 1995, when then seven-year-old Bobby wanted to add a personal touch to the brand new shelter that appeared at the end of his road. That it remains intact and carefully updated, never mind untainted by vandalism or theft, is a credit to the little community that is so proud of it.

II: Northernmost temporary northerner

Waiting in the decorated comfort of Bobby's shelter for a bus that may never arrive holds a lot more appeal than taking on north Unst's hill country on a borrowed bicycle.

But at least for now, the elements are on my side, and with a strong southerly at my back, the climb out of Baltasound is over, if not before I know it, then at least before my legs give out on me completely. The crest of the hill reveals yet another coastal community, Haroldswick, that comes with legends attached. Its name means 'Harold's Bay', and is said to derive from the landing on these very shores by King Harald of Norway in 875 A.D., when he popped in with a few longships full of hairy men with swords to put a personal face on Norway's claims to Shetland.

On a windy grey October's day, Haroldswick looks abandoned, neat houses clinging to a coastal bay with not one ambulatory soul in sight. And sadly, today it offers the casual visitor nothing more than its picturesque location. The village's two visitor attractions — a Boat Haven museum devoted to sailing craft through the ages and a Heritage Centre with displays on the history and culture of north Unst — are both closed for half of the year. Adam Smith would have grasped the supply-and-demand rationale, but surely, if an isolated location is to draw the very people who seek its isolation, at least parts of it ought to remain open for business.

To the north-east of Haroldswick lies the tiny bay community of Norwick, and beyond that, a solitary house at a coastal point called Skaw lays undisputed claim to being the northernmost home in Britain.

Norwick is known in local legend for the story from 1700 of a baby girl, Mary Anderson, plucked from her crib by a passing sea eagle and taken to the eagle's nest high on a cliff face. The child was rescued, unharmed, after a brave young lad called Robert Nicholson was lowered down the cliff on a rope. Naturally enough, Robert and Mary eventually married and of course lived happily ever after. It is a lovely tale, no less so for the fact that an almost identical story — complete with benign sea eagle and eventual marriage between bairn and cliff-dangler rescuer — is a part of the popular folk history of the island of Fetlar, south of Unst.

The real inspiration for such stories was surely the size and power of the sea eagle, whose metre-long body and 2.5-metre wingspan (over eight feet) must have made people wonder 'what if one of those was to.' Sadly, sea eagles, found throughout the British Isles since as far back as 1000 A.D., were hunted to extinction by farmers, overzealous gamekeepers and taxidermists working to meet the insatiable Victorian demand for stuffed animals.

The last remaining sea eagle in Britain, an ageing albino female, was shot in Shetland in 1918, but efforts since the mid-seventies to re-introduce the species to different parts of Scotland by bringing young birds from Norway have at last resulted in a fragile but growing population of around forty pairs dotted around our coasts. But even now, they remain heavily reliant upon protection from cursed egg-collectors and gamekeepers stuck in Victorian mindsets.

From Haroldswick the road narrows as it forks north-west. Fields here are defined not with fence lines, but by drystone walls of great beauty and even greater strength. A feature of Unst drystone dykes is that the heaviest stones form the top course of rocks, surely a function of needs dictated by weather on an island lashed by some of the fiercest winds found anywhere in the British Isles.

Dwellings recede in number until they are almost non-existent as I close in on yet another location called Burrafirth, this one at the secluded innermost end of a north-south voe of the same name. The fiord-like inlet is a half-kilometre wide corridor that stretches four kilometres north towards open sea. At its innermost point, a perfect arc of golden sand sits barely disturbed. In summer, with near-complete shelter provided by the twin tall shoulders of the coastal voe landscape and when the northern waters are relieved of just a little of their year-round chill, this must be an idyllic playground.

From east of the beach stretches a rocky coastline peppered with offshore stacks that throw shadows across cliff faces climbing ever-higher the further they reach towards open sea. Above the cliffline soars a hillside that reaches up towards the source of much of the island's employment for nearly half a century. Ever since the peak Cold War paranoia of the 1950s, the summit of Saxa Vord, at 290 metres the tallest point on Unst, has been host to an RAF radar station. With the Cold War receding rapidly into the past, the role of the station has been slowly fading away, and now, the announcement that it will soon be officially decommissioned brings with it fears for the economy of the entire island.

[I am on Unst in October 2005; Saxa Vord closes in April 2006 with the loss of 115 full-time jobs, causing the island population to drop by almost one-third. Not for the first time, Unst's population and economy are under serious threat.]

Saxa Vord entered the record books in 1962 when its wind speed measuring equipment logged winds at 285 kph, or 177 miles per hour. This was an unofficial British record, and speculation about even more powerful gusts will forever remain speculative, since moments after registering the record, the equipment blew away.

I pedal around the bay and up an undulating hill that follows the western coastline of the firth to the former Shore Station of the offshore Muckle Flugga lighthouse, a few kilometres north of here, and once the northernmost populated spot in all of Britain.

The word 'northernmost' crops up time and again on an island that sits above the rest of the nation. Northernmost home, hotel, bar, shop — even northernmost golf course (an undeveloped and facility-free nine-hole course only metres from where I cycled alongside Burrafirth beach. Enthusiasts be warned: if you do not bring a lawnmower, at least bring your own flagpoles).

The Visitor Centre at the old shore station is closed for the winter, so I push on to the rudimentary Hermaness car park and leave the bicycle leaning on a post.

Hermaness National Nature Reserve was founded in 1955, and today remains under the stewardship of Scottish Natural Heritage. That an unpopulated headland at the tip of Britain even needs stewarding is down to one thing: its incredible avian population. In peak breeding season, the headland is home to 100,000 birds, some species of which have come back from the brink of regional extinction.

In the mid-19th Century, local land-owners the Edmonstons hired a birdwatcher to protect the last three remaining pairs of great skua. Known to Shetlanders as the bonxie and renowned for the vigour with which it protects its nests by dive-bombing hillwalkers, during the 19th Century the great skua's numbers were depleted by egg-collectors and taxidermists' suppliers. Today, thanks initially to the Edmonstons and to organisations that have since taken up the fight, in the region of 650 pairs breed on Hermaness between May and August before dispersing south for the winter, some of them migrating as far away as West Africa.

This being October, I am much too late for the grand summer show of mass feathered residents, but in any case what draws me here is the coastal landscape and the lure of a glimpse of Muckle Flugga. But first, I have a strenuous walk across energy-sapping terrain, over a landscape so unforgiving that wearing the wrong kind of trousers can kill you. A sign at the beginning of the trail warns of the danger of wearing waterproof overtrousers, because so much of the walk is around steeply-pitched coastal slopes that are often slick with run-off. Lose your footing when wearing shiny waterproofs, and before you can arrest your slide you are over the edge of a precipice so tall that its height becomes irrelevant.

For forty-five minutes I dodge rocks and bogs and puddles and marshes and streams that threaten to mock expensive waterproof boots by running over their tops and soaking me from the inside out. The slog is uphill and over boggy peaty dale, offering up little in the way of scenery.

Quite suddenly the terrain switches to downhill. I have crossed the spine of the headland, and laid out in the distance is a seascape, only marginally less grey than the sky or even the land I trudge across, but with at least the prospect of seeing the west coast of Unst's northernmost headland. I trudge onwards, eyes down, choosing every footfall with care, scanning the greys and muted post-autumnal greens and boggy browns of the land underfoot. Suddenly my frame of sight is invaded by the stark black and white of a young dog so brimming with youthful kinetics that it flashes like a photographic strobe.

'Lovely day,' says a voice, thankfully not the dog's. Owner of both dog and voice is a young man wearing binoculars. One strong hand almost controls his young canine companion, and under the other arm he clutches an easel.

Apparently he is a birdwatcher, hiker, artist and dog lover who can't quite decide what to concentrate upon, and here he is on cliff top Hermaness embracing all of his passions at once.

'There are a load of goldcrests about,' he says helpfully.

He has divined from my binoculars, purchased specially for

Shetland less for their optic qualities than their waterproofness, that I must be a fellow birder.

Despite my mini-apprenticeship with the Fair Isle bank robbers, the sum of my birding knowledge could be written in ink marker on the back of a postage stamp, so the chances of stumbling across any area of mutual understanding with this nice young guy are at best slim. Confronted by a likely convergence of personal ignorance and mutual confusion, my instinct is to change the subject.

'How much further do I have to walk to get a view of Muckle Flugga?'

'Not far. No more than ten minutes.'

He heads off in the direction I have stumbled in from, and as I consider my options, I take in the sights.

All around me are vistas to die for, or to die from, if my overtrousers were not in my backpack. The grass at my feet is waterlogged slick and runs steeply downhill for only a few metres until it drops off the edge of the world.

Cliffs all around me are chillingly vast, bay-window-like coastal curves, a hundred metres or more tall, with craggy offshore skerries the size of London office tower blocks. The sense of scale is at once enthralling and fearful.

It is decision time. If I go back the same way I came in, the borrowed bicycle is less than an hour away. If I continue on an outward leg to a point where Muckle Flugga hails into view, that return time could double. It is late afternoon and night falls early in these northern parts at this time of year — so common sense gets thrown aside and I walk on.

What the young dog walker failed to consider when he said 'ten minutes' was our comparative states of strength and fitness. Ever wary of dizzying vertical drops that hover just three or four paces over *there*, I take to a contour line sheep trail across the tussocky landscape which, combined with some distinctly unfair uphill slopes, makes for very hard going. Ten minutes gets me nowhere near the next crest, so I pause for breath and look back at the seascape.

Spend a few days hiking around Shetland and the scenic treats it presents are so routinely fabulous that you start to get blasé about them. But one look back at the Hermaness coastline blows away all such thoughts. My uphill struggle has brought into view kilometres of precipice cliff faces, some at least 150 metres tall — or about as high as a fifty-storey skyscraper.

With the main breeding season over, the cliffs are not quite teeming with birdlife, but closer inspection brings out nests on every nook and niche, thousands of them occupied by wind-rustled seabirds. Fulmars hover in the gusting wind, awaiting the precise conditions to make landing on nest sites barely bigger than themselves at least a little less perilous. Fulmars are notorious for their projectile vomiting defensive skills, when they voluntarily erupt dense oily muck from their throats. A similar phenomenon is common all around urban Scotland after the pubs close late on Friday and Saturday nights.

A sheer-sided rock stack that looms off the coast is white with gannets and the broad-brush splash marks of gannet guano. One such stack used to lure birdwatchers from all around the country, binoculars and telescopes poised to spot 'Albert', a solitary black-browed albatross who roosted on the same cliff ledge almost every year from 1972 until 1995. Albert has been a celebrity in bird-watching circles for over forty years, having first been spotted in 1967 in the Firth of Forth near Edinburgh. A recent BBC news report tells me that Albert's solitary vigil continues on another uninhabited Atlantic rock. Sula Sgeir, sixty-five kilometres north of the Hebridean island of Lewis, is home to five thousand pairs of gannets — and one albatross called Albert.

I have still not set eyes upon Muckle Flugga, and from here the waymarked path leads straight up the steep slope towards the highest point on the headland. Darkness is less than two hours away, and I have more than ninety minutes' hiking to get back to the bicycle; getting stuck out here after dark is not an option, so pushing on uphill and further inland is rationalised by how at least it takes me further from the cliffs.

Darkness is not my only enemy up here, and I keep a wary eye on the south, from where the weather is arriving on the back of a steady southerly. It continues to look overcast and possibly rain-laden, but not too daunting. Not so long ago, a tourist couple were caught out on this headland by a sudden storm so powerful that it became too dangerous to contemplate trying to get back to the car park. They opted to ride out the tempest in a hut-like shelter, but it, and they, were swept over the cliffs.

By now I am reduced to mincing, grandma-in-a-tight-skirt paces up a slope so sodden with run-off that it washes over the toes of my boots. Concentration alone gets me from one waymark post to the next; far too tired to be so far from civilisation, I pause to catch my breath and look back once more.

Visibility to the south and west has improved beyond belief. I can look out along an imaginary line that runs directly south-west across the rippled North Atlantic to kiss the northernmost points of both the island of Yell and the tip of Fethaland.

The sky is a mottled grey curtain that obscures all sign of a sun that dips towards the horizon, a curtain unbroken save for two perfectly placed openings that send fat golden *goko* beams downwards — one each to fall precisely upon the tips of Yell and Fethaland. This is what they used to call a Kodak Moment, and here I am, camera-free, because I was certain it was going to rain today.

Legs like overcooked noodles, I trudge along a soggy sheep track, eyes on wherever boots land lest I go over on an ankle. Break an ankle now, and if I am lucky, Eve and Patrick will raise the alarm in a few hours, meaning I could spend the night up here.

By now, gaps between stops for breath are decreasing, and at the next such pause, I raise my eyes from the trail — and there she is. Muckle Flugga Lighthouse, first built by Robert Louis Stevenson's father Thomas Stevenson in 1854 to lend protection to troop ships headed for the Crimean War. There is a horrible irony about a government concerned for the safety of troops in transit towards a hideous conflict that will cost so many of them their lives. The 1854 tower was a temporary structure, and the present one, twenty metres tall and perched sixty metres up the jagged rock island, has cast its beam across some of the wildest waters in Britain for nearly one hundred and fifty years.

In his wonderful book Art Rambles in Shetland, published in 1869, artist and author John T. Reid described a storm that lashed Muckle Flugga lighthouse in January 1868.

*'The waves of the North Sea were breaking over it, although
the rock on which it is built is two hundred feet in height,
and the light-room stands sixty feet higher.'*

One last hilltop sits between me and the return route to the
bicycle. My compass tells me that the waymark posts now point
south, reaching up a slope not far short of forty-five degrees from
horizontal. It goes on and on, and the change of direction invites the
strong southerly wind to do its spiteful best to impede every step, to
make each uphill pace a trial for legs and lungs that are already close
to their limits.

It slows me to the point that ever-more frequent stops are
required to heave at moist salt-laden air, pauses which allow me to
turn and re-savour the view of Muckle Flugga and beyond it, Out
Stack — the British Isles' final geological punctuation mark.

At last, a wind-damaged climber's cairn breaks the skyline, and I
seek out a neat striated stone triangle, which I sit near the cairn's top
so that one apex points directly down the slope I have just weathered,
due north to Muckle Flugga.

When trekking, a firm safety rule dictates that if you wait until you
feel thirsty it is too late, and by now I am seriously dehydrated. But at
least here, on the top of the headland, the landscape levels out just
enough for water to lie. I fashion a drinking vessel from a plastic bag
and scoop peaty-brown fluid from a table-top-sized rainwater pond.
Ignoring all thoughts of sheep droppings, I slurp long and deep at
water so chilled that it makes my teeth ache.

Nothing, no drink consumed anywhere in over forty-five years
and as many countries travelled, *ever* tasted better, and months later, I
can still summon up the taste of the peat. At least, I hope it is peat.

Beneath the cairn, the land bolts downwards to the north coast
and dives off the cliff face into North Atlantic waters. A few hundred
metres out, standing proud upon massive rock slabs that themselves
teeter at steep angles forced upon them millions of years ago by
tectonic shifts, is the lighthouse whose beam reaches out, weather
permitting, thirty-five kilometres in all directions. When the light was
built, it was such a challenge that it cost £32,000 in 1857 money —
something like £20 million today. I call that a small price to pay for
150 years, and counting, of lives saved.

Back then the island it perched upon was known as North Unst, and not until 1964 was it changed to Muckle Flugga, from the Old Norse *Mikla Flugey*, a name whose romantic ring is at odds with its translation of 'large, steep-sided island'.

From the completion of the temporary lighthouse in 1854 through to the automation of the light in 1995, it was the northernmost populated point in the British Isles. Which right now makes me the northernmost soul in the nation. It is a solitary experience worth savouring while, for a few short minutes, every single one of sixty-odd million Britons is, well, *beneath* me.

Now darkness is coming in like a raging storm, and fired up by peat bog water, I cut a downhill dash straight into a southerly gale, towards where I hope a borrowed bicycle awaits.

Of course it is still there, but so too are more than ten kilometres of cycling into that southerly, in near-total darkness and without lights. Long before I reach Baltasound I bear the physical imprint of what marathon runners call 'the wall', after which I slip into a fatigue fugue state. When I pull into the empty car park of the village shop in desperate need of nutrition, it is a few minutes past six o'clock, and I am glad beyond belief to find the lights on and the door unlocked. A lady behind the counter looks at me with kindly bemusement.

'I was hoping you didn't close at six,' I say.

Her smile wears what I interpret as a hint of self-indulgence.

'I close when I feel like it.'

III: Out of the closet and into the brewery

After more than three weeks wandering Shetland at a time of year when there are fewer tourists than trees, I am well inured to spending breakfast alone. Today, as the sole guest at Ordale House, things are no different until Patrick surprises me by inviting me into a cupboard.

'This is very interesting,' he says as he disappears behind a door in the corner of the dining room. He pops back out to wave me after him, and I leave cornflakes to soggy fate and follow. The door leads not to another room, but to what my grandmother called a 'press', a shallow, full-length door-sized indentation lined with solid wooden shelves, a walk-in store-room without the space to walk into. The shelves are stacked with B&B dining room crockery, but Patrick wants me to look, not at the cupboard, but at the inside of the door.

Ordale House was built in the 1850s, possibly for an aunt of the then Laird, a Mr Edmonston, quite likely the same Edmonston who did so much to save the great skuas of Hermaness. The 'press' door seems to have hung here ever since, for marching up its unpainted inner surface are the progression of pencil marks so much enjoyed by families watching their young grow. Leaps in height of young Edmonstons are recorded over a period of about twenty years from 1879 onwards. It is a touching little piece of local history, valued and preserved by Ordale House's latest tenants.

Patrick clearly has a feel for local history, as he tells me, in a gentle accent that is somehow still redolent of his north-east coast roots never mind intervening decades spent wandering the globe, of the tough times this part of Shetland suffered in the first part of the 19th Century.

Still trapped in the Truck System, crofters lived subsistence-level existences while Lairds like the Edmonstons prospered. But if local Lairds' business models viewed their crofters as profit centres, authorities in distant lands saw them for their true potential. Patrick tells me of the coastal village of Colvadale, a few kilometres south of here, that was abandoned almost overnight, totally de-populated by working folk eager to snap up the chance of working for themselves instead of for a landlord, even if it meant picking up everything and travelling to the other side of the world.

Iniquitous it may have been, but the cunning in the way landlords controlled local economies to their own benefit was not lost on at least one Shetland emigrant, who exported the economic model all the way to a very different archipelago — the Cocos Keeling Islands, adrift in the Indian Ocean, mid-way between Australia and what today is Sri Lanka. In the 1820s, the uninhabited isles were settled by Shetland adventurer John Clunies-Ross, who set up coconut plantations that were tended by imported Malay workers. Granted ownership of the islands in perpetuity by Queen Victoria in 1886, subsequent generations of Clunies-Rosses embraced the self-styled mantle of 'Kings of the Cocos'. Malay workers received their wages in Cocos Rupees — minted by their self-appointed Kings, and redeemable only at the island store which, in a direct reflection of the ways of the Truck System, was operated by the plantation company owned by the King. Workers who left the island were even banished from returning, in much the same way as some Whalsay fishermen who left their island in search of work were barred from returning by the Bruces. Remarkably, Shetland-inspired Indian Ocean feudalism survived for a hundred and fifty years until 1978, when the combined distaste and wrath of the United Nations and the Australian trades unions finally forced the then King — another John Clunies-Ross — to sell the Cocos Keeling Islands to Australia.

Around the time that the first of the Kings set up his distant private fiefdom, on Unst the good people of Colvadale were plucked away wholesale by representatives of the New Zealand government, who dangled before them comparative riches and incomparable levels of independence. The temptations of free passage to the Antipodes and ownership, not tenancy, of fifty acres of prime sheep-rearing land turned Colvadale into a ghost town. Shetland's loss was New Zealand's long-running gain.

The numbers drawn away were so significant and continued for so long that I heard of a funeral of an old Shetlander that took place in New Zealand in the 1990s. A close friend of the dead man delivered a speech that harked back to the days before World War II, when they and many like them were young immigrants starting afresh. So many Shetlanders took the New Zealand option, he remembered, that more Shetlanders lived in New Zealand than lived in Shetland. Even today, a Shetlander browsing the telephone directories for New Zealand's South Island could be forgiven for thinking he may have stumbled across a secret Shetland island, so common are Shetland surnames.

I venture for a walk in what the radio says is a south-westerly, force 5 to 6. I soon get an idea how powerful this means when I put the binoculars on five geese struggling to fly due south, and being blown off course by sharp gusts. I see them react to one fierce flurry with an immediate doubling of effort that prompts a curious side-effect. Three out of five birds mark the sudden rise in exertion with synchronised bowel movements, simultaneous mid-air excretions. This inspires a light bulb-flash of understanding why, when flying in formation, each successive bird flies slightly higher than the one in front. Could this be Darwinist, evolutionary 'natural selection' in action? Learn to fly higher than the leading bird's *parson's nose* — or take the chance of wearing his waste?

Darwinist thoughts, *parson's noses* and all, I set off to talk beer with a Priest.

Unst may be steeling itself for the economic body blow of the impending closure of Saxa Vord, but for the people of Baltasound, such a set-back is nothing new. The last big blow to local employment came in 1995, when the island airstrip was closed down. Yet, for one man at least, this was the beginning of a new chapter of personal enterprise and self-employment.

I walk to the edge of town to visit Valhalla Brewery and meet up with its owner, Sonny Priest.

I later read Valhalla defined as 'a heavenly place where those who are favoured by the gods can go when they die' but when Sonny Priest's wife shows me into Baltasound's Valhalla, there is nothing heavenly about an oversized garage full of wooden tanks and fat piping that writhes like boa constrictors on an immaculately scrubbed floor.

For a man who makes quality beer for a living, Sonny Priest is surprisingly svelte of figure. He stands tall and trim in work overalls, has a web of dark hair that looks as if it may be difficult to control, and he holds up soggy rubber gloves by way of an apology for not shaking hands.

A native of Unst, he is a carpenter by trade, and was the manager of the island's airport when it closed down in 1995. The blow to the local economy was a harsh one, snuffing out steady employment to forty Unst residents, many of whom had to leave the island in search of work.

'It was the worst blow to island employment for decades,' he says in his soft Unst tongue. 'It meant a lot of folk had to leave the island to find jobs, but we had two girls in primary school here, so I was determined I wasn't going to leave, though I didna have a clue what I was goin' to do.'

One night, before the airport closed for good and after operations shut down for the day, Sonny and a few colleagues stayed behind for refreshments. A couple of beers led to another couple and a few more after that, until towards the end of a serious session, talk turned to what they were each going to do when their airport jobs were no more. When it came to Sonny's turn, he looked at his friends staggering around drunk, and said, completely off the cuff:

'I'll start up a brewery tae keep du in drink!'

It was a bold declaration based on nothing. Sonny had never before considered starting a brewery; the snappy comeback to his mates was born only of the alcohol swimming his veins, but he awoke the next morning with the seed of an idea that began to germinate. Over the following months a spur of the moment notion became a business plan which turned into a cottage industry, and in December 1997 Valhalla Brewery was in business.

The brewery still operates from an outbuilding, albeit a large one, at Sonny's home; and he continues to provide the vast majority of the labour involved in putting as many as 3,600 bottles a week out the shed door and onto the market. Twelve-hour days are the norm — and in summer, when demand peaks, eighteen is not unknown. Two local men work part-time on the bottling process, which is still done on a hand-operated machine, two bottles at a time. Mass production, this is not.

The five varieties of Valhalla beers are stocked in bars and shops all over Shetland, and the growing market for boutique brewery products on the U.K. mainland means Sonny meets demand from sellers of quality ales throughout the country.

But it takes more than a flash of entrepreneurial inspiration and a few thousand fifteen-hour days to make a business like this work, and in Sonny there is that extra ingredient, a passion for making the archipelago's only brewery — which, it should go without saying, makes it the *northernmost* brewery in all of Britain — something different, something identifiably from Shetland.

One way he has done that is by including in one of his recipes 'bere', a coarse barley that may have first been introduced to Shetland by Vikings in the 9th Century. With a canny nod to Shetland's history, Sonny named the beer 'Old Scatness' after the archaeological site in the far south of Mainland, and where the detection of barley bere inspired speculation that brewing may have gone on there, a thousand or more years ago. Old Scatness has been excavated every summer since 1995 by archaeologists from Bradford University, and therein lies the other reason for naming a beer after their summer workplace: English beer drinkers know their ales, and for years Sonny watched a surge in demand in south Mainland that coincided precisely with the months spent there by Yorkshire archaeologists.

'White Wife' takes its name from a ghost who appears on a lonely stretch of Unst road just a few kilometres from the brewery. She is an old woman who appears suddenly in vehicles, usually driven by men who are travelling alone.

But my favourite in name as well as flavour has to be 'Sjolmet Stout'. The naming of a strong dark beer with a light-coloured head after a breed of Shetland cow known for its strong dark body and light-coloured head is a mark of the man with the innate marketing nous behind Valhalla's success. When he offers me any bottle to take away, the choice is easy.

LERWICK

The second worst driver in the world

There was a period of about ten years when, from a home base in Hongkong, I flew all over Asia on photography assignments, jobs that regularly involved being met at regional airports by upstanding candidates for the title of Worst Driver in the World.

After years of deliberation, the dubious honour eventually went to a North Korean taxi driver who piloted an ageing Volvo at manic speeds along a four-lane mountain highway, navigating one blind bend after another like a racing driver intent on kissing every inner apex — two lanes deep into the *wrong side of the road*. Eventually I became so frightened that I abandoned the pretence of not speaking Korean. In the rear-view mirror, the driver's eyes widened as I compared him unfavourably with the smelliest underbits of a quadruped very low in the Korean social order, at which point he took both hands from the wheel and lashed out with a series of haymakers that were *never* going to hit me, if only because I was in the back seat.

So when, fifteen years later and a couple of continents away, an elderly man behind the wheel of an ageing Volvo actually admits that he is a bad driver, I laugh it off.

I am on the quay at Belmont, at the southern end of Unst, and the Volvo is one of only three cars in the queue for the ferry that is due in a few minutes. I arrive in Belmont well warned by the minibus driver that the public transport service that so impressed me on the way up because it linked ferries and local minibuses perfectly, does not work in reverse at this time of day. This means that if I arrive in Yell without a lift south to the next ferry in the transport chain, I could find myself at the mercy of regular road traffic running down the spine of Yell. And personal experience has already taught me that there is none.

I choose the one car with a single occupant and plenty of room for me and my bag — when hitching, or even scrounging, pragmatism is the only way to go — and wander over to have a word. The driver is a supremely neat man, I guess in his early sixties, white beard cropped very short, hair recently trimmed, open-neck shirt freshly ironed. He does that chin-down, eyebrows-raised trick that lets him look at me over the top of his finely-polished spectacles, and I say:

'Would you by any chance be going through Yell to the ferry for Mainland?'

He thinks about that for a second.

'God willing.'

A coherent response to which escapes me. I mumble something about a lack of public transport on Yell making it impossible to get down to Ulsta to catch the next ferry, meaning I would miss it and could he possibly—

'—I have to warn you,' he says, still looking at me over the top of his glasses. 'People who know me say I am the worst driver in the world.'

A few seconds later, he seems just a little nonplussed to find me sitting beside him, but as hitch-hiking techniques go, it is only one step up from basic: at the first sign of uncertainty or hesitation, jump aboard.

My new host's curiosity is piqued, and he grills me like a sergeant major firing one-liners at a new recruit, sweeping up details about what I am doing here without transport of my own. The stock line about travelling around Shetland to research a book inspires another thoughtful frown and a pause in his interrogation just long enough for me to get a question in sideways.

By now the ferry ride is behind us, and as we crest the hill outside of Gutcher, the road opens up and he lays on the speed. I remember something he let slip a moment earlier.

'Did you say the Sudan? You worked there?'

He takes his eyes off the road for long enough to get my pulse racing before deigning to reply. I expect another clipped one-liner, but instead I get a mini lecture that only serves to underline how, no matter where you are in 'isolated' Shetland, a local with first-hand experience of the world's darkest and most distant corners might only be around the next corner or, in the case of this fellow, clipping the next corner.

He tells me of being in the British military in colonial Sudan and of staying on after Independence in an advisory role to the new government. I meanwhile wrack my brain for faint slivers of general knowledge; didn't Sudan become independent in 1956? If so, it is time to raise my estimate of his age by at least ten years.

'I have heard that Sudan is a scary place,' I say, embarrassed by the lameness of the contribution to what had been an intriguing monologue. Still, it has the desired effect of keeping him on track, though what he says next is just about as far removed from heather-covered, wind-washed peat-bog-wrapped Yell as I can construe.

'I disliked Fridays,' he says. 'Fridays were the Muslim Sabbath, of course, and every Friday, they held public executions — hangings — and in my official capacity, I had to be there.'

A half century on from the events, he sounds distinctly more inconvenienced than outraged by what happened on mid-1950s Fridays. He takes his eyes off the road for long enough to trim the edge of a peat bog with two wheels and send a family of sheep running for the hills, and mis-reads the astonishment in my expression. His face takes on an instant chill.

'If that bothers you, if you're too *liberal* for that sort of thing, you can get out right now if you like!'

Get out right now? He has to be kidding. This is fascinating, his driving is merely terrifying, and in any case, I still have one more ferry to catch. Reassured that I am not quite so liberal as he momentarily suspected, he takes me all the way to Lerwick. By the time he drops me on Victoria Pier, we are the best of friends, and I have a new nominee for Second Worst Driver in the World.

I step out to discover Lerwick in a state of unease encapsulated in one image from the pedestrian shopping area of Commercial Street:

People are wrapped in collective confusion as they pinball back and forth along the street holding mobile phones at arms length, at eye level and higher. They live here, so they **know** the mobile signal should be perfectly strong. Yet they have no signal, so they hold phones as high as their arms will reach, as if maybe getting them that few centimetres closer to satellites rushing through outer space — or at least to relay antennae that blight the urban landscape of Shetland as they do elsewhere in the country — will do some good. Which, of course, it does not; I know, because I try until my arms go numb.

Thanks to a construction worker on the Scottish mainland slicing through a major communications artery, Shetland has suddenly found itself with no mobile phone links, no Internet, and very few operational landlines. At a stroke, he has put communications back fifteen years, and the shock of it is writ large on the faces of ordinary folk walking the streets. This would be a lot funnier if I could just get online and download my email, but along with the rest of Shetland, I am stuck in the communications Dark Ages of the dim and distant 1990s.

Uncertainty over the rest of my day is rescued by a low-tech blackboard notice announcing that *Hom Bru*, one of Shetland's finest musical outfits, are playing tonight at Flint's Bar.

Six months remain before anti-smoking legislation bestows a compulsory smoke-free status upon all bars and restaurants in Scotland, and for this non-smoker, it cannot come soon enough. I get a drink from the bar and try and fail to locate even a tiny corner that is not enshrouded in a nicotine fog.

Live music starts late here, so ten o'clock is long gone before a guitarist warms up with an astonishing solo rendition of the theme tune to The Muppets, melody, bass and rhythm all conjured out of one guitar.

From there it just gets better. Four middle-aged guys, two playing mandolins, one guitarist and a fiddler, rattle through everything from traditional folk to blues, bluegrass, country and jazz, all to a standard of proficiency that speaks of decades of playing together. Instrumentals are broken up by a Shetland song about the *Haaf* fishing and an old Chet Atkins number followed by another instrumental, Somewhere Over The Rainbow, with mandolins and violin sharing melody duties and the guitarist once more playing the role of three instruments at once. All of which goes on seemingly unnoticed by the pub's thirty or forty customers, and when the leader of the band announces a short break, applause is somewhere between thin and non-existent.

I grasp the opportunity to go over for a chat, and if they are disappointed that the only person to approach them is neither female nor good-looking, they manage to hide it well.

They welcome me to their table and I get a quick introduction to the line-up. The de facto front man and mandolin player (the banjo on a stand is also his) is founding member Gary Peterson, who explains that the band has experienced the personnel changes you might expect of an outfit that has been on the go since 1978, but that now, three of the four-piece outfit are founder members. Davie Henry (mandolin) and Brian Nicholson (guitar) are the two other founders, making fiddler John Robert Deyell the relative newcomer to the line-up.

In the early eighties, the band were based in Edinburgh and quickly gained a reputation that saw them playing gigs and festivals all over Europe. They have now been based in Shetland for over twenty years — all four have full-time jobs — but still manage to get over to the UK mainland or to the Continent to play major festivals. When Gary asks about my plans for the remainder of my Shetland stay, I say I still hope to get to Foula. He tells me that Davie Henry grew up on Foula, and that the man talking to him, Kevin Gear, still lives there.

Kevin is the quintessential man of few words who, when he discovers I am a writer, becomes a man of next to no words at all. Foula, like Fair Isle, has been the focus of uninformed broad-brush media rubbish in recent years from hacks who never let the truth get in the way of a good story, so I can hardly blame him for not opening up to me. Not that I exactly press him for much in the way of detail, though I do hope at least for some sort of insight into the lives of the fewer than thirty folk who live on the island full time. But Kevin is obviously not about to open up. Still, I take one last stab at conversation.

'If I get over to Foula soon, is there any chance I'll see you?' I say.

'If I'm there, you'll see me,' he says, with equal parts certainty and finality.

I head off into the cool night thinking about Foula. The island's silhouette has broken the western horizon so many times over the last three weeks, yet I am still no closer to visiting. With under ten days left in Shetland, the ferry option is becoming less and less likely — and the thought of it less and less appealing — so if I am to see Foula for myself, I will have to fly.

But before that happens, I have a date with the southern half of Mainland, down where the experts agree that the first human settlers on Shetland likely washed ashore on skimpy craft made of wood, bones and animal hide, more than five thousand years ago.

SOUTH MAINLAND

I: Betty Mouat's frown

When I leave for Scatness late in the afternoon, nightfall is only an hour away, and I am faced with either hitch-hiking forty kilometres in the dark or indulging in the rampant profligacy of a £2 ($4) bus ride. The decision is not a difficult one.

The bus is filled with commuters heading home from the capital. Every boarding passenger acknowledges the driver by name, and Colin seems to know most of his customers just as well. He also knows where they all live, because he occasionally makes special stops outside garden gates, and before the door hisses to a close behind them, every last departing passenger bids him a cheery farewell. This sense of community, never mind how spread out it is, makes me think of long periods of my life when I would have failed to pick my immediate neighbours out of a police identity parade. Yesterday, Gary Peterson of Hom Bru told me of the years that the band was based in Edinburgh and how the draw of home was so strong that, every time they came back to Shetland for Christmas, they always seemed to return south minus a band member. Homesickness is an affliction that I never suffered, but Shetland is beginning to teach me what makes it so painful for so many.

The route runs along the east coast of the long dagger-blade of south Mainland, which is never more than about four kilometres across. Place names along the route are a narrative of Shetland's Viking past, Norse roots evident everywhere. Places like Quarff (Old Norse *hvarf*, a turning place or a corner); Fladdabister (*flatibölstadr*, the flat farm); Hoswick (*hausvik*, a steep hill overlooking an open bay); and Hestingott (*hestennagardr*, a horse enclosure); every last one is rooted deep in the tale of a land over-run and not so much renamed as named for the first time in a new language by tough men arriving in open boats. Twelve hundred years on, those Viking connections live and breathe in the voices and daily lives of the people of Shetland.

Colin kindly drops me at my own front gate for the next few days, the entrance to Betty Mouat's, another of Shetland Amenity Trust's böds, this one named after a Shetlander who was at one time front page news worldwide.

The böd is beautifully crafted from stone on the site of Betty's 19th Century croft, and would sit in total darkness if it were not so close to the runway of Sumburgh Airport that it is streaked by the flashing lights of ground crew vehicles and the very occasional aircraft streaming overhead. I have the place to myself again, so I take the bunk nearest to the pot-belly stove. Some gracious soul has left behind coal and firelighters, and ten minutes later, it begins to radiate just enough heat to chip away at the deep chill of an empty stone building. Along with the required tinned fish and pasta, my rucksack yields a bottle of 2002 Merlot whose Romanian provenance might see purists wince, but under present circumstances, is more than acceptable. I settle back in a creaky armchair, revel in the warmth from a stove that pings as it gains heat, and raise a chipped mug to Betty Mouat. She looks on, with just a hint of a frown, or perhaps a forced smile, from above the fireplace.

When celebrity swept into the life of crofter Betty in 1886, she was already sixty years old, had been lame in one leg from birth, and following a mild stroke, decided to see a doctor in Lerwick. One hundred and twenty years ago, grim roads made the reverse of today's fifty-minute bus trip miserable, and so Betty decided to make her first journey to the capital in fourteen years by sea. From the port of Grutness near Sumburgh head, she set out as the only passenger on the weekly trip to Lerwick aboard the *Columbine*, a 15-metre sailing cutter with a crew of three. Betty went below decks, carrying with her forty shawls that she was to sell to merchants in Lerwick on behalf of herself and weavers from neighbouring crofts.

Not long into the voyage, a violent swing of the boom broke the main sheet (which, despite the designation, is of course a rope), and during attempts to make repairs, the Skipper, James Jamieson and the mate were swept over the side. The mate managed to clamber back aboard, and with the other crewman, set out on a rescue mission in the *Columbine's* tender, but failed to locate the Skipper. To make matters worse, the two in the small boat were unable to regain the fast-drifting *Columbine*. Meanwhile Betty Mouat, ignorant of the tragedy unfolding above decks, was alone on a sailing cutter adrift in the North Sea, amidst the winter chill and swollen seas of late January.

That Betty survived eight days and nights with little or no food or drink (she had brought with her only a bottle of milk and two biscuits) was remarkable enough. But that the *Columbine* survived to drift onto rocks at Lepsoy in north-west Norway was nothing short of miraculous. The island of Lepsoy lies behind innumerable reefs and land barriers that the drifting *Columbine* somehow evaded without incident. A blind man would have as much chance of negotiating a dense forest without brushing against a single branch as the Columbine had of reaching safety on its own.

The celebrity spotlight in Victorian times may not have been quite so intense as in these days of 24-hour news stations, but when she passed through Edinburgh on the way back to Shetland, the woman who had probably never seen a real crowd before had to contend with strangers asking for a souvenir hair from her head. She wisely resisted offers to become an exhibit in a travelling show, but after returning to her Scatness croft, continued to entertain curious visitors. Among them must have been the portrait photographer who produced the stern image that looks down at me in a building on the site where Betty lived until she died in 1918 at the grand old age of ninety-three.

The face that frowns at my Romanian Merlot is that of a vaguely masculine-looking woman in her sixties. Despite the photographer's charade of posed wool and knitting needles, she is done up in her Sunday best in an austere tunic buttoned all the way to her throat, and her finely-parted hair is smothered by a crocheted woollen cap; she struggles to freeze her expression and to hold the needles still for the long exposure required in the 1880s.

This is a lady who had lived a hard anonymous existence for sixty years before finding herself thrust into the public eye, and the sharp relief between harsh humdrum reality and fleeting accidental fame is written all over a face that, years after the event that brought overnight renown, might still be basking in what remains of the limelight.

She is still looking down at me when I stoke the stove and retire to my sleeping bag, while around me the big empty room rumbles with echoes real and imagined.

Heavy layers of wine-weighted sleep are peeled away by insistent thumps that first pick their way through the remains of an early morning dream before assuming the real-world urgency of workmen wanting in to use the kettle. Despite my weeks in Shetland I am still in town-dweller mode, so I locked up before going to sleep, and failed to notice the sign that warned of workers from the neighbouring Old Scatness archaeological dig needing daytime access to the böd.

The böd and my morning are instantly besieged by a double act. A dry but garrulous middle-aged Scot from near Edinburgh, and an Anglo twenty years his junior who only stops talking when the other guy speaks.

Even though they are hard work on a red wine hangover, I soon warm to my invaders. Here to do 'consolidation' work to protect the neighbouring archaeological dig before the onset of the long winter, these two sooth-moothers have lived in Shetland for years. Jim Keddie is the drystone wall master who built the böd, and Gary is an ex-army man from Wolverhampton who shed the constraints of uniform to take a degree in history before seeking work in archaeology — but only because he knew that the academics in the archaeology world would never take him seriously without a degree.

Tea-break over, they go back to consolidating the Old Scatness site, and I follow Jim. He explains that in 1975, when excavation was being done for a new airport access road, the remains of an Iron Age 'broch' were discovered. Brochs are coastal towers of drystone construction that only exist in mainland Scotland and its northern and western isles; Shetland alone has well over one hundred sites officially designated as brochs or broch remains. This alone might explain why it took two decades after the Old Scatness structure's discovery before a curious mound near the broch — more than five metres tall and eighty metres in diameter — began to be excavated by archaeologists from Bradford University. Almost immediately, they struck an archaeological gold mine: evidence of three thousand years of habitation, some of that buried under sand for well over a thousand years. Excavations have since revealed intact structures as well as trace evidence from the Bronze Age through Pictish, Viking and Medieval times. Since 1995, painstaking excavation has taken place every summer, seasonal activity that gives Sonny Priest's Valhalla Brewery such a perceptible spike in sales, and today Scatness remains one of the largest on-going archaeological digs in Europe.

While Jim is telling me all this, we stand outdoors, mere metres from the lingering warmth of the böd stove — and face north, straight into a wind armour-plated with Arctic chill. His enthusiasm for three millennia of multi-layered history that lay for decades undiscovered under Betty Mouat's doorstep bubbles in his language and his speech. Jim is a man whom many would envy; he views his work and the history it is wrapped in with obvious passion.

While we talk, I notice a strange thing. Jim has a very slight stammer that pops up in the usual places, minor dysfluencies that occasionally slow the enunciation of first syllables, but do nothing to prevent an eloquent and avid talker from getting his message across in exacting detail.

It is what I notice *next* that qualifies as bizarre. Completely involuntarily, I too begin to struggle with the first things out of my mouth and suffer what feel like interminable p-p-pauses before a word f-f-f-finally takes sh-sh-shape and appears. The more it happens, the more self-conscious I become; is this some sort of misplaced empathy with Jim? The idea that Jim might gain the impression that I am taking the mickey only makes things worse, so I resort to nods and 'hmmm-mms' for a couple of minutes before taking a gamble on regular speech one more time, and blessedly, the simplest of solutions to the short-lived mystery falls into place. My face is frozen harder than pork chops in a butcher's freezer. What affects my speech is nothing more than the pre-onset of frostbite.

Back indoors, I eventually regain sufficient communication powers to ask Jim what he likes about living in Shetland.

'This is a superb part of the world to bring up a family,' he says. 'Shetland has got so much going for it, that I get angry when locals lose sight of what makes it such a special place, and when they start moaning about their so-called problems — like how it is so expensive to travel to and from the Scottish mainland.'

'Take the prosperity delivered to Shetland by oil in less than a generation,' he says, 'In the space of the same generation too many Shetlanders have lost sight of those huge benefits. They are blasé about things that would be the envy of just about anywhere else in Britain.'

On big, rock-gnarled fingers, he ticks them off:

'Nearly full employment; superb care for the elderly; great roads; grand leisure centres in even tiny communities; some of the best schools in Europe with the lowest pupil/teacher ratios imaginable.'

Now he is on a roll.

'Shetlanders want to talk about problems? I'll show you problems. I'll put you in a working class housing scheme just about anywhere else in Scotland, and you'll soon change your mind about what constitutes *problems.'*

II: The Braer bullet dodged

The main road running south past Old Scatness kisses the inner shore of Quendale Bay, a scimitar of sand and rocky shoreline that curves north and west towards the cliffs of Fitful Head which, at 300-plus metres, are tall even by Shetland standards. Before the bay gets there, it passes the point on the coastline that became the focus of worldwide media attention on January 5th, 1993, when the MV Braer, a Liberian registered tanker en route from Norway to Quebec, lost engine power during a Force 11 hurricane and ran aground at Garths Ness. Predictions about the environmental fall-out were understandably doom-laden, since the 260-metre-long tanker carried 85,000 tonnes of crude oil — or twice the load of the Exxon Valdez that foundered off Alaska four years before, with disastrous effects. Commenting to the BBC on the likely environmental consequences of the Braer's sinking, a Greenpeace spokesman said it would be 'virtually impossible to avert a major ecological catastrophe.'

He and other commentators did not reckon on two factors that were ultimately to save Shetland from the horrific degree of damage that the Exxon Valdez inflicted upon Prince William Sound. The first was that the 'Gulfaks' crude carried by the Braer was an atypical variety of North Sea oil, being lighter in consistency and considerably more biodegradeable than other crudes. And secondly, the Gulfaks leaked from the stricken Braer straight into seas thrashed by some of the worst storms in living memory. Soon after the Braer ran aground, the region experienced the deepest atmospheric depression (909 millibars) ever recorded in the north-east Atlantic, after which came eleven days of almost constant hurricane-force winds.

At a speech delivered to an Anchorage conference to mark the fifth anniversary of the Exxon Valdez disaster, Shetland author, journalist and environmental activist Jonathan Wills said of the fall-out from the Braer:

> "We had at last discovered how to disperse an oil spill. All you have to do is arrange for your tanker to break up in a semi-circular bay about 100 feet deep; then you throw a two-week hurricane at it."

In the end, less than one percent of the Braer's payload was washed ashore, and nature's powers alone saved Shetland from an ecological disaster of frightening proportions. Even so, seabird deaths were in the thousands, and with oil concentrations in coastal waters twenty thousand times higher than normal, the salmon fishing season was ruined and fishing suspended for several weeks.

Shetlanders still chuckle at the stories of the world's media queuing up to film from crucial viewpoints over the broken Braer, and first having to pay eye-wateringly stiff fees to the farmer who owned the land.

There is anger, too, at what locals view as legal manoeuvering devised to cloud the true state of affairs on the ship at the time of the incident. Investigations by Jonathan Wills backed up the contention that the Braer's engines failed because of sea water contaminating its diesel fuel tanks, but also revealed that there was more to the story. Tankers do not normally run on diesel, but the ageing Braer had suffered a breakdown in the steam boilers vital to the thinning process required to render heavy fuel oil usable. Without steam, its fuel oil was entirely useless, and so the ship was running on diesel reserves that most likely would have run out long before Quebec. That the Braer was already booked in for major repairs on its arrival in Canada indicates that the ship's crew were aware of serious problems that almost certainly played key roles in the loss of the ship and its vast cargo of oil.

The sense of relief over the near-catastrophe is tempered by anger that this was a disaster waiting to happen — and that nothing much has changed in the intervening years to make it significantly less likely in the future. Shetland dodged a bullet, but with safety systems as fatally flawed and international regulations on ships' seaworthiness not much less porous than they were in 1993, some Shetlanders are rightly fearful of their ability to dodge the next bullet to come along.

III: ViKing, Hunny Bear and the Ness of Burgi

Scatness peninsula is like south Mainland in miniature. North-south oriented, many times longer than it is broad, with coastal plains that flow down to meet curved beach bays, cliffscapes and offshore skerries, baas and islets and deep-cut inlets, but with everything carved out on a smaller scale. At the landward end of the peninsula sits the small settlement of Scatness, a generational mix of old stone farmhouses, new modern bungalows and a procession of cereal-box homes on identical rectangular plots. The hamlet takes seconds to leave behind, and I soon have an ever-narrowing peninsula completely to myself, save for a few contented sheep and the occasional boxy WWII gun emplacement in angular reinforced concrete so hardy that not even nearly seventy years of northern climes have smoothed its edges.

The peninsula slims sharply until it becomes a tight waist of grey stone cheese-wedges where a stout chain arcs between solid metal posts. The hand line is the sole concession to safety, cold metallic links to a rockscape polished to a sheen by generations of slithering footfalls. It traverses only a short distance until the land again fattens out to become misshapen postage stamps of fertile green perched atop yet more ragged cliffs speckled with nesting seabirds.

From next to one cliff edge I watch fulmars fly regular ovoid circuits that intersect the cliff line, swooping skywards on updrafts from the rock face, out to sea a short distance, a casual twitch of wingtips swinging them effortlessly back in precisely the same aerial groove, accurate to within centimetres. It finally dawns upon me that I stand only a few metres above the birds' cliffside nests, and my presence is the root cause of these protective circuits; I might as well be on a different island for all the threat I pose to a nest clinging to a tiny ledge on a vertical cliff face thirty metres up from where surf batters incessantly at the rocky shoreline, but the fulmars don't know that.

Further south, the last thing I expect to happen upon is a house, but at Ness of Burgi, a two-thousand-year-old blockhouse is set into the hillside, and was excavated and partially restored in the 1930s. The robustness of its drystone construction may have been due to a defensive purpose as a promontory fort, or might simply have been what it took to survive on top of a tiny spit of land slap bang in the middle of where North Sea meets North Atlantic. Whatever its long-forgotten purpose, it is yet another example of the accessibility of history on Shetland.

From its lee I watch aircraft hum over the giant cliffs and the Stevenson lighthouse of Sumburgh Head, gliding inland to Sumburgh Airport where, a few hours from now and from the comfort of Betty Mouat's böd, I may hear them roaring away again. Despite the chill wind, the seas are calm and visibility is as sharp as the pictures in a photographer's window. To the south-west, Fair Isle squats in such plain view that I can pick out Sheep Rock with the naked eye despite it being forty kilometres away. I turn to look north-west, and sure enough, Foula's dark outline, dramatically sidelit by the setting sun, occupies its near-permanent place on Shetland's western horizon.

Watercolourists' delights of backlit pre-sunset clouds in deep burnt orange accompany me on the short walk back. The empty böd, stove or no stove, loses out to the allure of a cold ale and the possibility of some company, and where Scatness rejoins south Mainland, I turn east.

Beyond the far end of a crescent beach that glows post-sunset warm is a Victorian mansion that might be the Sumburgh Hotel, so I set off across castor-sugar sand so pure that it puts me in mind of some of the finest beaches I ever got sunburned on.

Viewed from at sea, the beach must shine like a silica welcome mat peeking out from between the dark no-go zones of Scatness and Sumburgh Head. As the most invitingly accessible point in south Shetland it also appeals to historians who speculate that the islands' first ever settlers (more than five millennia ago, and perhaps in coracle craft fashioned from tree boughs and animal skins) are likely to have first set foot on Shetland somewhere close to where I now struggle with sand so fine that it flows like water through the eyelets of my boots.

The Victorian hotel is a former Laird's mansion, dating to 1867. Access is by way of a long driveway that in a car would take seconds, but that on foot demands and allows time to appreciate the setting and marvel at the quality of the workmanship that went into the neatest of drystone boundary walls. Just as I make a mental note to ask Jim Keddie if he deserves credit for it, my eye is snagged by what may be the ugliest building extension in all of Shetland.

The grand baronial mansion is crafted tall from local materials, with multiple gables and peaked eaves of stepped stone and soaring bay windows overlooking the West Voe of Sumburgh. This grandeur is blighted, alas, by a boxy white modern addition that may well have doubled or tripled the room count during oil industry boom times while, at a stroke, it buried a knife in the heart of the building's Victorian appeal.

The hotel offers the only watering hole for miles around, and after hours of wandering alone, I am ready to rub shoulders with my fellow man. When the door swings closed behind me, the bar now has nine people inside, counting the barman and a short Scotsman spilling sand everywhere he steps.

Two young men hover earnestly over the most uneven of chess games, white outnumbering black by fifteen pieces to three. A solitary darts player fires arrows at a board while an expensive plasma television high on one wall emits the usual Saturday evening mind-anaesthesia; the program is hosted by an over-excitable woman with teeth like milk bottles, and an ex-professional footballer whose linguistic deficiency is so complete as to be shameful.

When he and the scary-toothed one eventually depart, things only get worse. Next up is 'celebrity' ballroom dancing where any participant who displays even basic ambulatory skills elicits rapturous adulation from a studio audience full of pasty faces and bad haircuts.

All of the female celebrities share a curious facial feature: streaky blonde hair and dark, monotone-brown eyebrows. Perhaps they breed them like this in TV WannabeLand, in carefully matched genetically-modified clutches of dull but bubbly souls whose collars don't match their cuffs.

When the latest B-list celebrity bimbo appears with an excrutiatingly fake flourish, the wind-weathered man at the next table announces in a thick Yorkshire accent:

'That one's had more pricks than a second-hand dartboard.'

As an opening gambit it takes some beating, even if I may have to take care when I use it myself.

He tells me he is a helicopter engineer working for a company that shuttles staff back and forth between Shetland and North Sea oilfields. Until recently he was flying all over Zimbabwe as the engineer to the presidential flight of helicopters of none other than Robert Mugabe. Every other day in Shetland, it seems, I meet someone else who has travelled the globe, even if some of them are not too bothered about who pays their wages.

Early the next afternoon I am back at the hotel, not in the bar, but standing in the grounds of the former Laird's house overlooking the famed archaeological site of Jarlshof — or 'Laird's house'. Even in a group of islands with archaeological sites by the thousands, Jarlshof inspires tweedy academics to unbroken streams of superlatives.

Less than two kilometres away, Old Scatness was re-discovered only after hiding underground for hundreds of years; Jarlshof, too popped up from beneath the surface with the powerful help of nature in the late 19th Century, when a series of massive storms blew away the sandy landscape. The sand had smothered and preserved evidence of thousands of years of activity stretching from 2500 B.C. through the Bronze and Iron Ages, on through periods of Norse settlement and medieval times until the Laird's house whose ruins still stand in front of me was finally abandoned in the late 1600s.

The house was almost certainly built in the 1570s by Earl Robert Stuart who, as the illegitimate son of King James V, benefitted greatly from a close association with his half-sister, Mary Queen of Scots. She granted him Royal estates in Orkney and Shetland, along with the powerful title of Sheriff of the two island groups. A bastard by birth, Robert Stewart the 1st Earl of Orkney was a man whose tyranny over Shetland extended to near-enslavement of Shetlanders for his own purposes and profits. The ruins before me were quite likely built upon the sweat and toil of Shetlanders enslaved by the Sheriff.

Over the coming centuries, wind and shifting sands completely buried the remains of over 4000 years' of continuous habitation, until even greater winds brought them back to the surface once again.

The name Jarlshof is in itself an ironic nod at history, being the one given by Sir Walter Scott in his 1822 book *The Pirate* to the ruins he saw ten years earlier when he toured south Mainland in the company of lighthouse builder Robert Stevenson (Grandfather of Robert Louis Stevenson). Not even the prolific Scott's imagination could have foreseen the astonishing discovery of an archaeological treasure trove beneath the ruins of the house he called Jarlshof, but the name lives on today.

The dearth of off-peak tourism in Shetland creates a self-defeating cycle, and in late October, although Jarlshof remains open to visitors, it is unmanned. The premier archaeological site in the entire region, and one of *the* historic jewels of Europe, is sadly only staffed for six months of the year.

But right now the exploration of several thousand years of Shetland history is the furthest thing from my mind because the real reason I am standing out here in the cold is that I have a date. With ViKing and Hunny Bear.

So well-chosen is the site of the Laird's lair that became the Sumburgh Hotel that it offers views deep into the Dunrossness peninsula of south Mainland, and I first catch sight of my visitors when they crest Ward Hill, still about eight kilometres away. From there, I track them with my binoculars all the way past the village of Toab, over the end of the airport runway (really; where the road clips the runway end there are traffic lights to warn drivers of oncoming aircraft), around the edge of West Sumburgh voe and up to where I await in the hotel car park. Several minutes pass before I finally hear the visceral rumble of powerful motorcycles torqueing their way up the hotel driveway.

ViKing and Hunny Bear are biker 'handles' that — for their sakes — I have to assume are at least a little tongue-in-cheek, even if Hunny's Harley is decorated with cute stickers of Pooh dipping paws in honey jars.

When I travelled up from Aberdeen on the Hrossey, I found a flyer for the Shetland Islands Cruisers motorcycle club that invited like-minded visitors to get in touch. It is decades since I last owned a motorcycle, but like most former bikers, born-again status is never more than a whiff of burnt hydrocarbons away, and for the last three weeks I have been in occasional contact with Colin and Carol Fraser — ViKing and Hunny Bear — trying to arrange a ride-out with the Shetland Islands Cruisers.

Attempting to impress upon the uninitiated the sheer joy of touring on a motorcycle is about as pointless as trying to describe the flavour of a fresh strawberry to a poor soul who has never tasted one. Mere minutes after we meet up in the hotel car park, I am smiling from the pillion seat of Colin Fraser's behemoth of a Harley-Davidson Road King (hence the 'King' in 'ViKing').

Two not very tall blokes plus one full-dress Harley tourer makes for half a tonne of man and machine that Colin takes through rural Mainland with relaxed skill, allowing me to sit back and soak up the sights. The throaty burble of expensive custom exhausts, only two of a hundred add-ons Colin has fitted to his beloved machine, may well be registering on faraway seismographs, but do not seem to bother sheep or occasional locals encountered along the way.

After a few minutes, Colin swings west at Boddam, and the deeper we go into south-west Mainland, the narrower the road becomes, until eventually we follow a neat single lane of bitumen with regular limpet-like passing places. Through rare, lowland sheep country the terrain lopes along like a rumpled carpet, the burbling of lightly-stressed engines broken only by the occasional *brrrrp* of cattle grid on fat tyres. This is a part of Shetland where four houses counts as a village. Loch of Spiggie borders the road for what seems a long way, until abruptly, only minutes after we left the North Sea behind us, the ragged rock shoreline and endlessly serried white tops of the Atlantic appear immediately to our left.

Bigton is anything but a big town, being about thirty neat houses haphazardly draped across a fertile coastal plain contrived by shelter from hills to the east and the warm embrace of the Gulf Stream sweeping in from the west. Signposts that point to 'Ireland' make me think of signs pinned high at Lands End and John O' Groats bearing precise distances to New York and Moscow, but this Ireland is another huddle of houses on the other side of fields north of Bigtown. Colin swings the Harley into a miniature car park that smells of very good coffee, and we all pile into the living-room-sized coffee shop with the notice on the door that says it is only open on Sundays. It is crowded with like-minded souls intent on enjoying the coastal views, aromatic coffees and encyclopaedia-sized slabs of fresh home-baked cake.

Geordie Jacobson and Joe Gray went through the Lerwick school system a couple of years apart, and both ended up at Aberdeen University studying Civil Engineering in the early sixties. They also share a lifelong fascination with motorcycles and magpie-like talents for collecting and holding onto old two-wheeled gems. Geordie's first bike was a 1955 Ariel that he still owns; Joe bought his first machine, a 1957 Norton, in Aberdeen in 1961, and it is still numbered among his collection of old British iron. Nowadays motorcycles are brought out of hiding for fun on sunny days, but Geordie and Joe remember when two-wheelers were basic transport for the working men of Shetland. A simple question about the quality of the roads back in the sixties inspires a detailed treatise from Joe that is far in excess of my needs. I only learn later that he retired as Director of Roads and Transport for Shetland Islands Council in 1997.

'I first started riding bikes in 1958,' he says, 'And back then, the roads weren't that bad.' Geordie nods in agreement as Joe goes on:

'The roads outside of Lerwick, in the south of Mainland and the western and northern areas of the island were what was called 'waterbound macadam', or 'mortar roads'. Not surfaced with tar, but hard-packed, well-made roads, perfectly good for motorcycles, which were very popular back then.'

In straightforward economic terms, life was harder for Shetlanders fifty years ago, with few year-round jobs and a lot of seasonal unemployment in the wet dark months of winter. But these were also the days when many Shetlanders went away for long periods to work as merchant seamen or, like Gibbie Fraser whom I met in Voe last week, to go whaling in the South Atlantic.

'They went off in the autumn and came back in the spring after working the whaling in the South Atlantic,' says Geordie. 'And a lot of them came back flush with cash, or even with a new motorcycle. A lot of bikes arrived in Shetland that way.' Geordie's Dad came back one year from a stint at sea to buy a Norton to replace his early 1930s side-valve BSA, 'A *horrible* creature of a motorbike.' Today these two enthusiasts own more than twenty bikes between them. Joe, known locally as a walking encyclopaedia of classic cars and bikes, has 'about ten, from a 1921 Rover to my 1957 Norton, though only two are registered for the road at the moment, the Norton and my Rudge.' He refers to the 1938 Rudge Ulster he is riding today, a jewel of a machine that he was gifted by an elderly man from Yell in the 1960s, and finally completed its full restoration more than thirty years later. Senior by a couple of years over his old friend Geordie, Joe is the eldest of the riders out here today, yet he is assuredly the only person in attendance who is a few years *younger* than his bike.

There is a good reason why so many very old bikes survived in Shetland that UK mainland buyers often arrive to pick up rare machinery for restoration and re-sale.

'People had to look after their bikes, because they were the working man's only form of transport.' he says. 'So they tended to get pushed indoors out of the worst of the weather. I think that's why so many great old bikes have survived in Shetland.'

IV: Solitude on St Ninian's

I sit soaking up the view of a perfectly-formed tombolo of eye-watering white sand that gleams like snow in the bright light of a blustery morning, and wait for Elma to finish her story. I may be here for a while.

Elma Johnson is a one-woman institution, a tour guide famed as much for the strength of her beliefs in what Shetland has to offer as for the volubility with which she presents them. So far as I am able to tell, she has been talking for the last ten minutes without drawing breath.

One of Scotland's favourite sons, the comic and raconteur Billy Connolly, is rightly renowned for the peculiar talent that allows him to embark upon a tale and digress down tangent after tangent until, after twenty minutes spent worlds away from where he started out, he miraculously finds his way back to the starting point, and delivers his punchline with a trademark flourish of comic genius. I sit in Elma's car entertaining the possibility that she might have taught the great Connolly everything he knows about narrative thread.

Without warning, Elma's tale reverses seamlessly from flower to bud to twig to branch to bough and back to the trunk source of a story that began so long ago that I have completely lost the plot until she underlines her original point with a triumphal note of hurrah. I grab the opportunity to leap from the car and take to the tombolo.

'Tak as long as you like,' she shouts after me. 'Ah'll be waiting back at the house, the awnly one wi' the orange roof, remember.' I wave my thanks and head for the beach before she embarks upon another story.

The tombolo is almost perfectly symmetrical, a tight-waisted shifting land bridge evenly cambered on each side of a soft crown. It rises no more than a metre above the twin fingers of Atlantic that wash against it on either side. At its far end squats St Ninian's, an island in name only for most of its existence, joined as it is to Mainland by the stripe of sand. When exceptional storm tides strike, such as during the storm that drove the MV Braer ashore ten kilometres south of here in 1993, momentous tides temporarily connect twin bays to the north and south — Bigton Wick and St Ninian's Bay. For centuries the bays have provided shelter to sailing vessels on the run from whatever the North Atlantic threw at them.

The tombolo is pleasingly clean, yet still suffers the inevitable detritus that washes up on all our shores. I pause to look down at the front pane of an intact television cathode ray tube that sits perfectly framed in sand. With nothing worth watching on Tombolo TV save for an arced reflection of the clouds above me, I re-set my sights on the island that rises up against the azure sky at the far end of the 500-metre silica isthmus.

St Ninian's is said to be a holy island named for the Bishop Ninian (c. 360 - 432 AD) who, depending upon whom you ask, might even have first brought Christianity to Scotland. This he apparently did in 397 AD by setting up church at Whithorn in Dumfries and Galloway in Scotland's deep south. However, this claim is pooh-poohed by adherents to the alternative notion that it was St Columba who imported the faith when he brought it to Iona one hundred and seventy years later. It is hardly surprising to see people of faith revert to factionalism, but what really makes me wonder is when a faction resorts to an argument that goes something like *'no WAY your guy got here first, because ours beat him to it, one hundred and seventy years later!'*

Bishop Ninian is said by some to have explored Pictish Scotland as far north as Shetland, a hypothesis once more poured scorn upon by others with interest-bearing investments to defend in their own saintly hero figures. Yet, whether or not he ever made it to Shetland, Ninian remains revered by some as the island group's unofficial Patron Saint.

Even if its links to a sainted Bishop who died nearly sixteen hundred years ago remain open to debate, the island of St Ninian's is famous for the ruins of a 12th Century church building, itself built atop a former chapel structure. Fame came about after a series of excavations by archaeologists from the University of Aberdeen that commenced in 1955. The visitors attracted a lot of attention over the years, and one Lerwick schoolboy called Douglas Coutts was so determined to be involved that he was assigned a part of the ruins to 'investigate'. *Away over there, laddie, out of our way.*

Imagine if you can the pursed lips of Aberdonian academia when the crème de la crème of the excavation's finds turned up at the hands of a local fifteen-year-old who, on lifting a stone with a cross inscribed, discovered a larch box containing twenty-eight priceless items of Pictish silver (and a porpoise jawbone) dating back to 800 AD. The hoard included eight bowls and silver brooches in a style known to be fashionable among Picts at the turn of the 9th Century.

Elma, who has lived all her life in Bigton and was a teenager at the time of the dig, told me her memories of the historic find.

> *"The dig on St Ninian's lasted from 1955 to 1958, the*
> *year the treasure was found. Wis lasses wis always around*
> *the dig, bit we were not that interested in it. We were more*

interested in all dis fine young boys that wis come about.

Before the dig started the ground was flat with some tomb stones. Rabbits would burrow and bones would come up, even skulls sometimes. I never mind wis thinking anything about it — it was just da auld kirk yard. We had always been told that the auld kirk yard was on top of a chapel.

Professor O'Dell was in charge of the students doin' the dig — they were from Aberdeen University. Every day at 11 a.m. and 3 p.m., wis lasses were sent across the sand with tea in a bucket, and pancakes or rock buns.

The day the treasure was found no one was told except the Budge family." (Mr and Mrs Budge were seniors in the village who were close to Professor O'Dell). "It was kept overnight at Bigton Farm, and the next day Professor O'Dell flew south with it."

There was evidence that the treasure, of such value and sophistication that it likely belonged to a local Chieftain, was buried in haste, but from there, the story goes cold and relies heavily on both informed historical context and old-fashioned guesswork.

Many Shetlanders today not only entertain, but widely embrace the belief that when the Vikings brought their longboats ashore, what followed was a peaceful colonisation of the islands. Other historians and academics find this picture of harmonious integration fanciful in the extreme, and instead paint the more traditional image of violent raiders engaging in rape, pillage and even complete extermination of the locals.

Around 800 AD at least one Chieftain, on catching sight of longships rounding the coast, is thought to have foreseen more pillage than harmony, and hurriedly buried his fortune under the floor of the church on St Ninian's isle. That his treasure remained there uncollected for centuries neither bodes well for the fate of its owner nor lends much support to the rather Disney-esque notion that the Vikings were welcomed ashore as genial colonists.

Today, St Ninian's is uninhabited save for sheep, but crofters used to live on the island until they stripped it bare of vital peat supplies and moved back to Mainland around 1700.

Not even the island's church graveyard has survived as a focus of the Bigton community. In the 1830s, locals tired of long funeral treks across the tombolo in all sorts of weather. Since then, a cemetery and a new Kirk in Bigton has seen local involvement with St Ninian's fade until today's foot traffic is restricted to walkers and sheep crofters.

What a stunningly beautiful walk it is. For an island that is no more than two kilometres from north to south and about half that from west to east, St Ninian's has an astonishing array of coastal features, most of them bludgeoned by the sea out of cliff faces that plummet into the North Atlantic. At its south-east corner lies a rash of rocky islands and stacks and skerries that provide welcome shelter to St Ninian's Bay, but which must have made seeking the bay's refuge in the days of sail a hellish game of chance.

Beyond the rocks and skerries the south Mainland coastline dives and weaves towards Fitful Head, eight kilometres away but so clear I might be able to reach out and touch it. Beyond its gigantic profile nothing breaks the jagged ocean horizon. But my map hints at more to see, so I trip westwards, skirting geos and gullies and a miscellany of coastal gashes, their rock faces speckled with nesting birds. Most are in pairs, usually with one doing all the squawking while the other sits impassive, feathered bum fidgeting on the cold rock of home. I can't help but think of my family's living room in the seventies.

When I get as far west as I can go without tumbling into the Atlantic, I turn the binoculars south once more, and *there*, I am rewarded when from the far-off sea haze appears the outline of Fair Isle, almost fifty kilometres distant.

The hike north is over verdant farmland criss-crossed with sheep tracks rising to a crown in the landscape where a tiny drystone shelter sits, little more than an 'L' contrived of local rock and so painstakingly crafted as to be almost windproof. A glance towards Mainland confirms my good fortune in wandering across the only shelter in sight, as the stern easterly drags a dark curtain of rain across the landscape.

From crouched in the lee of the enclosure I watch giant raindrops explode across the turf. Behind me, the landscape has turned battleship grey, with visibility so far reduced that it could be measured in metres. Yet in the opposite direction, the skyscape remains a startling sharp blue, and visibility is more than forty kilometres. I know this for certain, because to the north-west, Foula stands tall and lonely. I have marvelled at Foula from viewpoints all over Shetland, but now its stage-scenery look is embellished with texture and light and shade and even variations of colour draping the island's stirring outline.

Even on a bright day when waters here are protected from the easterly by Mainland, North Atlantic swells march tall and fierce, a fact brought home when, through the binoculars, I pick out the sole shipping activity in the entire seascape. The tough little ferry that I last saw nearly a month ago tied up at Walls pier struggles away from west Mainland, soaring and dipping through the Atlantic swell towards Foula.

As quickly as the rain arrived, it sweeps past, and the tough trek back across foot-swallowing soft tombolo sand is eased by short breaks to marvel at a perfect rainbow arc that dives into the heart of the miniature community of Ireland.

I am almost at the Mainland end of the beach and wondering if Elma's directions to her house will prove easy to follow when I look up to see Elma sitting in her car.

'I wis worried du wis getting awful wet,' she says.

Before we leave, I speculate that the bays below Bigton must have seen some shipwrecks over the centuries.

'Ohhhh, they most certainly have,' she says, as I sense a story coming on.

> 'A ship called the Atlas went aground below Ireland there, not even in such bad weather, in December 1806, it was. The Captain's wife wis onboard, and they all got into the jolly boat and started to row. When they got half way ashore, da wife wanted to go back to da ship for more dresses, but when they came onboard again there wis nothing left but the hoops from her dresses lyin' on the cabin floor.' Elma's laugh is so full of pleasure that she might as well have been there to see it happen. 'The Bigton men were verrry quick off the mark when a ship was wrecked,' she smiles again. 'It was said that the Bigton ladies wis all awful well-dressed at Kirk the followin' Sunday.'

IV: Brochs, Bruces and house-burnings

Elma picked me up at the böd this morning to show me around Dunrossness for the most unselfish of reasons: she believes passionately in the allure of her homeland and wants to convince me of the same. When I mention that I might like to see the ruined broch at Burraland, Elma does the natural thing, and ropes in another volunteer to help make it happen.

Jennifer is a neighbour and friend who, with her husband, works several small patches of croftland. At Elma's request, she arrives in her Japanese 4x4 pick-up, complete with obligatory sheepdog. There are no questions asked, and nothing sought in return other than the satisfaction of showing the visitor around her homeland.

Elfin in stature, indefatigably good-natured and every bit as much the born tutor as Elma is the natural story-teller, Jennifer shares with me everything she knows about this part of Shetland, which as a working crofter with decades of experience, is seemingly without limit. She takes us the short drive from the Atlantic coast across south Mainland to the North Sea coast, and soon the big 4x4 comes into its own while I leap in and out every few seconds to open and close farm gates. My ignorance of the niceties of crossing crofters' land is total, so I assume that Jennifer might personally know the owners of the farmland we are on, and in truth, she doesn't look too concerned. I would be shy of *walking* these fields without permission, and here we are in a two-tonne pick-up with (thankfully) enormous fat tyres impressing muddy grooves in the rain-saturated landscape. In a few minutes, we cover so much soggy ground that to walk it both ways might have taken the better part of the afternoon. Soon we reach the coast, and uninterrupted views of two brochs in very different states of repair.

Between us and the first broch, farm building ruins squat under the grey skies, totally timberless and devoid of any signs of long-gone roofs, every square centimetre of stone walls enveloped in leafy lichen in the softest of powder greens. The purer the air, the leafier is the lichen, which means the air here is so free of sulphur that the growth clinging to the ruined walls is more like turf than algae.

Jennifer explains that the houses must be at least two hundred years old, since they are of the long-gone design where the animal byre butts directly onto the residence, making it possible to access the animals from the living quarters by way of a connecting door, without having to brave the outdoor elements.

These modest structures are crafted from a local stone that might have been manufactured by nature for the purpose of building houses, so parallel are its lines and so tidy are its right angles. Slate-like in that it splits into perfect-edged blocks of an almost infinite range of thicknesses, the outer wall surfaces it creates are so smooth that they give the impression of being machine-made. Inside, the thick walls are marked only by tidy storage recesses crossed with shelves as neatly shaped as if they were cut from wood, but which are planks of stone that have survived the elements undisturbed for a century or more.

The beautiful old ruins inspire an obvious question. Where did all that lovely building stone come from? The answer lies only metres away, in the spectacular ruins of just one of Shetland's more than one hundred brochs.

What remains of Burraland Broch is a perfect illustration of the omnipresence of Shetland's history, and of how its archaeology sits out in the open, there for all to see and enjoy, to investigate and interpret and, hopefully, preserve.

Iron Age brochs are striking fortified towers with circular footprints, intricately wrought from drystone without the use of mortar, and which from around 300 BC to 100 AD stood at key coastal points not only all over Shetland, but throughout Orkney and the northern mainland and western isles of Scotland.

Historians and archaeologists are unable to agree on the purpose of these imposing structures, with the pendulum of opinion swinging from 'defensive castle-like buildings' to 'status symbols of the land-owning classes'. Nowadays, there may even be something of a consensus that the towers possibly combined both purposes. In times of perceived threat from invaders — or indeed rival neighbours — they could well have served primarily as defensive structures, only to evolve later into status symbols.

Amazingly, even after far more than a thousand years of abandonment and centuries of being robbed for construction materials — the adjacent, long-ago-deserted farm buildings being an obvious case in point — what remains here is easily identifiable as a coastal broch. Built of twin concentric drystone walls with space between them to allow a circular corridor and stairways and small rooms to exist suspended between the two rock skeins. Of the twin walls, shallow stretches remain in place. What would surely have been a central living area is now the repository for much of the remaining debris that once made up the surrounding tower.

Outside the main broch ruins are archaeological ciphers so obvious that even I can pick up on them, identifiable elements of exterior buildings and complex structures that used to butt up to the broch and spread across the small coastal plain that it once commanded. Ten or more metres away from the main ruin, bulky cuboid blocks in the turf form a near-circle that are surely the remnants of another structure of impressive girth and importance.

Frustratingly close but completely out of reach across a few hundred metres of Mousa Sound towers the real thing, Mousa Broch, quite likely the most complete example in existence of a two-thousand-year-old broch. At fourteen metres tall, even from its position on the inner island coastline it commands views over Mousa and out to sea. Its base measures fifteen metres in external diameter — yet only six metres internally, so thick is the double-skinned wall-cum-corridor at the bottom of the tower. As well as being nearly completely intact, Mousa broch is unique in that it stands alone, rather than surrounded by other structures associated with it, in the manner of the ruined broch across the strait here at Burraland. Mousa Island is privately owned, and the pier there is for summer use only by the family-run company that has operated ferry visits to Shetland's most famous man-made attraction every summer since 1971. At the end of the season, part of the island's pier is removed, not, as Shetlanders are wont to speculate mischievously, to prevent non-paying visitors from making use of it, but to stop winter storms from reducing it to matchwood.

Back at the car, Jennifer's sheepdog remains in its place in the back of the truck. Jennifer explains that as this is not her own land, out of respect for the landowner she has not allowed her dog to get down, and since the dog never received an instruction to leave the truck, she remained where she was.

Knowing that her dog will likely need a toilet break, she gives it the signal to jump down, which it does in an instant. Then Jennifer adds an order to pee, and the dog does exactly that before vaulting back into the pick-up bed on command. I make no effort to hide my astonishment, and despite her best efforts to disguise it, Jennifer lets slip what may just be a glimmer of proprietorial pride.

For the rest of the day Elma gives me a tireless tour of her home region's past and present. We stop at a Croft Museum, a thatched cottage that might bemuse Shetlanders as much as it informs visitors from outside Shetland, so fresh and personal will be the memories it invokes of elderly relatives' homes in not-so-distant times. This was an actual crofter's home until the 1960s, when it would have looked, not like a museum, but very much like a regular rural household of the period. It was not until the late 1970s and the oil industry brought steady well-paid work that homes like this dark cubby-hole, with its stone floor, open peat fireplace and box beds, began to be supplanted by the modern face of today's Shetland.

We scuttle from chilly croft house to the warmth of Elma's car, and for the next two hours she delivers a vocal torrent of historical facts interwoven with anecdotal hearsay, some of it dating back centuries, all delivered with certainty and passion.

On the way to Sumburgh Head, we pass the Sumburgh Hotel, the former Laird's mansion where Elma points to a giant bay window and says,

'The auld Laird, Mrs Bruce, had big mirrors put by the windows o' her bedroom so's she could keep an eye on her farm workers without gettin' out of bed.'

At the miniature natural haven of Grutness harbour, Elma indicates the small marina and tells me that her husband Laurie's grandfather George Johnson was a famous boat builder who worked here from 1900 to 1925, and was known for being able to build a yoal in thirteen days. 'From larch wood so fine a man could feel the water through the hull with his bare feet,' she says. The last yoal George made, *The Highland Belle*, built in 1925, is still in the marina where it was built, and remains in fine working order.

When the road dives south, we get a glimpse of the Laward of

Grutness, a low headland that defines the south shore of Grutness Voe, and is a fantastic illustration of the climatic extremes that play such a regular role in Shetland life.

Mention to Shetlanders the great storm of February 16th, and watch brows knit and heads shake. A week of gales developed into a south-easterly hurricane that battered much of east Shetland, sinking at least five ships and causing many deaths by drowning. Here at Grutness it came ashore with such force that an existing storm beach was swept inland, leaving a coastal field evenly peppered with boulders the size of tea chests. Storms as momentous as this one remain in the local consciousness for a very long time; the February 16th hurricane that gave the Laward of Grutness a fresh coating of giant boulders took place on February 16th, 1900.

From the visitors' car park, which Elma drives past as if it is not there, the road up to the first of the Stevensons' Shetland lighthouses — it entered service in 1821 — is a zig-zag of single-track tarmac to make vertigo sufferers blanche, separated from cliff drops only by low drystone walls.

The view from Sumburgh Lighthouse is one to treasure. I lean on a drystone wall and do the stand-on-tiptoes and peer-down-the-nose-without-leaning-forward trick, and my suspicions are confirmed. On the other side of the weather-battered mortar-free stone wall lie a few square metres of steeply-pitched tufted grass, followed by a hundred metres of sheer drop into the waters that wrap around three sides of Sumburgh Head. In season, the cliffs present visitors with a chance to get within a couple of metres of thousands of nesting puffins, but this is the wrong time of year, so while I try not to think of the precipice that lies just *over there*, I content myself with the view of Dunrossness.

A coastline that looks ripped from a thick blanket of geology juts and weaves its way to where old Ma Bruce spied on her workers without getting out of bed, on to the boot-invading soft sand of West Voe, inland over the airport and up the hill towards south Mainland that I watched the Cruisers' motorcycles ride down on their way to meet me. To the west, Scatness Peninsula contrasts sharply with the looming frown that is Fitful Head. Between the two rests lovely Quendale Bay, and when I clamber back into the car, where Elma has sensibly remained with the engine running and the heater blowing, she tells me 'We'll tak a run to show you Quendale.'

The view from the fertile farm land of Quendale is the reverse of what I took in from Sumburgh light. It looks south-east across Quendale Bay towards Betty Mouat's böd and the airport and beyond to the twin sprawling land fingers of Scatness and Sumburgh.

The lush green landscape next to the bay may now be serene, but in 1874 it was the scene of an episode when the scourge of the Clearances that swept Scotland's Highlands and Western Isles for over a century came to Dunrossness. When a Lerwick landlord by the name of Andrew Grierson decided that he could make more money if small crofts were broken up and his land turned over to blackface sheep, he had twenty-seven families in four small communities driven from their homes in the middle of a cold November night.

Homes were put to the torch for the most brutally pragmatic of reasons: thatched roofs made for fires that left nothing worth coming back to.

While some of families managed to re-settle elsewhere in Dunrossness, others added themselves to the growing Shetland diaspora, sailing off in search of new lives in the Antipodes and North America. I can only speculate that, insecurity about what lay ahead of them aside, these emigrants may one day have grasped that they were the lucky ones.

Much later, I ask Donald Robertson, chairman of the south Mainland Community History Group about the conditions in the region during the Clearances.

'The people were living in terrible poverty at the time. There had been a population explosion in the 1800s due to excellent fishing, aided and abetted by the Lairds, who owned the land and insisted on the poor tenants fishing for them and retaining almost all profits for themselves (the Lairds).... and when crops failed, the tenants fell even further into debt to the Laird.'

Elma points out the remains of farmsteads that once provided warmth and shelter on land that often supported three generations of local crofters who had lived and worked here for centuries. All of this was torn apart by an already well-off landlord. The famed Shetland dialect poet, Rhoda Bulter (1929-1994), wrote in her poem, *'Da Clearance'*:

Noo dey aa hae equal portions o aert ta tak dir sleep.
Tell me, wis it wirt it aa for twartree extry sheep?

aert: earth; twartree: two or three

As Elma tells it, the clearance was never to benefit any one of a succession of Lairds. She firmly believes that this was due to a curse placed on the estate by an old woman forced from the land. Storyteller Elma tells me what happened after the working folk of Quendale were forced out of their homes:

'Da folk wir walking tae Hillwell an Gord, der nearest neighbours, ta seek shalter. Some o' da auld folk an bairns wir havin ta be kerried. Whin they wir on tap o' da brae, an auld wife turned aroond, and looking down on the estate, she laid on a curse. She said 'May never ever a son's son son's son ever inherit.' An' it came true, for to this day, for one reason or another, no one who ever owned da Quendale estate wis able to pass it on to a son.'

LERWICK

Different strokes

When I was in my late teens, a close friend called Roy had a pet trick he pulled every time we encountered pairs, always pairs, of well-groomed young men, almost as white as their neatly pressed shirts with the giveaway black name badges. A large Mormon church in the neighbourhood meant we locals regularly encountered American missionaries. This occurred usually while we engaged in the long hours of aimless street-wandering that, I am told, has been rendered, like you-know, soooooo *last year* by MySpace and something called an Xbox.

Roy's pet trick was to watch the approaching Americans very carefully and, at the precise moment he saw them start to move, he would beat them to it, and throw out a big sunny flat-palmed wave and yell a very un-Scottish 'Hi!' Oh, how we laughed at the confusion in their innocent faces, how we reveled in the devilish cunning with which Roy play-acted an overworked imitation of their affable ways.

It was an embarrassingly long time after adolescence waned that it finally dawned on me that by mocking the courteousness of the young Elders, we showed ourselves up for the intolerant, unwelcoming swine that *we* really were.

This is a humbling set of thoughts to embrace as I find myself in an anteroom of the Lerwick Church of the Latter Day Saints, every query that I direct at two young men — white shirts, black badges, disarmingly sincere smiles and all — being met with courtesy, consideration, candour, and more than a little humour.

Lerwick is small enough that in the last few weeks I have seen these young men around town. An enquiry to the church to request the chance to sit down with them for a chat brings me to this meeting and my miniature, if momentary, crisis of conscience.

Young Mormons are encouraged to serve a full-time 'mission', a year spent spreading their faith, often in lands very far from home, and under almost military-like conditions; it is not unusual to be told of a foreign mission only days before it happens. While abroad for a year, though, they *are* allowed to phone home. Twice. Which, in the days before email, must have been tough on nineteen-year-olds separated from their families for the first time in their lives.

Their religion holds no fascination for me whatsoever, but I am curious about how, as definitive outsiders — foreigners promoting a minority faith in a society already chock-full of churches — they find life in Shetland.

Brandon is the more talkative of the two. Twenty years old, he is the real deal, a native of the Church's Utah homeland, and from a family with multiple generations of Mormon faith behind them. He is a confident young man and an absolute ringer for Donny Osmond, circa 1978. Fellow missionary Ashley is more reserved, perhaps content in a role as the quiet foil to his more outgoing companion; we are well into our conversation before I find out that he is not actually American, but from the English Midlands, which helps explain the mid-Atlantic tenor to his speech.

Both of them have spent time in towns on the Scottish mainland, after which, they tell me, Shetland is a breath of fresh air.

'There is something about Shetland,' says Brandon. 'The peacefulness, the cleanliness, even the lack of billboards. It is so much more relaxed than other parts of Scotland I have visited.'

It is so relaxed that they liken Lerwick to a retirement community, its streets silent after dinner time, and worry that the young people here lack direction. Brandon says, concern written all over his face:

'One young guy said to me, "I can't wait until I can get into pubs and drink"!'

They look genuinely worried for 'young guys' who might be all of two or three years their junior.

As part of their mission, they spend ten hours a week knocking on doors asking if anyone needs 'help'. When one woman joked that she was behind with her ironing, Brandon did it. They have done electrical work, decorating and even tended gardens for elderly Lerwegians.

'There is a feelgood factor from helping people,' says Ashley, 'We enjoy it.'

The closest to animosity they ever experienced was when they attended a cross-faith Christian gathering, and were stopped at the door by someone who denied their right to call themselves Christians. I may not share these lads' faith, but I do share their discomfort at the narrow-mindedness of the snub.

He and Ashley have another appointment and I have been demanding enough of men whose weekly allocation of free time is only seven hours (on Tuesdays, they tell me), so after an exchange of email addresses, we shake hands and, having enjoyed their company, for once I manage not to squirm at the laser-like soul-seeking eye contact so beloved of people of faith. Before I leave, Brandon pushes a small gift into my hand. *The Book of Mormon*. When I qualify my thanks by saying that I cannot promise to read it, he smiles with wisdom far beyond his years.

When I think back on the meeting, perhaps Elder Brandon Osmond was a little nonplussed by me not mentioning word one about his famous Dad Donny, nor any other of his Osmond Family relations. And of course it must only be a coincidence that months later, my website (that did not even exist when I met Brandon and Ashley) began to receive regular pop-in visits from a high-powered law firm in Utah — visits that continue as I write this, more than a year after I enjoyed my meeting with the two young men in Lerwick.

In terms of contrast between interview venues, going from the caffeine-, alcohol- and naughty-word-free Mormon chapel to the Up Helly Aa Galley Shed on a weekday night is just about as extreme as it gets.

The annual Up Helly Aa fire festival that lights up mid-winter Lerwick lies very close to the surface of Shetland public consciousness. In a month of wandering the islands, I have lost count of how many folk from disparate sectors of the community have encouraged, nay *exhorted* me to be sure to see the great event for myself. The underlying question, not always expressed outright, is obvious: how on earth could someone write a book about Shetland and not include Up Helly Aa? I am forced to take repeated refuge in the indisputable fact that I am here in October, and Up Helly Aa is held on the last Tuesday in January.

Eventually even I become chastened by too many looks of bewilderment from Shetlanders who fail to grasp why I am not particularly intrigued by a fire festival, the centrepiece of which is a squad of men dressed as Vikings torching a 'Viking' galley ship that took months to build. So, in an attempt to discover just what makes Up Helly Aa so special, I visit the Galley Shed where the Galley is built.

Roy Leask knows a thing or two about building the Up Helly Aa Galley, having been in the Galley Squad, the group of men who gather in the Galley Shed two nights a week for nearly half of the year, since 1968. Now the squad foreman, he shows me around the shed and does his best to fill the considerable gaps in my Up Helly Aa knowledge.

He leads me past the wooden structure that, fully three months before the big event, is already recognisable as a stylised longboat. We go upstairs to the *sanctum sanctorum* that is the Up Helly Aa Committee Room, a windowless vault dominated by a long table, and crowded by walls that groan under the weight of oversized, framed photographs. With only faded colours and the occasional archaic parked car to hint at their period origins, the photographs show frame after frame of men in wild beards and wilder, quasi-Viking costumes, merrily brandishing axes, their eyes shining with adrenalin and the buzz from being the centre of attraction for all of Shetland on a day that they have been labouring towards for years.

The Committee who meet here, as well as being the organisers of the annual event, are all future *Guizer Jarls*, or central kingpin figures of Up Helly Aa. On the big night, the Jarl leads his own Jarl's Squad of invitees who are the figureheads of the festival, the gang of bearded enthusiasts who delight in custom-designed and custom-crafted 'Viking' outfits, pointy helmets, shiny axes and all, and who lead the Galley through the streets of Lerwick at the head of the torch-lit procession that is the main public event. Behind the Galley march nearly a thousand torch-bearing guizers — in squads of twenty, each sporting fancy dress costumes unique to their squad, outfits that run the gamut from the visionary to the puerile.

'You have a thousand guys all carrying burning torches and having a dram, and there is never such a thing as a disturbance,' says Roy. 'If any one of the thousand guizers steps out of line at any time during the night, they will be discussed here' — he waves a hand at the long committee table — 'and could be banned from taking any part in future festivals.'

The fact that nearly one in five adult males in Shetland takes part on the night may explain why the threat of being barred is spectre enough to keep folk in line, free-flowing alcohol or not.

Elevation to the top table as a committee member means you are in line for the top task as Guizer Jarl; but this will not happen for about fifteen years, since there are that many others at the same table. Roy Leask joined the committee in 1995, and has already known for more than a decade that he will finally step into the role of Jarl for Up Helly Aa 2008.

Back downstairs, the odorous mix of woodshavings, toxic solvents and testosterone is confused by delicious cooking smells as the squad settle around a table for the next of the evening's rituals, a feast of smoked fish so beautifully prepared it crumbles on plates packed with gigantic quantities of mashed potato yellowed by rivulets of melting butter.

The room feels to me like a meeting place for overgrown boy scouts, but only because it is precisely that, a regular gathering place for like-minded males who combine industry and creativity with ritual, humour and even the odd song. Teenagers whose faces never saw a razor blade jostle for space with grizzled characters who long ago tired of shaving.

A stout table bows under the weight of plates packed high with food, elbows poking from rolled up worksleeves, and enough alcohol to float a pub full of Irishmen. Piles of beer cans embraced by lattices of plastic loops, an array of full bottles of spirits that would be no disgrace to any public bar's gantry, and the very occasional, lonely-looking non-alcoholic beverage. The room buzzes with the banter of men with the intimacy of workmates who spend a lot of time together, the younger faces doing their best to keep pace with the scything wit of their seniors, their inevitable failures to do so only adding to waves of laughter that shake the room's fittings.

Tonight the clubhouse has another guest, one so welcome that his wife is the sole token of femininity in a room where male bonding is not only the order of the day, it is written into the fabric of Up Helly Aa. Unlike at the smaller, regional fire festivals hosted elsewhere around Shetland, the Lerwick Up Helly Aa procession sticks rigidly to its men-only rule. When a thousand guizers take to the streets in the January murk and chill, there are no women among them.

The guest tonight is a former Jarl from the festival of 1990. His name is John, and although his surname escapes me, he carefully spells out for me the tag he adopted as his Jarl name, Svein Asleifarson. He now lives outside Shetland, and pines visibly for the camaraderie of the Galley Shed. When I ask how important to him was his night as the Jarl, he says, without hesitation:

'It was the most important day of my life.'

All around him, heads nod in complete understanding, and I am surely alone with my wonder that his wife does not blink an eye at the certainty and gravity with which her husband puts their wedding day — and quite likely the birth of their offspring — in the shade of what was evidently *the most important day of his life*. It is little wonder that spouses of the sixteen men who gather around the committee table upstairs have their own, all-female, gathering. They call it The Forgotten Wives Committee.

FOULA ISLAND

1: Keeping the best to last?

When the Loganair Islander pulls its low-velocity gravity denial trick at Tingwall Airport, in control is pilot Marshall Wishart. Just as on the flight out of Fair Isle three weeks ago, the privilege of sitting up front in the co-pilot's seat is mine. Marshall takes the Islander up to about two hundred metres, and as the stubby little aircraft's cloud-softened shadow zips across west Mainland, he stares intently out to sea. Where I might reasonably expect to glean at least a trace of a horizon, there are only a thousand different gradations of dense, grey cloud.

'It'll pop up soon,' he says, with equal measures of confidence and good cheer. I try to pull off the role of a passenger without a care in the world, but right now, the notion of Foula Island 'popping up' anytime soon inspires only disquiet. Foula's daunting cliffs, at not much shy of four hundred metres, tower to twice our current altitude, and as we fly towards them at over two hundred kilometres per hour, we cannot even see them.

After nearly a month of eyeing it from afar, and more than four weeks after my first encounter with the Foula ferry captain on the pier at Walls, I am finally on my way to the island whose outline has always been *just out there*. And now it has disappeared.

Twenty-five kilometres out in the Atlantic and somewhere amidst an endless canvas of perspective-altering cloud formations, Foula (pronounced 'Foolah') is the last habitation between Mainland Shetland and the Americas. Marshall, flying as Shetland pilots always do, on a precise combination of instruments and gut instinct, soon plucks the island's jagged silhouette from among pregnant clouds, and minutes later, we flash over the tiny exposed inlet that serves as Foula's harbour. A handful of houses, separated by broad stretches of treeless terrain more brown than green, dot a landscape that streaks towards an angular peak, only the beginning of the north-leaning hilltop range so visible from all over Shetland.

Marshall puts the Islander down on a wind-washed gravel airstrip and taxis to a halt in front of the assembled reception committee. As locals clamber from battered cars the fire crew unloads luggage, and from under one fireman's helmet I get the briefest of 'told you so' smiles from Kevin Gear, the man of few words last encountered in a bar in Lerwick, when he told me that if I was coming to Foula, I would certainly bump into him. He resumes his ground crew duties without a word.

With a population of only twenty-eight, the wearing of multiple hats on Foula is a plain necessity. Today, crofter Isobel Holbourn is also Island Ranger and B&B operator, and she plucks me from the mini crowd of four arrivals with such certainty that I am momentarily impressed. Until, that is, it occurs to me that she could likely quote me the other three passengers' middle names and birthdays.

Nowhere is far on an island only five kilometres by three, and not long after she points out the contrast between the ruins of a cottage that for decades served as the island school and the angular, tall-windowed structure nearby that houses the new community centre and school, Isobel stops on a hillcrest overlooking north Foula.

This is no place for the agoraphobe. Sweeping coastal plains and soaring sheep-flecked slopes reach out for cliff ranges that merge into a land and seascape stretching across huge areas of ever-moving, white-streaked waters. Of only three houses in view, the white one is Freyers, Isobel's croft and B&B.

It takes twenty stumbling boggy foot-soaking minutes to walk from Freyers to the cliff overlooking Gaada Stack, a colossal pinched rock doughnut set on edge amidst the boiling North Atlantic.

Between it and the shore are twin outcrops called Brough, formerly linked by a bridge span that disappeared one stormy night nearly forty years ago, leaving two rock stacks marooned by foaming seas. Wide open to an arsenal of elemental forces, coastal Foula is nature's ongoing work-in-progress.

A patchy trail turns north towards the cliff edges of Soberlie Hill. To add to the discomfort of the boggy terrain, slate-grey clouds open up with a rain barrage that rattles against my jacket like pebbles, and has me peering from a hood drawn so tight that line of sight is restricted to a dripping tunnel of Gore-Tex.

Any newcomer to Freyers will creep up on hundred-metre cliffs with caution verging upon paranoia, Isobel's stern caveat about *the flaan* ringing fresh. Before setting out, I apologised for running off without a proper chance to sit down and talk, but after fifty years on Foula, there is nothing Isobel can learn from a newcomer about grabbing outdoor opportunities whenever the weather cooperates.

On my way out the door, she delivers a school madam-like warning about *the flaan*. Foula's pitched, angular topography, she explains, makes it possible to face directly into a steady gale, yet still be caught from behind by a powerful gusting *flaan* that bounces off the island's hillsides to catch you unawares. I advance warily along a steeply canted cliff top promontory that points north into the Atlantic until I stand surrounded on three sides by cliff edges that dive a hundred metres into the seething Atlantic. Isobel's warnings, meanwhile, ring loud and clear.

I want the view that a cliff edge position will provide, but do not want to leave myself open to wind blasts of any sort, so I am as delighted as I am confused by the sight of a rock that hugs the cliff edge. Delighted because it is about the size of a small family car, which makes it big enough to hide behind, but confused as to how on earth it ever got here. This is the high side of a steeply canted promontory that may have been formed by a humungous collapse of the cliff line — but if so, how did a rock so huge end up here?

However it came about, the rock provides welcome sanctuary and a lookout point from which I can take in the view, the promise of which drew me to this spot.

It is a view that is hard to take in. My location atop a dizzying cliff top is at less than half the height of the adjoining cliffs of the North Bank, a mind-altering expanse of perpendicular geology that rockets directly upwards from wild North Atlantic waters to a height of over two hundred metres. It is awe-inspiring and frustrating at once, since around the cliff corner and out of view, the rock face nearly doubles in height again at the Kame, the highest cliffs in occupied Britain.

A day when raindrops propelled by gusting winds take on the properties of flying needles is not the time to wander alone towards the tops of yet taller precipices. Instead, I turn south along the coast, back past Freyers towards a spacious flat-topped headland where, after the extremes of the North Bank, cliff faces of a mere thirty metres exude a deceptive air of harmlessness.

Nestled among a beach of stones the size of dinner plates languish the corroded alloy remains of a seaplane that put down in the bay in 1943 with engine trouble. Foula folk were well-versed on the threat from Hitler's forces, so when the sole crofter resident saw the strange, boxy-framed seaplane bob towards his land, he did precisely the right thing. He met the flyer's unintelligible cries with a dark-eyed stare from the business end of a shotgun.

The flyer had to stand pleading with the shotgun's owner for a long time before it finally dawned upon the islander that what he was listening to, rather than the guttural barkings of an officer of the German Luftwaffe, were in fact the pukka-toned entreaties, almost as alien, of an officer of Her Majesty's Royal Air Force.

Isobel tells me this story later, in the comfort of her croft living room, with its views over the stoney bay where the Supermarine Walrus amphibian came ashore more than sixty years before. But so close-knit is Foula's community that she will not divulge the name of the crofter who confronted the airman, because she does not want to embarrass fellow islanders who are related to the man. Centuries of being unjustly derided by outsiders have made Foula people assume, not without some justification, that outsiders will twist any story to make the islanders look like idiots.

South of Isobel's croft sit the ruins of a house looking out towards the rocky shore. Stone walls at least a metre thick first make me think 'insulation', but closer inspection reveals them to be made from odd-shaped stones without mortar. Foula rocks are boulders, so ill-suited to drystone construction that to remain stable and avoid crumbling in on themselves, the walls had to be a metre thick.

A few hundred treacherous metres of bog land suck relentlessly at my boots until a 'Look out behind you!' moment makes me turn to see brooding rain clouds scud over the tip of the North Bank like smoke from an industrial accident.

On the headland of Strem Ness, fifty metres inland from thirty-metre-high cliffs, rock shards are sprinkled across the terrain like pepper grinds on a pizza. Some of them fist-sized, they could only have arrived in the wash of enormous waves swamping the headland, a theory backed up by unbroken limpet shells amidst the rock shards. I remember something that geologist Allen Fraser taught me at Eshaness, and pick up a rhomboid rock striated with, count them, *seven* parallel geological strata. Its geology is interesting enough, but more exciting is that the diamond-shaped imprint on the turf beneath the rock has not yet begun to turn yellow. This suggests that the storm that hurled it over the cliffs and into the middle of a hundred-metre-wide headland had to have been very recent. If Foula's wind-driven raindrops feel like needles fired from a shotgun, I would hate to be out here when jagged half-pound rocks soar in front of a gale.

II: Glacially or overnight –- things *do* change

Late at night, the wind drops, the rain stops battering the windows, and in a crofthouse whose nearest occupied neighbour is ten minutes' walk away, sleep is shrouded in absolute silence.

Over breakfast, Isobel talks about Foula and Fair Isle, and how she is certain that the islands are marked more by how they differ, than by characteristics shared.

'Foula has always had it harder than Fair Isle,' she says. 'We had no National Trust and no Summer Camps of volunteer workers.'

So is it fair to suggest that Foula folk might envy the deep involvement of the National Trust in Fair Isle's day-to-day business and economy?

'Absolutely not,' she says. 'Foula folk are much more independently-minded, and would not have responded well to the set-up on Fair Isle where everything is done only by permission of the National Trust.'

She acknowledges the irony of Foula being worse off for not having the involvement of a powerful organisation like the National

Trust, but being better off for not having had to deal with what Foula folk would view as its stifling bureaucracy.

She also points out that historically, unlike Fair Isle — or the rest of Shetland for that matter — Foula was never on international shipping routes, and so failed to benefit from centuries of passing vessels' trade and cultural influences.

Isobel is absolutely certain that Foula has long suffered from being ignored by or put to the back of Shetland Islands Council's priorities. When she first came to the island in her early teens, her father was the church minister and island schoolteacher, and she remembers how repeated requests for pencils for the school went unanswered for so long that he ended up writing a letter to his brother in Oxford, who bought pencils with his own money and posted them to Foula. The package arrived long before the Council got around to dealing with her father's urgent requests.

It is but one tiny, half-century-old example, but nonetheless illustrates how the seam of resentment over the perceived lack of outside help runs deep.

The most glaring illustration is the island airstrip, which only came into being in 1969. For far too long the Council argued that the island population was too small to justify the expense of an airstrip. Faced with what they saw to be a threat to their community's very existence, the folk of Foula quite literally took matters into their own hands. A community with fewer than fifty residents, many of them too young or too old to wield a hoe or a shovel or drive a tractor, got together and built their own nine-thousand-square metre airstrip, with no outside assistance whatsoever. At a stroke, emergency access to the island became a reality, and five thousand years at the total mercy of the sea was consigned to history.

Ringing fresh in the memories of the islanders as they toiled to create the airstrip would have been the longest 'dearth', as they call being completely cut off from the rest of the planet, in living memory. In the winter of 1960-1961, ferocious storms raged so incessantly that the island was cut off from the outside world for more than two months.

'I can easily remember how long it was,' says Isobel, 'Because when at last a fishing boat made it to Foula it arrived with food supplies and thirty-three sacks of mail, and I got eleven copies of my weekly comic.' The island was completely deprived of outside contact for precisely seventy-seven days.

The lack of movement by the Council on the need for an airstrip was not just bloody-mindedness. It reflected conviction at local government level that Foula was doomed to abandonment, and that throwing more money at its tiny community was pointless.

The island has a plentiful supply of superb fresh water, but in 1961, when civil servants looked into constructing a mains water network, they rationalised their refusal to do so with a prediction that the island would be abandoned within a decade. In 1971 they rejected the plan once more, again with the same rationale. It was not until 1982, more than a decade after the islanders built their own airstrip, that the authorities reversed their stance and installed a tap water system to Foula homes.

'Foula came out of the Middle Ages into modern times very, very quickly,' says Isobel.

Despite outsiders' assumptions that Foula is living on borrowed time, assumptions that have prevailed for a century or more, the backbone that is a population with its own deeply imbedded characteristics survives intact — and from that, Foula derives its will to continue. On Papa Stour, the long-running exodus of island families has all but killed off the local culture; and even Fair Isle's decades-long dependence upon entire families of incomers to keep its future secure has almost certainly diluted that island's cultural strengths. But Foula's case story has differed significantly.

'Outsiders often came to Foula to marry their Foula partners, bringing with them their own ways and ideas, but adapting to Foula ways as well,' says Isobel.

Not that everything can possibly be rose-tinted in a village community so small. Nowadays, she tells me, with only twenty-eight people on the island, silly feuds build up between families, often over land use or sheepdogs straying; these disagreements can run on for months, she says, 'but then at Foula Christmas everybody gets together and differences get sorted.'

'Foula Christmas' is a term that has resonance on the island, as Foula is one of the few remaining communities in the world — outside of the Russian and Greek Orthodox churches — to continue to observe the Julian Calendar.

Introduced and named after Julius Caesar in 45 B.C., the Julian Calendar broke the year into 365 days, but added a day to February once every four years, making the average year equate to 365.25 days. When it was devised, this was doubtless thought to be close enough, but it failed to take into account a discrepancy of eleven minutes a year that separated the Julian Calendar and the astronomical solstices. Caesar's astronomers, understandably enough, deemed an astronomical incongruity that added up to one day every 134 years to be insignificant.

For sixteen centuries, the ever-growing disparity was ignored until, in 1582, Pope Gregory XIII decreed that the calendar should be shifted to match the equinoxes. So, under the new Gregorian Calendar, Thursday, October 4th was followed by Friday, October 15th. Credit card companies of the day must have rubbed their hands together with glee; at a stroke, bills that yesterday still had ten days to pay were now subject to late charges.

Nations disinclined to be seen following the lead of the Catholic church, Britain among them, ignored the need for a new calendar until finally they had to face up to its scientific accuracy, and in 1752, throughout Britain and its Empire, September 2nd was followed by September 14th.

Everywhere, that is, except Foula, which continues to adhere to the Julian Calendar even two-and-a-half centuries on. So when Isobel talks about 'Foula Christmas', she means January 5th. Likewise Foula's New Year's Day — 'Newerday' in the local dialect — falls on January 12th.

Relations among the twenty-eight inhabitants can get fractious, she acknowledges, especially near the end of winter when, despite lengthening daylight hours, the weather can remain hellish, causing spirits to wilt and tempers to fray.

But on the flip side of such fractiousness is a concrete unity in the face of threat or tragedy, when differences, no matter how deeply scored, mean zero and even near-enemies stand together for the common Foula good.

'What binds Foula folk more than anything is an almost tangible passion for the island,' says Isobel.

Apparently word has yet to reach Foula about the destruction that I brought upon the Fair Isle bank robbers' Peugeot, because Isobel suggests a walk in the southern part of the island, and lends me one of her 'Foula cars' to get down there. Foula is one of only a small number of British islands whose road network is so limited that it is exempt from laws that enforce annual vehicle inspections. This means that much of the island's traffic, such as it is, consists of old steeds in varying but visible states of decay. Yesterday at the airstrip a fine selection of bashed bangers lined up to meet the plane, some of them held together with sticky tape and seat belt webbing. On an island with a road network you could walk every metre of inside a couple of hours and no repair shop this side of a fifty-kilometre round trip by sea, expedience, rather than bureaucracy, prevails. Isobel loans me a fine little hatchback. 'Just ignore the oil warning light,' she says, before I drive off.

I take the little car, oil light flashing merrily, to Hametoon in the south of the island, which is not to be confused with Toon o' Ham in the middle of the island, and which I pass on the way. Neither name has anything to do with the popular Scots dialectic 'toon', for *town*. Derived from the Norse 'tún', for an enclosed cultivated area, it would have been applied in days when the túns were an hour apart on foot.

I leave the car on a piece of firm turf in the 'Y' of one of the island's few intersections — keys dangling in the ignition, since there is no cause to lock houses on Foula, let alone cars. Camera to hand, binoculars freshly polished and sandwiches packed, I hike into an expansive valley that runs east-west, straight across the island.

To the north-west is the long run-up towards first Hamnafield and later the Sneug, angular peaks whose silhouettes I have so often admired from Mainland, and at the Sneug's 418 metres the highest point on the island. South-west, Noup hits 248 metres, and in between nestles the gigantic curved valley that is the Daal.

Gouged out by the slow-motion passage of a corrie glacier during the last Ice Age when ice fields over two hundred metres deep scored the landscape, the Daal sweeps across the southern half of the island in a half-pipe of such evenness that it has the effect of an enormous tunnel with a startling blue sky for a roof.

I arrive well-warned about the marshy perils at the valley's floor by Isobel, whose depth of knowledge of the island, combined with an innate understanding of exactly how I am likely to go wrong, surely mark her as an ideal Island Ranger. And so I find my way onto an animal trail that cuts a muddy traverse across heather and scrub on the Daal's northern flank.

Planticrubs, the little stone seedling enclosures I first saw near Walls in west Mainland, perch ahead of me on the north slope, some nearly intact, others crumbled by decades of standing up to everything the northern climate hurtles at them.

Across the valley the Noup, backlit by the sun, casts a monster shadow that glides across the brown-green tapestry of the valley floor. Lurid flashes of green flag the boggiest of bogs and crooked fingers of miniature streams gleam wherever the sun curves around to reach them.

The narrow animal trail, muddy or not, makes for easier going than the heathery turf on either side, but with the trail comes a succession of animal droppings that present hazards of ever-varying proportions. After a month of tramping across Shetland landscapes, I am attuned to the variety of animal ordure that decorates my path. From the glazed black-marble sheen of tightly-packed sheep droppings to the scattered musket grapeshot of rabbits to the fibrous excretions of Shetland ponies, I separate and identify them with self-assurance like a quiz contestant far too confident for his own good — *'For my specialised subject on Mastermind I will take Shetland Animal Droppings.'*

The walk across the landscape is lit up with assured mental observations and evaluations.

Sheep — so fresh it might even be steaming; sheep — dried but not yet crumbling, so perhaps yesterday's; sheep — in need of a laxative, by the looks of it; rabbits — a whole warren of rabbits; Shetland pony — hoof-marks to support the identification thereof; more sheep; then: whoah! what the hell could have produced **that?**

Spread all the way across the skinny trail and spilling beyond its limits into turf and heather is a monstrous land-mine of intestinal emission. If it is the product of a pony, the poor animal is not only very poorly, but might also have shed about a quarter of its body weight in one rank excretion. A few more seconds' nose-twitching observance of this bio-hazard in all its foul vastness convinces me that it is far too expansive to have erupted from even the sickest of ponies. Which, of course, begs the question, what did do this? Cue the inner-ear screeching of Hammer House of Horror violins.

I put thoughts of the Beast of Bodmin Moor to the back of my mind and plod on, dodging as I go the deeper bog waters that cross the animal trails with irritating frequency.

Walking in Shetland has many rewards, but the ever-present boggy underfoot conditions can make it very hard work, not to mention a little disquieting when an unidentified beast lurks somewhere in terrain almost entirely absent of hiding places.

But in a landscape without plant life taller than ankle-high, the eye quickly adjusts to isolate anything bulkier than a heather clump. The two facing slopes of the Daal are dotted with sheep. And there, high on the northern horizon atop the rising slope of Hamnafield, where rocky hillcrest meets puffy clouds, the origin of the monster emission stands majestic. A stocky brown and white cow, roaming as free as the hill country sheep.

The walking at last becomes easier, the land underfoot simpler to negotiate, the terrain more smooth grass than heather tussocks, while the views open up to give me a better understanding of the heights of the two slopes that contain the west end of the Daal.

At my feet the turf is as close-cropped as a cricket pitch, if a mite less predictable, and very soon I find myself standing over one of the reasons I took the time to wander across to this uninhabited part of a nearly-uninhabited island, *da Sneck ida Smaallie*.

The Sneck is a freak of geology, a dauntingly-deep (at least sixty metres) rock ravine so perfectly parallel-sided with inner walls only three metres apart that it resembles more a tower hotel corridor minus the floors and ceilings than a natural feature on a coastal landscape. At its inland end, a thirty-metre-deep rock corridor drops from the pasture floor and heads, die-straight, to a point where it plummets yet deeper under a giant boulder jammed in its maw, to emerge more than a hundred metres further out as a tall slotted opening high on the one long cliff face that is Foula's west coast.

Local folklore says that Da Smaallie was a 'trow' (Shetland for troll) who called the Sneck home, and when the mood took him, he brewed up bad weather in the depths of the Sneck. Later, Isobel explains how such a legend could have gained credence:

'If you look west along the Daal on a bad day, the huge quantities of upthrown spray from the westerly swells look as if they are brewing up out of the Sneck,' she says.

I stand above its inland end, savouring the solitude but wishing for knowledgeable company; there is a way down and through the rocky corridor and under the boulder to where it emerges through the coastal cliff face. It is said to be a relatively manageable scramble, but to undertake it alone and without the benefit of a local guide would be madness. So I have to make do with creeping cautiously up on the vertical drop that is the coastline, where I settle flat on the wet turf and take in coastal scenery so brash and brutal and yet of such beauty that it makes my eyes water.

In 84 AD, the Roman General Agricola reached the northernmost point on his circumnavigation of Britain. There, he reputedly stood atop a hill in the Orkney Islands (between Shetland and the Scottish mainland), and cast his eyes yet further north, where he claimed to see *Ultima Thule* itself. Farthest Thule, the edge of the habitable world.

From north Orkney, weather permitting, three tall land formations would have stood before Agricola: Fair Isle in the middle of the strait between Orkney and Shetland; mighty Fitful Head on Shetland's south Mainland; and furthest away, the island of Foula.

I lie atop a vertical precipice one-hundred-plus metres above where the North Atlantic reduces itself to foam on coastal rocks the size of bungalows. In both directions, a five-kilometre-long cliff face ascends dramatically, spread out in the painfully sharp northern light. Agricola surely had Foula in sight when he declared *'dispecta est et Thule'* — also seen is Thule.

The cliffscape panorama is so stunning, and I feel so blessed to be seeing it in weather conditions so close to perfection that I opt to spend a few minutes enjoying the novelty of photographing the antics of cliff-face nesting seabirds from above.

Fulmars, as I have seen elsewhere on Shetland cliffs, do not actually fly *to* their nests, presumably because of the inherent difficulties in performing an emergency stop in mid-air. Instead, they fly to a point offshore and above the nest and ride the wind currents, every square millimetre of wingspan spread wide and feather profiles undergoing intricately complex adjustments to compensate for myriad fluctuations in wind speed and direction, until at the precise correct moment, another trimming of feathers plops the bird's rump firmly to ground, precisely where it should be, on a ledge only marginally bigger than the rump that lands on it, a dizzying height above the shoreline below.

West of me lie five thousand kilometres of Atlantic swells before the first landfall in Canada. A kilometre to the south, the Noup's peak elevation of 248 metres appears to almost coincide with the coastline, making the soaring cliff that sparkles backlit by the sun as high, and every bit as vertical, as an eighty-storey building. In the other direction, yet taller front-lit cliffs clamber skywards and, close to the point where they disappear around a corner towards the elusive Kame, a sprinkling stream crests the rocky wave and is aerated by wind gusts until it falls as miniature tumbling rainbows towards the roiling Atlantic, nearly three hundred metres below.

I settle down to a bespoke picnic lunch in as grand a location as I have savoured in many a long year.

III: Through the ages

On the return trek through the Daal back to the east coast, I steal wistful glances up the slopes of Hamnafield towards the Sneug that hides the Kame from view. Conditions are near-perfect for a hike up to the north slopes of the island, but I have an appointment for a guided coastal walk with Isobel's fellow Island Ranger. This means that any chance of seeing the Kame from above before leaving the island will depend on the weather being unseasonably beautiful two days in a row. In late October. In the middle of the Atlantic. I am not optimistic.

The little hatchback awaits me, keys still glinting in the ignition barrel, and minutes later, I pull up at the island post office to meet with Sheila Gear.

People by the name of Gear (it rhymes with 'dare') have played a significant role in the island's story, but crofter Sheila, who took the surname when she married into the Gear clan, has another ancestral claim to modern Foula history, as she was born a Holbourn. (Isobel, on the other hand, married a Holbourn). Holbourns are, in historic terms at least, newcomers to Foula, since they only popped up on the local radar in 1901, when Professor Ian B. Stoughton Houlborn, according to Liv Schei's finely-researched book *The Shetland Story*, 'took a fancy to it when sailing by and later bought it at an auction in London' — in one impetuous moment, adding whole new depth to the phrase about 'taking a passing fancy' to something.

For twelve centuries before the new Laird's arrival in 1901, Foula's experiences at the hands of a variety of empire-builders largely mirrored that of the rest of Shetland. The Vikings dropped in during the early part of the 9th Century, and the island remained a part of their empire for hundreds of years, leaving behind an almost complete set of place names derived from Norse.

Unlike most of Shetland, which was eventually returned by the Danish royal family to Scotland upon the default of a royal wedding dowry in 1469, Foula (like Papa Stour) remained in the control of the 'Lairds of Norway' for nearly three more centuries.

Sheila starts my tour at the spot on the coast without which even Foula's long struggles would never have occurred. Ham Voe is not only the island's harbour, it is the sole spot on the entire coastal landscape to offer anything like the protection demanded of a port. Being little more than a gash in the east coast, even Ham Voe has often been found wanting; when the weather hails from the south-east, the Voe bears the brunt of batterings that used to require the 'mail boat', as island ferries were always known, to be manually hauled far above the highest watermark to prevent it being reduced to splintered ruins.

On Fair Isle I saw one modern solution to such worries, a steeply-canted ramp high on dry land onto which the *Good Shepherd* is winched at the end of every voyage. Here on Foula, the solution is even more drastic; the *New Advance* dangles from stout davits, metres above the voe's waterline, and protected on three sides by a bunker-like concrete enclosure. Viewed from the concrete pier that reaches protectively across the mouth of the voe, the tough little 11-metre ferry hangs proud in its protective lair, washed only by the warm glow of the afternoon sun, like a ship's lifeboat dangling ready for emergency deployment. There is a beauty to its fish-out-of-water presence at the end of those davits, but it is a beauty inspired by necessity.

Sheila explains that for decades at the end of the 19th Century, Foula's entreaties to the government for help to build the pier to protect Ham Voe and its tiny complement of vessels were ignored completely, never mind that in the most dangerous of conditions, the mail boat arriving from Walls often found itself with no option but to return to Mainland, so impossible was it to land safely.

But it was not until World War I inspired fears of sea-borne invaders that the pier at the mouth of the voe was at last constructed, at least in part to support gun emplacements to thwart potential invaders whose need for the island's only safe landing point was somehow an easier concept for the authorities to grasp.

In the calm waters within the voe, common seals, some bobbing in the bay, others lolling on small patches of foreshore, watch us with what might even be suspicion.

At the mouth of the pier inlet, Sheila points out an eroded slope that from time to time delivers up shards of pottery and other artefacts from a Neolithic homestead. One-hundred-and-forty kilometres to the south-west, Skara Brae in Orkney is one of the most celebrated Neolithic homesteads on the planet, while here on Foula, unexcavated and slowly giving itself up to the combined might of the climate and the ocean, evidence of Foula's own Neolithic history sits unmarked and unexplored.

In my readings about Foula I encountered a propensity among outsiders towards looking-down-the-nose scorn for the faraway, little-known island and its inhabitants. I saw the same slights and slurs and half-truths regurgitated and exaggerated until they took on the gravity of accepted knowledge. Unsubstantiated mockery is something that Foula folk over the generations have become *very* sensitive to.

A few metres from the harbour of Ham Voe is the Hàa, or hall, for more than two hundred years the island Laird's residence and for the better part of a century the focal point of fun over what was supposedly a turret built into it by the Laird of the day. When Sheila points out the unprepossessing Hàa, I make the mistake of mentioning the book references to the turret, a mistake on at least two counts. One, there is no damned turret; and two, the Laird in question was my current guide's grandfather.

Not only is Sheila adamant that the turret is a figment of a malign travel writer's imagination, but she has the evidence to prove it: a modest little building with what might be the aborted remains of a minor architectural affectation affixed to one corner.

Whatever the true story, the building modifications' beginnings, constructed of sandstone brought by boat from the northern part of the island, remain incongruously swallowed up in the Hàa's roofline. At most, the aborted modification was an innocent attempt by the Laird to add to his charmless home's aesthetic appeal, but the travel writers of the day blew it so far out of proportion that 'castle turrets' on the Hàa, which never actually existed, became just another story gleefully re-told to make Foula folk look stupid.

Nearby is the building that for many years was the island shop, but which closed for business in the 1970s. Sheila is curiously adamant that there is a positive side to having nowhere to buy anything. When the shop was there, she says, people depended on it to keep them supplied with essentials. (A little like how the rest of the planet exists, I imagine). But now, folk look after their own needs more carefully, and if anything is in short supply in one household, its shortage can easily be alleviated with help from another. It has to rank as the best, or perhaps the most fanciful 'glass is half full' rationale I have ever heard, even if there is no doubting the sincerity with which it is delivered.

Just over the way from the Hàa and the former shop are centuries-old signs of the fishing trade that was central to the livelihood of Foula folk for centuries. Outlined in stone are the walls of the old salt store, and embedded in the shore are deep rectangular basins cut into the rock, where fish were washed before being dried and salted. All of which would have been in everyday use in the 18th and 19th Century days of the Truck System.

Sheila indicates orange lichen clinging to the mica schist rock that runs down to where dark blue water foams against the shoreline. She tells me that in various parts of 17th Century Scotland where textiles were produced, this lichen was gathered up, soaked in human urine for two to three weeks, rolled into small balls that were dried in the sun and then exported as a source of textile dyes. World-famous Harris tweed, produced in Scotland's Western Isles, was coloured in this way.

What I want to know is who on earth came up with that idea, and by what sort of process of elimination?

> *Damnation, Angus, the sun-dried sheeps' gonads and the ground chicken-eyeballs didna work. How about we just pee on that wee plant an' see if that does it?*

At a nearby croft, an outbuilding squats low to the ground and is shaped exactly like a narrow boat. It is an illustration of down-to-earth ways forced upon the island by its location and environment. Buildings were constructed according to the materials available, and on an island with no native wood sources, such availability was often down to fate. In the case of this outbuilding, an old *sixareen* boat that washed ashore after one of the many late-18th Century *Haaf* fishing tragedies was co-opted to serve as a roof, and so a *sixareen*-shaped shed was built to fit the available 'roof'.

In another outbuilding Sheila demonstrates a hand-operated millstone made from mica schist because, unlike sandstone, it was so soft that stone particles which found their way into the corn mix would not damage teeth. Foula mill stones were widely exported throughout the region, and ancient examples are found all over Shetland and Orkney.

Outside the shed sits a 'quern stone', its deep bowl-like indentation speaking of years of manual labour while cereal was mashed using a wooden mallet of cartoon-comic dimensions to produce 'barley bere', a coarse cereal that was eaten roasted.

'It was said that the best thing about barley bere was the smell,' says Sheila, with a wry smile. She leads me to a smaller, broken quern stone built into a drystone dyke, and explains that landlords used to encourage islanders to build water-powered mills, then impose a tax upon anyone using them. The landlord or his hated factors stopped islanders from employing the age-old quern stone method by breaking the querns, forcing locals to opt for devious means, such as building quern stones into walls to keep them from prying eyes. The one we look at now evidently failed to escape the factors — and *still* it ended up being built into a wall.

In Sheila's own kale yard at the head of Ham Voe, kale grows sheltered by lichen-encrusted drystone; huddled next to one wall, a fifty-year-old sycamore tree stands like a bonsai miniature, its perfectly-proportioned but dwarfed dimensions a fraction of those of a normal sycamore, its branches barely peeking over the top edge of the protective wall. Anything growing higher than the wall gets 'burnt off' by the wind.

Outside the yard is yet another quern stone, a giant example, broken apart to reveal a cross-section of the deep bowl. Even to my eye it looks old — and with good reason. It dates from the Bronze Age, which makes it between three and four thousand years old, and it sits unattended on a pathway. Sheila tells me that she leaves it upside down so as not to draw too much attention to it when there are tourists around.

We cross a wooden footbridge that spans Foula's largest river, little more than a stream running into the innermost point of the harbour inlet, and hike past a field dotted with Shetland ponies. Foula ponies are valued by foreign breeders for their purity of lineage, which keeps prices high, and doubtless puts smiles on the faces of Foula breeders.

Sheila points out an island rarity, a solitary white sheep among a flock of many colours ranging from dusty beige to coal-black. I do my best, but fail to resist speculating that it must be the white sheep of the family.

Sheila then leads me to clear traces of runrig farming, never mind that the system disappeared nearly two hundred years ago. Remains of furrows mark out the small narrow field plots that were rotated among farmers for centuries until land reform created crofts in the 1830s.

The farmland here is some of the best in all of Shetland, but what looks perfectly natural to me is in fact only two or three centuries old, as Foula's entire arable land area was crafted by hand. Fertile soil occurs naturally only around Foula's coastline, so these fields were created using earth carted by crofters in wicker backpacks called 'kishies'. A frightful amount of work was involved in giving birth to every runrig plot, and now the land is used only to feed sheep.

Crumbling around the edges of the old runrig fields are ancient peat banks, and Sheila breaks a handful out of the ground to show me clear traces of the wood vegetation that became peat. These are no more than perfectly-preserved twiglets, but deeper down, stout branches survive intact, and, like the broken quern stone over yonder, can be dated to the Bronze Age.

'Without peat, Foula couldn't possibly have been inhabited for so long,' says Sheila.

A fisherman's böd squats dug into a headland overlooking rocks running down to the choppy mouth of Ham Voe. Snuggled into the landscape, two hundred and more years ago, the böd was inhabited every summer season by visiting *Haaf* fishermen from Shetland. Even stretching the mind's eye to put a turf roof back on the small structure, it is hard to imagine six or seven men living and sleeping in a cramped interior no larger than a present-day garden shed. This one was last used at the end of the 18th Century, when its crew, racing a Foula boat back to the harbour in a popular game of one-upmanship, struck a rock only metres from where we now stand. In those days, nobody could swim (how would they ever learn in these climes?), and by the time the men in the Foula boat realised what had happened, all the Shetlanders had drowned, mere metres from safety. It is a tragedy that remains undocumented, and has survived through the generations for over two hundred years, purely by word of mouth.

Sheila pulls a handful of waterlogged sphagnum moss from the earth at her feet. Famous for its natural sterility and for its sponge-like qualities, sphagnum finds many uses around the world. Sheila tells me that North American native Inuits used it for baby diapers. I hope they dried it first.

At the bay of Ham Little, a cliff shoreline modest by Foula's standards is thick with puffins in summer, nests so close to the cliff paths that walkers can get almost to within touching distance. In late October, there are only fulmars in residence. Although ever-present now, the first fulmars only arrived on Foula in the 1880s before spreading throughout Shetland and the rest of Britain. Local legend says they floated here aboard the carcass of a dead whale.

When I ask what she thinks about the theory that recent downturns in seabird populations are due to global warming, Sheila snorts with what I interpret to be derision. The real problem, she tells me, is a shortage of seabirds' diet of sand eels that are actively fished commercially, mostly as feed for salmon farms, and are caught using a net so fine that a matchstick cannot pass through it.

'It's just unsustainable,' says Sheila, her head shaking with disbelief.

I barely manage to desist from leaping into the air in fright when snipe explode, screeching in high-pitched alarm, from the watery undergrowth at my feet. Sheila identifies them for me, then names bramblings and snow bunting with the casual certainty that a city-dweller applies to variants of the Ford Mondeo. Both the bramblings and snow bunting are temporary migrants on trans-oceanic layovers, she tells me, which is not something you often hear said about Ford four-wheelers.

From the swaying waters of the bay, a grey seal performs an effortless slow-motion pirouette to maintain glassy eye contact with our course around the cliff edge.

We finish up at the tall war memorial to five Foula men who died in World War I, two brothers and three cousins. The memorial is a favourite spot in the summer, when the fields are awash with more than two hundred types of wild flower, and families can enjoy the grand views of much of the east side of the island, with the central peaks looming in the near-distance.

Only two kilometres offshore from here are the 'Terrible Shaalds', a rocky reef that lurks unseen a bare metre below the water's surface. The Shaalds have been the ruination of many ships over the centuries, but none more famous than the HMS *Oceanic* which, only two weeks after being pressed into naval service to patrol the waters around Shetland, ran aground there on 8th September, 1914, when a navigational blunder in thick fog resulted in the ship sailing up the wrong side of Foula. Oops.

Formerly an ocean liner that worked the transatlantic route for the famed White Star Line, the *Oceanic* was launched in 1899 at the eye-watering cost of one million pounds Sterling. She was hailed as 'the greatest liner of her day', and so she remained until her sister ship sailed out of the same Belfast shipyard twelve years later. That sister ship was called the *Titanic*.

Remarkably enough, one of the two masters of the *Oceanic*, Captain Henry Smith, was himself already a survivor of the *Titanic* disaster of April 1912; this time he, and the entire *Oceanic* crew, were rescued by boats that rushed to her assistance. They left the mighty ship — at 17,272 gross tons, it was the length of two football fields — parked high and nearly dry on top of the reef, according to witnesses, almost as if it were laid up in dry dock.

When Captain Smith was brought ashore at Ham Voe, he reportedly looked out at the Oceanic, only three kilometres away, and expressed the view that she would stay on the reef like a monument, since 'nothing would move it'. A Foula man who overheard him is said to have muttered:

'I'll give her two weeks.'

Foula wisdom prevailed, even if the local's prediction was out by a few days. After an overnight storm on the night of 29th September — three weeks after she ran aground — the giant *Oceanic* disappeared, swallowed up in her entirety by the mighty seas that hold the island in their clutches, and that the Foula man knew so well.

IV: Eric's wide world

Yesterday I looked up to hills that from under pristine skies winked and crooked an alluring finger, and brooded that my one decent chance to see the Kame up close might be about to pass me by.

How right I was. The morning arrives to violently blustery conditions, with intermittent wind-whipped showers that shake the walls of Freyers, and a thick mantle of pea soup cloud curdling the mid-slopes of Soberlie Hill. Conditions are so severe that a back-up plan to view the Kame from sea level aboard the Aith lifeboat, whose coxswain had kindly agreed to pick me up at Ham Voe and include me in exercises off the west coast of the island, is also blown away by the weather. I feel like a Dolly Parton devotee who went all the way to Tennessee and didn't do Dollywood.

Foula folk know all about having to re-think their days to suit the vagaries of the climate, so while I scowl at weather so inclement that it puts the kibosh on any worthwhile outdoor activity, Isobel morphs seamlessly into the role of producer and firms up an appointment for me.

When I park her little Foula car in the muddy yard of the southernmost house on the island, a thick-set man waves from the croft doorway. I tiptoe through the mud and he apologises for his untidy house, but welcomes me to a living room whose every square inch of wall surface is filled with books, charts, CDs and long-playing records. Eric Isbister is in his early sixties, and has spent his whole life in this, the family croft. He is, as I am about to discover, that rarity, a bona fide eccentric who genuinely cares not one jot what the rest of us think.

Perhaps it is in his blood, as Eric's parents were stalwarts in their resistance to change. When their fellow islanders welcomed the long-overdue comforts and convenience of plumbing and electricity, the Isbisters held out, content for things to remain just the way they were. Eric's father, who for many years was the island shopkeeper, died nearly twenty years back, but his mother passed away only three years ago, and Eric is yet to instal any of the luxuries eschewed by his parents. Which makes him the only person on Foula still to live without mains electricity (paraffin Tilly lanterns do just fine), and to make do with a chemical toilet and well water. The only concession he makes to what a century ago passed for cutting-edge modernity is having a telephone so that he can keep in contact with an elderly aunt on the island.

Eric tells me he is not in the least averse to change, but has lived this way for so long that he is in no hurry to fall into line with the rest of Foula, let alone the rest of the developed world. Everything in its own time, is the message I get, and so what if some people have a different idea of time from others?

In the meantime, he has his interests to pursue, and he pursues them with a passion. When not tending to his croft or checking in on auntie, Eric has no trouble keeping busy. Decades of shipping industry periodicals that form teetering towers all around the crowded room are evidence of a lifelong fascination for ships. Eric, with the help of powerful telescopes, has kept a register of every ocean-going vessel that he has seen passing Foula since 1957. And during the long winters with their short days, he hand-crafts wooden models of ships that have visited Foula over the decades. He shows me several; they are built from his own sketches (some of which have appeared in the shipping bible, Janes Merchant Ships) and completely by eye, with no plans or records to help him with perspective or proportion, yet they are incredibly realistic. I am not surprised to hear that his reputation as a model-maker has spread far, and that he occasionally receives special requests from abroad for recreations of vessels long ago consigned to scrap.

The airstrip that the islanders created within sight of his croft led to another of Eric's passions: a comprehensive log of every aircraft to land on Foula since 1973.

Eric can be certain of the comprehensiveness of his logs for the simple reason that he has spent almost his entire life on Foula. It is a subject that I do not want to press, and when I ask if he has lived on Foula all of his life, he replies:

'I hope not all of it, not yet.'

But Eric is by nature expansive, and he soon fills in the gaps. When he was born in 1943, all expectant mothers travelled to Mainland to give birth, which meant that Eric spent the first two weeks of his life outside Foula. Since he arrived on the island as a two-week-old, he has left Foula precisely once, in 1976, when he spent a week touring Mainland Shetland in the company of his father.

Yet there is nothing remotely insular about this man's fascination for the wide world beyond the reach of his telescopes.

He has his logs and his huge collection of books and periodicals as well as friends around the world with whom he exchanges letters, and then there is a vast accumulated wealth of music, on both vinyl and CD. Like his transport-spotting hobbies, Eric's love of music is somewhat focussed, and started when he bought his first ever record in the late 1950s, the 78 rpm single of 'Does your chewing gum lose the flavour on the bedpost overnight?', by the Glasgow-born skiffle maestro, Lonnie Donegan.

'I have every track released by Lonnie Donegan, bar two,' he says.

Should anyone have a spare copy of either 'Wasn't I the lucky one' — recorded in Australia, perhaps in the 1960s; or of the 45rpm single version of 'Midnight Special', recorded live in Belfast — please wrap them carefully and post them to Eric Isbister, Foula, Shetland.

Eric listens to his music on a system powered by car batteries, though by the time you read this he may have embraced mains electricity. But then again, he may not.

When asked about how things have changed on Foula in his lifetime, he points to a fondness for more sociable times gone by.

In the 1950s and 1960s, he says, people were far more sociable, and used to visit each other of an evening, something that does not happen much any more.

'People seemed more contented then, and only grumbled about the weather,' he says. 'Folk nowadays grumble a lot more, even though they probably have much less cause to.'

Eric has very fond memories of the 1960s, when he remembers people on Foula were far more self-sufficient, raising cows (for meat, milk, butter and cheese), growing a range of vegetables for their own consumption and catching and curing fish for the long winters. The 1970s and the new airstrip saw people quickly become dependent upon the air service to keep them supplied with things they once supplied for themselves. Gone forever were the days when Foula folk produced almost everything they ate except for sugar and flour.

Not too surprisingly for a man with his hobbies, Eric returns to the subject of transportation, and how changes there have had a huge effect upon Foula, and almost all within his own lifetime. Before he was born, his family had the only horse and cart on Foula, prior to which, he recalls, the closest thing to 'transport' on the island was a wheelbarrow. After the movie The Edge of the World was filmed on Foula in 1936, the island's first car was left behind by the film-makers. Another twenty years passed before the second car arrived on the island, when in 1957 the Church of Scotland gifted the island a Land Rover.

'Now, there are probably more cars than people,' he says.

The addition of the air service, he concedes, has been a big boost to the island, in particular how it has saved Foula from being completely cut off when the seas are too rough for ferry passages. He recalls how, a few years before flights started, his mother needed treatment at the hospital in Lerwick, where she was a patient for ten days. Then, when she was discharged, she had to stay with relatives for more than two months until the next boat crossed from Mainland to Foula, so bad were weather conditions. It occurs to me that he is almost certainly thinking back to the same 'dearth' that saw a teenaged Isobel deprived of her favourite comic for eleven weeks.

But not even regular flights mean guaranteed access to the island. In the 1980s, a relative of Eric's from the USA managed to come to Shetland for three days, but never got closer to Foula than Mainland. She could see Foula and talk to Eric's family on the telephone, but her Shetland stay coincided with three days of violent westerlies when flights could not possibly operate. In a case of so near but yet so far, and after travelling thousands of kilometres, she had to return to New Jersey without managing to set foot on her ancestral homeland.

When we somehow get onto the subject of our shared fascination for maps, Eric tells me how, with his late Dad, he copied a map of Foula and added to it all the local place names that have never appeared on maps produced outside of Foula, many of which are disappearing from usage even among the islanders. When I ask if he has a spare copy, he disappears to an upstairs room, and after what feels like a long time listening to noises of furniture being moved around, he re-emerges triumphantly holding his last spare copy, which he promptly parts company with for what strikes me as not exactly a bargain price. Did I get done? Of course I did, but it is a lovely one-of-a-kind map that some day will merit framing. I leave the Isbister croft clutching my new acquisition and thinking that I have met, probably for the first time, a true eccentric — and my life is the better for it.

That night, back at Freyers, Isobel pulls out another surprise. A DVD of the movie that Eric mentioned, the 1937 classic written and direct by Michael Powell, *The Edge of the World*. Up until now I have only seen reference to it in books and heard mention of it from people here on Foula, where in 1936 Michael Powell and his cast and crew spent four months over the summer of 1936 shooting an astonishing 33 miles (53 kilometres) of film.

In his introduction to a book by Professor Holbourn — who died the year before Powell and crew arrived on Foula — Powell said:

> '... the real star of my film is the lonely island of Foula —
> and the real makers are its people.'

Noble words, maybe, but not so far from reality, as the film was shot almost entirely on location on Foula, and was released with no studio footage whatsoever.

The film was inspired by events six years earlier in the even more remote Atlantic community of St Kilda, when after years of below-subsistence misery, the St Kildans capitulated and sent out an SOS request for immediate evacuation. Eager to craft a dramatisation of the tale but denied permission to film on St Kilda, Powell instead turned his attention to Shetland, and eventually set out to make a film with a cast made up of only nine professional actors, and virtually the entire population of Foula.

A drama set in a familiar urban location is entertaining, but watching *The Edge of the World* while seated in a croft in the north part of the island is enthralling. Powell was right — Foula is the star of the show, and the island I have barely scratched the surface of is instantly recognisable throughout, so much so that even I can detect *changes* in the landscape — like the Brough, only a few hundred metres from where we sit now, its span connecting the two rock towers still intact.

The cinematic tale is poignant to the point of being over-sentimental — this was the 1930s, remember — but glorious cinematography takes me to places on the island that I recognise instantly, and to others which have so far eluded me. The cliffs of the west and northern shores command their own dramatic roles, with cast members clambering around and dangling from their peaks.

Even having stood at the top of some of the smaller cliffs, it is hard to comprehend that for centuries Foula men routinely lowered themselves down these gigantic rock faces to harvest vital bird eggs and even tufted grass for cattle-feed. Isobel told me of one crofter in the 1840s who, when driving in the steel pin at the precipice edge to attach his rope, felt himself sliding into the abyss and fainted in terror. He regained consciousness, dangling over the edge, saved by a moleskin patch on his trousers that had caught on the pin.

In a key scene in the movie, the menfolk of the island hold 'parliament' on the shoreline at Ristie, the very shoreline so clearly visible from Isobel's living room window. The parliament is in session to debate evacuation of the island, the inevitability of which resonates throughout the film's plotline, and which sees the people of Foula flocking to the pier at Ham Voe, laden down with their scant possessions, to board the waiting boat and leave their homeland forever.

Seventy years on, this association with St Kilda continues to cast ill-informed doubt upon Foula's sustainability. Doubt that unaccountably ignores the colossal significance of the island's unique heritage and landscape.

V: Between weathers

The very last day of my journey around Shetland dawns with weather so perfect that it pains me to think how much my travels would have benefitted from experiencing these sort of conditions just a little more than I have. But perhaps, in October, at a latitude equivalent to parts of Greenland, to harbour such thoughts is to ignore reality.

Before I go to the airstrip, Isobel drops me at the island school. Kathleen Gardiner is the temporary supply teacher at a valued institution which currently has a grand roll of two primary kids and one nursery infant, who is absent today.

The two lads welcome the distraction from their regular lesson plan and show me around with bubbling eagerness and not a little pride. Robert is eight, and Daniel is nine. Daniel's fizzing enthusiasm for everything around him is infectious. He wants to be a pilot, specifically on the Foula plane, where he tells me he has sat up front with Eddie Watt (in the same seat in which I sat when I flew with Eddie from Fair Isle to Tingwall; I really am beginning to feel like a local); Daniel's love of transport extends to the New Advance ferry, and he tells me proudly of having been allowed to 'take the helm' during trips to Walls, and narrates to me, in sequence, the entire complicated berthing procedure at the little pier in Walls. A month ago, I watched through my binoculars as the New Advance performed this very procedure, and I recognise its intricacies from Daniel's description.

Robert is a quieter soul who this morning lives a little in the shadow of Daniel's exuberance, but who makes a point of telling me with some certainty that he wants to be a policeman.

The school is part of a purpose-built community centre building. There is only one classroom, but what a classroom it is. Floor-to-ceiling windows look out at Hamnafield Hill and upon mixed-brown Foula sheep grazing only a few paces from where the lads sit doing their lessons. The room is open-plan, with low tables and ultra-modern facilities that teachers in more fashionable postcodes still can only wish for. In a neighbouring room, latest-model computers that are hooked up to the island's own broadband network allow the lads to be in regular contact with schools all over the world. I am taken next door to the community hall, where games are played, and where the picking of teams must have a certain element of predictability.

When Isobel arrives to take me to the airstrip, the boys escort me to the door and deliver farewells and handshakes with formality and sincerity. On these young mens' shoulders rests at least a part of the island's future, and I leave convinced they are the right men for the job.

At the airstrip the Islander arrives a half hour late to considerable grumbling from a small number of residents leaning on battered cars. The skies remain clear; visibility is as good as at any time during the last five weeks, and could present one last opportunity of seeing the Kame, just so long as the ever-resourceful Isobel can arrange it. She has a quiet word with Marshall Wishart, who by way of response waves me into the co-pilot's seat. Persuasion is not required, and so I am seated, buckled in and camera at the ready, before I notice the salt that encrusts the outside of the window; and of course there is no door on my side of the plane. Marshall unbuckles his seat belt, climbs down, rounds the front of the Islander and takes great care over cleaning the window for me. You wouldn't get that from a Captain of a Jumbo bound for New York, and right now I wouldn't change places anyway.

Marshall decides he does have time to show us (myself and teacher Mrs Gardiner's husband) the back of the island. Over the radio he informs air traffic control that he will be 'doing a quick circumnavigation' for the benefit of his two passengers. There is no need to seek permission from a line manager in Lerwick or Sumburgh, just a need to keep air traffic control informed for reasons of safety and common sense.

The Islander takes off to the south, and within seconds we swing past Eric Isbister's croft and over the deeply indented south-east coast before Marshall puts the Islander into a long slow right-hander. As we level off parallel with the coast, the view is an astonishing illustration of how, west of the peaks that hog centre stage and dominate all views of the island, one entire side of Foula plunges abruptly into the North Atlantic. It looks as if the back half of the island was summarily ripped away, and whether this came about by the merest twitching of tectonic plates or by a million years of erosion, the effect is truly spectacular.

As we pass the Noup, the glacial half-tube of the Daal and my picnic point next to the Sneck of the Smaallie sit bathed in glorious sunshine. From there the coastline climbs inexorably towards a new high point in the shadow of the Sneug, where Marshall hangs a right turn — and there it is at last. The Kame, so blindingly backlit that it looks like something from a Sci-Fi special effects department. Flying at about two hundred metres, we are in line with only about the mid-point of the tallest cliffs in occupied Britain, and in nearly thirty years of travelling, I have never set eyes on anything like it. The scale is beyond comprehension, the North Atlantic setting so profoundly dramatic that no photograph could do it justice. Which is at the very least convenient, as the intense northern backlighting makes a mockery of this photographer's attempts to capture the scene.

All too soon, the visual feast is over, and as Foula disappears behind us, we proceed towards Mainland in the clearest visibility I have experienced since I arrived on the *Hrossey*, five weeks ago.

A few minutes later, in a taxi bound for Lerwick, I comment on the beautiful conditions, and the driver nods and says,

'It's a day atween waddirs.'

Between weathers. If ever a phrase was made for Shetland, this is it.

Back in da toon, a few minutes wandering along Commercial Street is broken up by three conversational encounters with people I know, and nods in the directions of others who look familiar, and who nod back in a way that only seems to confirm our acquaintanceship. A man could get used to this sense of belonging in a small, close-knit community.

Unseasonably warm weather for the first day of November makes taking lunch on the pier a possibility too good to pass up. A bollard next to the RNLI lifeboat *Michael and Jane Vernon* makes for a slightly bum-chilling perch and a fine spot from which to scan the harbour. The Bressay ferry nips back and forth across the Sound as if on rails and a big grey seal lolls back, face pointing towards the blue sky as if trying to draw the last few rays of autumnal warmth before the long inevitability of winter closes in.

I say my goodbyes to the kind folk at the Tourist Office, and at the modern ferry terminal, lug heavy bags across the interminably long footbridge, only to be met half-way by a NorthLink crew member with a luggage trolley. He waves away my breathless thanks and assures me in his Shetland dialect that it is nothing. It is an act of simple kindness that still strikes me, even after weeks of exposure to the ways of the islanders, for its stark comparison to the cold-shoulder treatment we accept as normal elsewhere.

After weeks of mostly sleeping bags and pine bunks, the cosy ferry cabin no longer inspires thoughts of budget Japanese hotel rooms or 1970s caravans; I fill it with luggage and head up on deck for the few minutes before we cast off. Winches creak, ropes splash into frigid crystal waters, the bow turns south, and just as the lights of Lerwick flicker into life, we leave them behind. I blame the chilly south-easterly for the water in my eyes that turns street lights into exaggerated starbursts.

As we steam south, a meal in the restaurant offers up an unexpected sideshow; outside the window a winchman from Oscar Charlie, the Shetland Coast Guard helicopter, floats at the end of a line, perilously close to the speeding back deck that would be lit by nothing but the stars were it not for the helicopter's fierce spotlights. A restaurant worker dismisses it as a routine training exercise, but just how routine can it be for the man who swings wildly amidst the solid steel perils of thousands of tonnes of ferry steaming ahead at full speed, miles from shore? As if to free me from my concerns, he retreats skywards like a neon-striped spider and Oscar Charlie veers off towards Mainland, its exercise over. For a moment I envy him, but only for a moment, before attentions return to the more mundane matters of a rapidly-cooling baked potato and a pleasantly dry white wine.

EPILOGUE: LERWICK FOR UP HELLY AA

I: Traditions ancient and freshly-painted

It is the afternoon before the Big Day, and a sense of rectitude pervades the speech and body language of everyone involved in what is evidently Shetland's most eagerly anticipated event of the year, one that is seemingly of unquestionable importance. My scepticism hidden, hopefully, from the sharp questioning eyes of my Shetlander hosts, I nod a lot and say very little.

The men who show us around the Galley Shed do so with unerring courtesy and humour. In pride of place is the newly-completed Galley which as we speak receives loving attention from a man perched high on a step ladder. He brushes and trims the dragon figurehead's whiskers with such care that suggests he *knows* it can feel every snip of the scissors.

Showing me around is Andy Angus, a project engineer from Sullom Voe oil terminal who became a Committee Member in 2002. This means he can look forward to many more years of toil before the honour of donning a Jarl's costume of his own design in 2017. Galley Shed tour duties completed, he hands me over to next year's Jarl, Graham Nicolson, whose role today is to give the assembled media, all six of us, a formal Press Briefing, complete with a walk through some of the key locations of tomorrow evening's procession.

Up Helly Aa is overloaded with traditions, fundamental to which is the wearing of beards by the Jarl and his squad. A calendar year before *his* big day, Graham is already resplendent in facial hair going haywire; by next January, it will be something to be proud of, but right now, combined with a well-cut business suit and tie, complete with secret-service-like lapel button, it has a handsome incongruity about it; and at the moment it may be the lapel button that makes the man, for he talks with the finality of a secret service agent. The clear impression I receive is that the media are to be tolerated, whether the organisers like it or not. It is an impression gained while he gives a briefing made up mostly of 'Do nots'.

'Do not even think about standing here, or there — or there — for you *will* be moved.'

'Do not get in front of the procession — because we do not stop, and if you fall, we *will* walk over you.' From the look in his eye as he says it, he might not be joking. The gravity of the event in his mind is obvious, and the implication that there will be no tolerance of anything seen as media interference, crystal clear.

It makes me think of a quote I noted down from the book *The Shetland Story* by Liv Schei, and who might have been right when she wrote, way back in 1988:

> *'While Up Helly Aa is a wonderful spectacle for a visitor to watch, it is definitely not a tourist event.'*

Later, the briefest of episodes lends present-day credence to words penned nearly twenty years earlier.

The torchlit procession and the burning of the Galley are only the opening acts of a night-long drama, the long meandering tail of which plays out in 'the Halls', twelve gatherings around town, hosted often by partners of men at the heart of the event — no women are allowed in the main procession, remember — and where people get together to eat, drink, dance a great deal, and welcome the visits and party pieces of each of the fifty squads who marched in the procession that kicked off the night's events.

At a meeting with the Tourist Office, a suggestion that I might drop in on a few different Halls over the course of the night causes the normally unflappable Director to blanche. The procession might happen in public and be fair game for promotion by the tourist authority whose activities contribute enormously to Shetland's image and economy, but the Halls, hosted by Shetlanders and attended in the main by their relations and acquaintances, are, well, *different*. Ever-helpful Stephen Simpson whispers in my ear that a problem arose last year when one group of journalists thought they could stroll into any Hall they wanted, without first seeking invitations. Wherever they blundered, they doubtless encountered courteous welcomes, but umbrage among the community over the perceived slight was instant and deep-felt, and the tourist board is still dealing with the fall-out.

So there are not only rules to follow, but local sensitivities to consider carefully. Could it be that, at least at certain times of year, the politics of isolation apply not only to truly remote island communities such as Papa Stour, Fair Isle and Foula? Perhaps Shetland has something of a chip on its shoulder when it comes to outsiders crashing its biggest party?

The deep sense of ancient tradition that surrounds the mid-winter festival is at least a touch misleading, since its roots go back only to the mid-19th Century, when young Lerwegian men, still reeling from the excitement of the Napoleonic Wars, brought seasonal mischief-making to the narrow lanes of Lerwick.

They did so by dragging 'tar barrels', wooden sledges bearing half-barrels full of rags and combustibles, lathered with tar and set aflame. Commonly employed in 19th Century sea ports as sources of heat and light, tar barrels took on a rowdy festive role, as teams of alcohol-fuelled working class lads, many wearing masks, hauled them up and down narrow Commercial Street. Protests from the establishment were met with open defiance; when joint Procurators Fiscal (public prosecutors) James Greig Snr and James Greig Jnr issued threats against tar-barrel activities, small bombs, powerful enough to shake houses and break windows, were set off on their doorsteps. Other pranks were surely calculated to cause outrage, like in 1855, when dead cats were fired from two of the Fort Charlotte cannons.

In the 1870s, Socialist and Temperance movements embraced the event with agendas of their own and introduced new ideas, including more sophisticated disguises — the 'guizing' element that continues today — and, for the first time, a torchlit procession. At this point there was still no Viking ingredient to Up Helly Aa; that developed gradually over the years, with the first Guizer Jarl appearing in 1906, and the earliest Jarl's squad of Vikings fronting up after World War One. A resonant chord must have been struck, because ever since, the torch-lit procession has been led by a squad of 'Norsemen', and today Up Helly Aa is almost indelibly linked in peoples' minds with the Vikings.

When it comes to views on their Viking forebears, opinion among Shetlanders is polarised into mutually-exclusive schools of thought which can be categorised, simplistically or not, as the Romantics and the Realists.

The Romantics number many scholars among them, and take the view that the Vikings colonised Shetland as a supply depot from which they could source food and other essentials for longboats heading for points as far away as Iceland and the British mainland. This line of thought embraces the notion that the Vikings were tough but fair, benign colonials under whom the indigenous people of the islands lived and worked in something approaching harmony. One well-read couple with a passion for history whom I spent time with were adamant that there could not have been *any* strife between the Picts who occupied Shetland in the early 9th Century and the Viking incomers.

'There are no signs whatsoever, of battles between the Norsemen and the Shetlanders,' they told me.

Others I met took an opposing, and possibly more realistic, view.

'Shetlanders celebrating the Vikings is like the French celebrating the date the German Army drove their Panzers into Paris, or like the Jews holding a Happy Hitler Day,' said one man I talked to. 'The Vikings were robbers and rapists and murderers everywhere they went — so why on earth do Shetlanders celebrate by dressing up as Vikings every year?'

I seek the views of author and historian Brian Smith, who is well-known in local circles as a vocal critic of those who view all things Norse with dewy-eyed sentimentality.

'Scandinavians who came to Shetland in the 9th Century were one hundred percent successful,' he says. 'They colonised the islands and ousted or slaughtered the local population.' Among locals and academics, he maintains, 'there are sentimentalists, especially archaeologists, who refuse to believe that this happened.'

If this were not so, he argues, at the very least some of the old Pictish place names would have survived, yet next to no non-Scandinavian place names exist in Shetland today. Smith points at Australia, where Aboriginal names live on throughout the country, with the ominous exception of the island state of Tasmania, where the wiping out of the Aborigines was nothing short of genocidal. Hand in hand with the extermination of the Tasmanian Aboriginal went the disappearance of Aboriginal place names. Brian Smith sees a direct parallel between modern Tasmania and present-day Shetland, where pre-Norse place names are notable for their near-total absence.

Brian is well-known too for his views on Up Helly Aa. While not being in the least against the event *per se* (he writes an article every year on the history of the festival for the much-sought-after official programme), he is openly contemptuous of implied historical revisionism regarding the Norse invaders, and of how it seems to have been conveniently forgotten that Up Helly Aa in its present form actually began with the Temperance Movement and the Socialists, and that it has since morphed, over the course of a century, into something very different, and very much soaked in alcohol.

Excessive drinking, a thousand flaming torches marching in procession, and heavily bearded men sporting skirts and waving blunt instruments in a celebration of genocidal invaders who wiped out their Shetland predecessors. What's not to like about that?

That night, Radio Shetland previews the big day by broadcasting short interviews with members of the Jarl's Squad — among them, two Australians and one Kiwi — and indulging their requests for songs to be devoted to Squad members and their families. Thin Lizzy's 'The boys are back in town' is almost predictable; Slim Dusty's 'I like to have a drink with Colin, 'cos Colin's me mate', and Village People's 'Macho Man', less so. The programme winds up with Dr Feelgood's riff-driven 'Milk and alcohol' — and a last-minute urgent request for anyone who has a spare Hawaiian shirt to please get in touch with a squad member whose costume for tomorrow night is still lacking that vital floral element.

The last Tuesday in January dawns bright and clear; there is a collective sense of relief on the faces of Shetlanders on the streets of Lerwick as they exchange glances at the chilled blue sky and 'fine day for it' comments ring out loud and often.

A steady trickle of Lerwegians rumbles towards Fort Charlotte, whose stout walls are already peppered with folk waiting for their first view of this year's Jarl's Squad. I fail miserably in an attempt to hoist myself up onto the fort's chest-high wall, and suffer the ignominy of having to take a leg-up from a friendly soul who is easily twenty years my senior. He and his wife occupy one of the prime cannon-notch viewing points, and lean against a weapon that might have once fired dead cats towards the harbour. He soon tells me he is originally from Aberdeen, a fact ably backed up by his accent:

'Ah kem up tae work in Shetland in nineteen-fifty-fower, goat the heather stuck atween ma taes an' ah'm still here yit.'

Below us, the north end of Commercial Street is a narrow tunnel of bodies, necks craning south towards an approaching rumble of anticipation and applause. On the other side of the street, the Galley sits tall on its trailer, dragon-whiskers stirring in the breeze, lovingly-polished varnish and silvery fittings firing starbursts of reflected sunlight.

Anticipation crackles through the crowd like static electricity accompanied by the parp-thumps of a marching brass band interspersed with quaintly old-fashioned cries of 'Three Cheers!' and, even more out of place, Uggy Uggy Uggy! — Oi! Oi! Oi!

Bystanders break into applause in welcome of the Jarl's Squad. Upwards of fifty bearded men brandish gleaming axes above their heads and bellow from the depths of their lungs. It is ten o'clock in the morning, and the squad have another twenty hours of this ahead of them.

For most of Lerwick, this is the first chance to see the Squad in a full set of regalia specially designed and hand-crafted, at a reported cost of fifteen hundred pounds per squad member. Fashion cognoscenti nod approvingly at the cape of pure sheepskin that blends neatly by way of a black leather mantle and extravagant buckles into intricate chest armour of shining metallic circles. Lurking behind the circles sits a one-piece woollen ensemble in burgundy that envelopes the wearer from crook of the arm to just above the knee, where a tidy skirtline is accentuated by an interlocking pattern with a heavy hint at Nordic origins. Dark leggings reach down to black boots that rather smack of the 21st Century, and the whole ensemble is topped off with stout decorated circular shield, even more stout shiny axe, and the requisite metallic helmet, complete with ear and nose protectors.

Mercifully, the Squad's helmets lack the upturned horns which no self-respecting Viking would have been seen dead in, and only ever appeared in movie theatres and vapidly unfunny syndicated newspaper cartoons.

The Squad assembles in and around the Galley for the taking of yet another official photograph, and bask in attention directed at them from land, sea and air. In the waters behind them, a seal watches the proceedings with customary curiosity, an Irish trawler slows its trip towards the North Sea to get a better view, and even the Coastguard helicopter makes a cameo appearance, luminous-costumed crew clustered in the open doorway.

Photographs taken, the Squad form tight ranks and march off, a full day of appearances at schools, hospitals and old folks' homes ahead of them, before night comes down and the real fun starts.

My own day passes at a less frantic pace, enjoying the mild weather and browsing the library before dropping in to speak to the harried folks at the Tourist Office, where Stephen Simpson introduces me to a lady who will host one of the Halls tonight. What she tells me inspires panic. With a firm gaze that any headmistress would be proud of, she tells me that dress at the Halls is most definitely formal, and that neckties are expected. I try to pull off the illusion that this comes as no surprise, but I can count on one thumb the number of times in the last decade when I wore a tie, and a worried glance at my watch says it is three minutes past four. Lerwick shops close early on this Big Day. A sprint into Commercial Street gets me to a charity store that is clearly shut; by five minutes past the hour, a second charity shop is also closed for the day, but my pained expression draws a grandmother figure to unlock the door, and upon hearing that the Halls beckon, yet here I am without so much as a collar and tie, she ushers me in. Five minutes later and a mighty two pounds lighter in the wallet department, I leave, my new shirt and tie carefully folded in a charity shop bag. Even if the shirt is a putrescent shade of green, and the tie a skinny thing that hails from the 1980s, my mission is accomplished. Formal attire, after a fashion, achieved.

II: Men in skirts, bearing blunt instruments

The atmosphere on the dark streets of Lower Hillhead feels testosterone-heavy, as when football supporters gather for the bus to an away match, or the menfolk from a wedding party grab time out for a smoke and an exchange of ribald digs at the in-laws. Squads of guizers in full costume flank the route, impatiently awaiting the arrival of the Galley and distribution of the all-important torches. At the business end of the snaking lines, the Galley is at last towed into place by a pick-up that creaks under the weight of hundreds of torches — long square-section wooden staffs with bulky, paint-tin-sized lumps of tightly wrapped fabric and inflammable wax. One spark out of place, and . . .

First to march behind the Jarl's men will be a squad whose costumes put the cow into cowboy. Hats, waistcoats and leggings are in faux-fresian black and white. The man at the head of the squad, face swallowed by pantomime whiskers, tells me this is his thirtieth consecutive year at Up Helly Aa. His fellow squad members put up an ironic cheer, their outer spiritedness already owing something to sustenance drawn from unlabelled bottles that appear from belt pouches. It is only just after seven p.m., and the revelries in the Halls will endure at least until tomorrow breakfast time. As the Americans say: you do the math.

When the Jarl's Squad arrive to something akin to mass admiration, a tall, pale-eyed young man with the look of the Norseman about him threads through the throng, shaking hands and thumping backs. Magnus Thomson's Shetlander parents emigrated to Canada before he was born, and he is back to rediscover his roots. From the enraptured look in his eye, it has been an untrammelled success. The young Canadian has come home, and he knows it. In plain clothes today, he tells me he already plans to return next year to join a squad.

A flare courses through the inky black sky, drawing roars of glee from more than nine hundred guizers, and for long minutes Hillhead turns red as hand-held flares move between clustered torch heads thrust eagerly to the flame.

Torches flickering bright orange like gigantic tapers, the Jarl's Squad form up for more ritualised bellowing before the roars give way to singing and at last the procession is launched to a spirited rendition of 'The Up Helly A' Song'. Men in £1500 outfits, in Viking helmets, in Cowboy hats, Mexican sombreros and in Che Guevara costumes — even men dressed as sponges and as aircraft — head off into the night, chanting the words of Shetland poet and author J. J. Haldane Burgess (1862-1927), to what sounds rather like the melody of 'Mine eyes have seen the glory':

> From grand old Viking centuries,
> Up-Helly—A' has come,
> Then light the torch and form the march,
> and sound the rolling drum:
> And wake the mighty memories of
> heroes that are dumb
> — The waves are rolling on.
>
> Grand old Vikings rules upon the ocean vast,
> Their brave battle-song still thunder on the blast;
> Their wild war cry comes a-ringing from the past;
> — We answer it "A-oi"!
> Roll their glory down the ages
> Sons of warriors and sages
> When the fight for Freedom rages,
> — Be bold and strong as they!

I wonder if I may be the only person struck by the surrealism of these lyrics. In the course of a single verse and chorus, the argument so often put forward that the festival is really about celebrating the transition from darkest northern winter towards the cheery promise of springtime, and nothing *really* to do with celebrating the Vikings, is rendered moot. The singing continues:

We are the sons of mighty sires,
whose souls were staunch and strong;
We sweep upon our serried foes,
the hosts of Hate and Wrong;
The glory of a grander Age
has fired our battle-song;
— The waves are rolling on.

Never mind that most of the singers are in squads with names like 'Kinky Kong' and 'Horse Shit 'n Nappies', these are stirring, spirited lyrics, albeit ones that beggar belief. Vikings as a force of virtue, enemies of evil embracing a selfless campaign for the freedom of others? This is historical revisionism gone mad. Whatever happened to good old rape, pillage and mass slaughter?

The elevated view from my position at the raised corner that belongs to the Mormon Church is perfect, thanks to one friendly member of the congregation. After initial reticence that runs like a flag up a pole the moment she hears that I am a writer, she warms visibly upon learning of my meeting with the two young Elders, Brandon and Ashley. Then her expression chills again as it locks onto an arriving cameraman whom I recognise from yesterday's Press briefing. A media veteran who for many years was the BBC's man in Shetland, he must surely have done or said something in the past to draw the ire of Shetland Mormons.

'Quick,' she says, 'You get in there before *these people take all the best places.*' She moves aside and ushers me into the only available position with an unbroken view of the procession route.

Viking hero worship is difficult for this outsider to grasp, but the visual power of the torchlit procession is the stuff of universal appeal. Flickering flamelight reflects in the expressions of young kids that tell of deeply-engrained impressions being carved in their soul by the visceral thrill of nine hundred tall costumed figures firing up the mid-winter night.

Twin courses of torches form two ever-moving lines of flame

along St Olaf Street. The Galley heads the procession with Einar of Gullberuvik — Guizer Jarl Mark Manson — towering above the burning wicks, axe held high, soaking up the attention that he must surely have been dreaming of for fifteen years. He and the Galley sweep around the corner to a sequence of cheers from spectators standing four-deep on the pavements.

After refusing a sincere offer of hot soup in the church, I head off in search of the impossible, a vantage point overlooking the climax of the procession, the burning of the Galley. Good fortune and just a bit of bloody-mindedness sees me to a spot in the garden of the Catholic Rectory. Nobody, certainly not the generously-proportioned gent in a priest's cassock enjoying the procession streaming past his front gate, seems too bothered that the Rectory garden is being flattened underfoot. But I bet his gardener lives in dread of the day after the last Tuesday in January.

The Galley is wheeled to its final resting place in an area of parkland, and nine hundred-plus guizers, some of whose torches by now have to be held tip-down to keep them burning, form concentric lines around it and the Jarl's Squad lead the singing of The Galley Song, the final two verses of which go like this:

> Worthy sons of Vikings make us,
> Truth be our encircling fire
> Shadowy visions backwards take us
> To the Sea King's funeral pyre
>
> Bonds of Brotherhood inherit,
> O'er strife the curtain draw;
> Let our actions breathe the spirit
> Of our grand Up-Helly A'

Successions of three cheers go up for everyone involved in the festival, with those for the Jarl coming last and loudest of all. Then a bugle breaks through the hubbub of excited voices, and a vision of Valhalla breaks loose as swarms of guizers step forward to dispatch a tumbling parabolic chaos of torches into the Galley.

Up Helly Aa reaches its final chapter where it started for me much earlier in the day, at Fort Charlotte, in whose Hall is one of the key social flings that rumble throughout the night. I am reminded of the Fort's role as a Territorial Army Headquarters when I find myself in front of an armoured doorway fashioned of cold blue steel and with bold signs attached.

**This door is alarmed and
sensitive to heat and vibration.
Triggering the alarm will
Summon the police, who:**

MAY USE ARMED RESPONSE WITH DEADLY FORCE

Oh goody. A hall with an ever-changing roll call of hard drinkers on all-night benders, and it features a fully-equipped armoury with an alarm system hot-linked to SWAT armed response teams. Too much rattle and roll in the corridor — and heavily-armed men in black abseil into the yard from helicopters.

The Hall is alive with music, dance, laughter and the kind of banter that can only exist among an intricately-connected, village-like social group. I stand wrapped in an invisible social fabric that connects all around me by blood, by marriage, or by years spent in the same schoolyards or workplaces.

From a low stage in one corner a band — a real, Shetland band of accordions and fiddles — keeps the floor shaking with the dance steps of folk who swarm enthusiastically from the sidelines to form up as each dance is announced. Unsurprisingly, on a night when nearly a thousand of Shetland's adult males are trekking from Hall to Hall, the room is filled with single ladies, none of whom seem too bothered by being alone for much of the night, if the explosions of raucous high-pitched laughter is any measure of things.

There are no bars in the Halls on Up Helly Aa night; and so the strains of the band, the *whee-yeuch!* cheers of dancers and the buzz of conversation is accompanied by the near-constant clink of bottles moving around in plastic bags that lurk under every chair.

The format for the long night is simple. Dance a little, then retreat to the sidelines to drink and laugh loud at the acts put on by successive squads, who enter the Hall to fanfare and boisterous applause before taking over the dance floor to perform their cabaret party-piece.

The acts are mostly in the comedy-satire mould, and rely very much on the audience's knowledge of Shetland affairs.

The squad dressed as Che Guevaras are dedicated to an anti-speeding activist who for some unfathomable reason dressed as Che when he was arrested for his protests.

Another act lampoons the Shetland Islands Council in a sketch where a television game show host allows 'councillors' to gamble vast sums of Shetland oil revenue on a variety of follies. One cast member represents a council member by the name of Feather by dressing in a full canary outfit. (Later, the sight of the same character in full flight during an eightsome reel, the canary head flapping behind him like a still-strutting broken-necked chicken, has onlookers in tears).

The next squad's act would not have too many fans in the Tourist Board, as it pours scorn on overseas tourists who will buy anything 'traditional' — Fair Isle G-strings included.

No wonder Shetlanders jokingly call this Transvestite Tuesday. The number of acts that involve men in drag is striking, and as troupes of males in mini-skirts and wigs prance around the dance floor, the many women in the audience fold double in appreciation. The real women of Shetland are thankfully far more pleasing to the eye than their transvestite counterparts, even if one thing strikes me as a sign of the times: some of the characters in drag have visibly fewer tattoos.

One act has a gimmick straight out of a secondary school locker room. Inflatable boobs, blown up in mid-dance using an air tube reminiscent of inflight briefings when the air stewardess demonstrates how to top up a life-vest in the unlikely event of you not breaking into sandwich-sized pieces upon impact.

As the dancing squad blow enthusiastically into their busts, they draw attention to something that so far has escaped me. Apart from miniature kilts and pleated wigs, they all wear school blouses and ties. I look around the Hall. Apart from the drag act, I cannot see another necktie in the entire room. Except, that is, for mine. I spent two pounds on this token stab at formality, and apparently the joke is squarely on me. I am the only guy in the room dressed more formally than the mob in miniskirts and inflatable boobs.

The squad disappears to healthy applause and attention turns quickly to the dance floor when the MC announces a Gay Gordon's. My night is almost over, but I have yet to grace the floor — and the Gay Gordon's is one of the easiest dances of all. A grandmotherly figure stands alone nearby, and I pluck up the courage to ask if she would mind dancing.

'Mind? Not at all,' she says, and leaps towards the dance floor with such alacrity that I struggle to keep up.

As the introductory bars strike up, I warn her that it has been a very long time since I did this, but she just smiles, and leads me off with the expertise and confidence born of half a century's practice. She is a wonderful dancer, so good that no matter how many mistakes I make, her little feet fly in safety, far from my own blundering footfalls.

She is a talkative soul, and I soon find myself admitting that, after everything I had heard, I came to the Hall tonight not knowing what to expect. She asks what I mean, and I mention the furore that went up in recent years when a Guizer Jarl put multiple noses out of joint by proclaiming that Up Helly Aa was only really for Shetlanders, not for sooth-moothers and certainly not for members of the Press. Outsiders and writers were less than welcome, was the unsubtle message. When she shakes her head, lips pursed, I tell her I was concerned that I might be intruding on a private event, and not feel welcome.

In mid-twirl at the end of a Gay Gordon's set, she casts her eyes around the Hall, then locks them back upon mine, and says:

'Dis du **feel** unwelcome?'

Of course I don't. I feel as much at ease, every bit as welcome here, among comparative strangers in a distant northern land, as I ever felt anywhere.